T3-BGM-771

*Development Assistance
in the Seventies*

ROBERT E. ASHER

Development Assistance
in the Seventies

ALTERNATIVES FOR THE UNITED STATES

THE BROOKINGS INSTITUTION
Washington, D.C.

THE BROOKINGS INSTITUTION is an independent organization devoted to nonpartisan research, education, and publication in economics, government, foreign policy, and the social sciences generally. Its principal purposes are to aid in the development of sound public policies and to promote public understanding of issues of national importance.

The Institution was founded on December 8, 1927, to merge the activities of the Institute for Government Research, founded in 1916, the Institute of Economics, founded in 1922, and the Robert Brookings Graduate School of Economics and Government, founded in 1924.

The general administration of the Institution is the responsibility of a self-perpetuating Board of Trustees. The trustees are likewise charged with maintaining the independence of the staff and fostering the most favorable conditions for creative research and education. The immediate direction of the policies, program, and staff of the Institution is vested in the President, assisted by an advisory council chosen from the staff of the Institution.

In publishing a study, the Institution presents it as a competent treatment of a subject worthy of public consideration. The interpretations and conclusions in such publications are those of the author or authors and do not purport to represent the views of the other staff members, officers, or trustees of the Brookings Institution.

Foreword

THE NIXON ADMINISTRATION, when it assumed office on January 20, 1969, fell heir to an unenviable array of problems. This study addresses itself to one of those problems: What, if anything, should be done about the U.S. foreign aid program? It focuses on development assistance—financial and technical assistance from rich countries to facilitate growth and change in poor countries—rather than on military assistance or other kinds of foreign aid. It also discusses changes in U.S. trade and investment policy which have a bearing on the problem of development aid.

Although the study includes recommendations, its principal aim is to interpret and analyze rather than to prescribe and to ordain. It is assumed that the reader wants to know which are the principal alternative courses of action open to the United States and what the pros and cons of each alternative seem to be. Should the United States have a development assistance program? If so, about how big should it be, who should run it, and how long should it last? Where will the money come from? What will and what will it not buy? The reader does not want simplistic answers; he recognizes that in the developing world uncertainties, anomalies, paradoxes, and explosive side effects abound. Neither does he wish to be overwhelmed with details about these complexities.

Accordingly, the study begins with a brief résumé of changes in the domestic and international environment which make development assistance in the world of the 1970s a radically different enterprise than it appeared to be during the first postwar decade. This discussion provides background for a more detailed consideration of the rationale for development assistance from the United States—how that rationale has changed over the years and how valid and interconnected the various links in the chain of reasoning now appear to be.

The case for development assistance during the first postwar decade necessarily rested on a series of untested assertions; until then, sustained, large-scale resource transfers from rich countries to promote the modernization of poor countries were virtually unknown. Indeed, development assistance did not come into its own until the last half of the 1950s. Experience to date, limited though it is, has taught us at least a few lessons about the nature of the development process and the role of foreign aid in helping or hindering its evolution, lessons that must be taken into account in designing a development assistance program for the years to come. It is maintained in Chapter 3 that, though some of these lessons have attained the status of clichés, they do not yet govern policy. The chapter is therefore devoted to a discussion of lessons considered by the author to have important implications for aid policy.

Statistical information on the trend of U.S. aid during the 1960s and the growth records of aid-receiving countries is concentrated in Chapter 4, together with an analysis of the targets being set for the 1970s.

The remaining six chapters look ahead to the issues of the 1970s. Specific problems such as the indebtedness accumulated by the less developed countries and the burden of a rapidly increasing population are dealt with first. Chapter 6 considers aid channels and proposes a phased transition to a predominantly multilateral aid program. But there remain important questions concerning the future division of labor between multilateral and bilateral channels, the specific mechanisms for providing capital and technical assistance, the terms on which each is to be provided, the effects on the U.S. balance of payments, and the possibility of tapping sources of development finance not now being tapped, as for example the special drawing rights created by the International Monetary Fund as a new reserve asset.

Separate chapters are devoted to alternatives in the fields of trade policy and private investment policy which could reduce the need for aid and help build a better integrated community of nations. The principal recommendations and conclusions of the study are brought together in the final chapter as elements for consideration in establishing a legislative framework for development assistance during the 1970s.

The author, Robert E. Asher, is a Senior Fellow at the Brookings Institution. He is a co-author of two 1957 Brookings books, *The United Nations and Economic and Social Cooperation* and *The United Nations and Promotion of the General Welfare*, author of *Grants, Loans, and Local Currencies: Their Role in Foreign Aid* (Brookings, 1961), editor of and contributor to *Development of the Emerging Countries: An Agenda for Research* (Brookings, 1962).

The study was conducted as a part of the Institution's program of Foreign Policy Studies directed by Henry Owen. In that program, Brookings' long-standing interest in foreign aid and aid-related issues continues to figure prominently. The Institution is as grateful as the author to the readers of his manuscript and the other persons mentioned in the acknowledgements following this foreword for their constructive assistance at all stages of the work.

The views expressed in the book are those of the author and should not be construed as representing the views of those who were consulted during its preparation. Neither are they to be taken as reflecting the views of the trustees, the officers, or other staff members of the Brookings Institution.

KERMIT GORDON
President

December 1969
Washington, D.C.

Author's Note

THIS MANUSCRIPT WAS COMPLETED in late July of 1969—in other words, before any congressional action had been taken on the aid authorization or appropriation measures for the fiscal year that began on July 1, 1969; before major troop withdrawals from Vietnam began and their budgetary implications could be weighed; before the release on October 1 of the comprehensive and informative report of the Commission on International Development headed by Lester B. Pearson; before the presidential task force on the U.S. aid program chaired by Rudolph A. Peterson had been named; and before President Nixon's address of October 31 to the Inter-American Press Association on U.S. relations with Latin America. In the final editing, it has been possible to indicate at least an awareness of some of these events, but not necessarily to place them in proper perspective.

This study can be regarded as supplementing and complementing the report of the Pearson Commission, *Partners in Development*. The latter is the product of a high-level international commission and is addressed to the international community; the present study addresses itself specifically to the U.S. aid program and basically to an American audience. This study, for example, recommends a much more rapid multilateralization of the U.S. aid program than the

Pearson Commission considers feasible for the programs of major donors taken as a group. It also recommends more liberal terms for loan aid than the commission recommends. But the thrust of the two studies is in the same direction.

The Peterson Task Force will address itself to opinion leaders and policy makers in the United States and should issue its report at about the time this book is published, perhaps before then, but no forecast of its findings can yet be made. In any event, the recommendations and conclusions of this study constitute one man's opinion, not the conclusions and recommendations of an official task force or commission, aided by an expert staff. The book expresses a point of view—my own—but presents no new theory of development or of the role of foreign aid, peddles no panacea, and promises no miracles as a result of adopting its recommendations.

As author, I am deeply indebted not only to the writers cited in my text but also to a host of friends whom I have consulted while en route to conclusions that may in some cases dismay them. The list includes, although it is by no means limited to: John H. Adler, William G. Carter, Paul G. Clark, Harriett S. Crowley, Richard H. Demuth, Isaiah Frank, Theodore Geiger, Richard Goode, James P. Grant, Samuel P. Hayes, Michael L. Hoffman, James W. Howe, Albert H. Huntington, Peter Knight, Lawrence B. Krause, John P. Lewis, Abraham F. Lowenthal, Daniel F. Margolies, Edwin M. Martin, the late Max F. Millikan, Raymond F. Mikesell, Joan M. Nelson, Robert L. Oshins, John Pincus, Rutherford Poats, Walter S. Salant, Guy V. C. Stevens, Alan M. Strout, Irving Swerdlow, Albert Waterston, David C. Williams, and C. Tyler Wood.

Henry Owen, director of Foreign Policy Studies at Brookings, was extraordinarily understanding, helpful, and encouraging at all times. I should like to express my thanks to Rosemary Taromino and other members of the secretarial staff, who cheerfully and accurately continued to retype pages and passages that they had long since thought of as permanently "over and done with," and to Elizabeth Cross, who edited the manuscript, and Florence Robinson, who prepared the index.

With the characteristic fondness that authors have for the sound of their own words, I have reused some sentences, paragraphs, and ideas from my previously published writings, with the kind permission of W. W. Norton and Company, Inc., the National Planning Association, and the World Peace Foundation. The quotations from John Pincus's book, *Trade, Aid and Development: The Rich and Poor Nations* (copyright © by the Council on Foreign Relations, Inc.), are used with the permission of the McGraw-Hill Book Company.

ROBERT E. ASHER

Contents

CHAPTER ONE

The Changed Domestic and International Environment

IN LEARNING THE LESSONS of twenty years in the foreign aid business, the United States is still very much like Shakespeare's "whining schoolboy, with his satchel and shining morning face, creeping like snail unwillingly to school." Each year before the appropriation is voted, the program undergoes an agonizing but superficial reappraisal, the outcome of which is a stay of execution rather than a new lease on life for foreign aid.

The President asserts that the program is clearly in the national interest, that the sums asked for constitute a bare-bones request, and that the taxpayer is getting, and will continue to get, a good return on his investment. The Congress, however, wants proof and has become increasingly unwilling to provide the sums requested by the President. With respect to foreign aid, it persists in pulling up the plant by the roots several times a year to see how it is growing. In its never-ending war with the executive branch and its uninhibited pursuit of "truth," it appears to flaunt America's failures as norms and dismiss its accomplishments as aberrations. The public is bewildered and uncertain where to place foreign aid in a rational arraying of priorities for a nation with great but by no means unlimited resources.

The Foreign Assistance Act of 1968 provides the smallest appropriation since the program began in the 1940s. In recognition of the impasse that has been reached, the Congress in Section 502 asked the President "to make a thorough and comprehensive reappraisal of United States foreign assistance programs" and to submit by March 31, 1970, "his recommendations for achieving such reforms in and reorganization of future foreign assistance programs as he determines to be necessary and appropriate." The reference to future foreign assistance programs would seem to indicate that the Congress does not expect the United States to be out of the foreign aid business within the near future, but that it does look forward to fundamental changes in the character of the U.S. effort.

The range of alternatives is broad. My array assumes that the economic, social, and civic development of low-income countries—their modernization—is in the long-term interest of the United States and should be the principal current objective of America's foreign economic aid. If development is accepted as the objective, various assistance strategies can be envisaged. Choices can be posed in terms of categories of countries on which assistance should be concentrated or to which it should be limited: for example, those with which the United States has long-standing historic ties, those it considers closest to, or farthest from, the takeoff to self-sustaining growth, or those of greatest strategic importance.

The United States lives in a world of nations and tends to think— properly, I believe—of development assistance in terms of aid to India, to Korea, or to Bolivia, and what aid can accomplish in each of those areas. The choices, however, could be posed in problem-focused rather than country-focused terms. Aid proponents can and at times do think of global campaigns to wipe out illiteracy and malaria, to introduce the new, phenomenally productive rice and wheat strains, or to launch family planning throughout the low-income world, with results judged on the basis of progress toward global targets.

In terms of money, or real resources, or of proportion of gross national product (GNP), the United States can consider reducing, maintaining, or increasing present levels of aid. At each level, it can reduce, maintain, or increase the proportion of bilateral aid as compared with multilateral, the proportion of grants to loans, the proportion of technical assistance to capital assistance, the proportion devoted to particular activities such as education or agriculture as compared with other activities such as road building or industrialization, and, more generally, the emphasis on quality and effectiveness as compared with quantity or mechanisms. "Requirements" for aid, a rubbery term about which more will be said, will depend not only on the self-help efforts of the poor countries, but also on actions taken or not taken by the rich countries in the field of trade and investment promotion, military assistance, immigration, and cultural exchanges.

There is no point in stretching the list of policy alternatives to embrace every conceivable variant. If one assumes that the United States is not prepared to abandon the country focus of its bilateral program or end its participation in the activities of the World Bank Group, the Inter-American Development Bank, the United Nations Development Program, and other multilateral undertakings, an oversimplified list of the principal alternatives might include the following:

1. The United States can retreat—that is, reduce the scope, geographically, functionally, or financially, of its bilateral effort.

2. It can jog along more or less as at present—that is, without basic authorizing legislation, annually tightening the screws a bit here and occasionally loosening them a bit there, but not appropriating enough money or reorganizing its program in such fashion as to make a markedly different impact, economically or politically, than the program now makes.

3. It can enlarge its contribution, to attain by some specified date the 1 percent of GNP that has been recommended as a target level for the flow of long-term financial resources from high-income to low-income countries; and it can calculate that 1 percent (or any other target figure) much more realistically than the current practice of indiscriminately lumping together grants, loans, Food-for-Freedom, private investment, and other items of disparate real value.

4. Although the multilateral-bilateral mix can be changed in either direction at any aid level, the present program is overwhelmingly bilateral. The practical alternatives in this field are (a) whether and how much to alter the mix in the direction of greater reliance on

multilateral instruments, and (b) which multilateral instruments to use.

5. The United States can seek to integrate aid, trade, investment, and cultural exchange policy more formally into a broad, long-range strategy for promoting development in the low-income countries and obtaining a better integrated community of nations.

With respect to foreign aid (and most other aspects of foreign policy as well), the United States does appear to have reached the end of an era. Fresh perspective and program changes to match it are urgently needed. During the 1950s, the basic framework for American foreign aid was the Mutual Security Act as amended. Foreign aid was justified primarily as a national security measure, needed to strengthen allies and to build up low-income countries so that they would be less vulnerable to communist invasion or takeover. During the 1960s, security was more broadly defined and less emphasis was placed on the quest for military allies, although the support of potential aid receivers for the U.S. effort in the Vietnam war remained important in the eyes of the Congress.

In the 1960s, development itself was given a higher though by no means overriding priority, at least by the executive branch. On the more narrowly security side, emphasis was given to the internal threat to less developed countries from guerrillas and from operatives trained abroad. The basic framework for foreign aid has been the Foreign Assistance Act of 1961. Dwindling appropriations have made it less important, both absolutely and in relation to other sources of assistance, while restrictive amendments and provisions considered offensive by self-respecting nations have made this country's bilateral development assistance program progressively more difficult—almost impossible—to administer. Further amendment of the much amended Foreign Assistance Act of 1961 is one of the least attractive policy alternatives.

At present, economic aid is still expected to serve a variety of contradictory purposes. It is an arm of foreign policy, but increasingly ill adapted to fulfill various short-range objectives of American policy and not yet well adapted to serve the long-range goal of expediting balanced development in low-income countries. Although it is an economic instrument, the ultimate end it serves is political. Its relationship to such other economic instruments as commercial policy and investment policy is loose and poorly understood. Foreign aid continues to be viewed as a voluntary, annual, emergency program, but virtually everyone expects it to be with us through the 1970s, and beyond.

That the United States got into the international development business somewhat haphazardly via Lend-Lease, the United Nations Relief and Rehabilitation Administration, the European Recovery Program, the Mutual Defense Assistance Program, Point Four, and various military alliances and that it has been learning by doing rather than waiting until it had all the answers are consistent not only with the pragmatic, action-oriented temperament of this country but also, in my view, with the exigencies of the situation abroad. The foreign aid program, however, began in a world environment fundamentally different from the one in which we live today. Before policies appropriate for the 1970s are considered, it would be useful to reconsider, with the benefit of hindsight, the import of certain developments since the close of World War II. These developments involve changes in the global political and military landscape, in the economic scene, in the domestic situation of the United States, and in worldwide understanding of the nature of the development process. The summary that follows is intended to be suggestive and impressionistic rather than comprehensive and probing.

The Political and Military Landscape

When the guns were stilled and the bombing and killing of World War II were brought to a halt, the second most productive workshop in the world—Western Europe—lay physically devastated and deeply damaged economically, politically, and psychologically. Half a world away, a terrifyingly potent new source of energy had been revealed in the atomic bombs dropped on Hiroshima and Nagasaki; Japan's "co-prosperity sphere" had been split asunder. The Kuomintang of Chiang Kai-shek was losing its grip on China and communist forces under Mao Tse-tung were tightening theirs. An aggressive and truculent Soviet Union seemed bent on expansion.

The United States stood at the pinnacle of its power and prestige. Physically undamaged, enormously strengthened economically (both absolutely and relatively), sole possessor of the secret of the atom, father of the United Nations, filled with missionary zeal and determined not to relapse into the isolationism of the interwar years, it appeared to be a formidable bulwark against the forces of totalitarianism and chaos. Nevertheless, building a new world order of the kind implicit in the United Nations Charter—a collectivity of sovereign nation-states collaborating in the maintenance of international peace and the promotion of the general welfare—was not going to be easy in the divided world that was emerging.

For the United States, the containment of communism and the reconstruction of Western Europe and Japan soon claimed top priority. Although the dissolution of colonial empires was creating power vacuums, the pace of dissolution during the first postwar decade seemed to the United States far from headlong.

In 1949, the USSR exploded an atomic bomb. In June 1950, communist forces invaded South Korea, and the United States, under a United Nations umbrella, responded to the challenge. Hostilities continued until July 1953, by which time South Korea was a devastated area. Now, sixteen years later, a promising economic recovery is under way, but South Korea still receives American aid and 50,000 American troops are still stationed there. Korea remains a divided nation; frequent border incidents threaten to touch off more general hostilities.

During the early years of the Eisenhower administration, a network of military alliances involving some forty-two nations throughout the "free world" was built up by the United States and military bases in far-off lands were acquired. Initially, economic aid commitments to less developed countries were more often than not the sweetening believed necessary to make the military pact more palatable. Regardless of the rationale, subsequent investment was invariably required to protect the initial investment. Since both military and economic assistance were forms of foreign aid, subsequent allegations that foreign aid had "entrapped" the United States, or overextended it, or involved it in commitments not required by more current assessments of the national interest, could be made without specifying the kind of aid and without regard to the relationships between military and economic aid. In addition to 50,000 troops in Korea, the United States in mid-1969 had more than 500,000 in Vietnam, 300,00 in Europe, 50,000 in Thailand, and smaller contingents in Japan, Okinawa, and many other areas. The cost of maintaining its overseas bases was estimated to be between four and five billion dollars a year.

As the 1950s wore on, Western Europe and Japan, with generous American aid, rose to new heights of prosperity and productive power. This triumph of American policy was not unalloyed. France, America's oldest ally, became singularly uncooperative, and other high-income allies grew more inward looking, more preoccupied with the domestic problems of affluent societies, more confident of the validity of their own assessments of the risks the future held in store for them. The European Economic Community survived a series of crises and emerged as a major economic force in world affairs.

The communist world ceased to present a monolithic facade, if indeed it ever did. Polycentrism, to use recent jargon, has steadily undermined the power of both of the superpowers (the United States and the USSR). Nationalism in Eastern Europe refuses to succumb to a communism that gives top priority to the interests of the Soviet Union. Among the communist giants, the split between China and Russia appears to be a fact of historic importance. China, though internally convulsed at present, has come forward fast as a nuclear power. Further proliferation of nuclear weapons can probably be expected. Intercontinental ballistic weapons and other developments in what is ironically called "national security" have reduced the military necessity for overseas bases; resurgent nationalism has increased the political hazards in maintaining such outposts.

The low-income world has ceased to be merely a passive battleground for rival great powers. It has become a restless, vocal constellation of more than ninety sovereign states, each of which is eager for a voice in the world of the twentieth century. Almost all of them are in the grip of revolution (in the historic sense of the term) and revolutions are, by definition, disorderly affairs. Violent overthrows of existing governments, military takeovers, and periodic breakdowns of law and order continue to occur. The relationship of economic growth to political stability is far less direct than it once appeared to be. To expect stable or democratic regimes and friendly relations with the United States as early corollaries of economic growth has been revealed as naïve. A militant attitude toward the rich countries is fast becoming a prerequisite for the political survival of leaders in poor countries.

Three times in the Middle East war has broken out between the Arab States and Israel. India and Pakistan, and India and China have marched against each other. Numerous other threats to the peace have erupted in both the more developed and less developed regions of the world—in Berlin, the Congo, the Formosa Strait, Quemoy and Matsu, Cuba, and elsewhere—particularly in the low-income world.

Saddest of all for the United States has been the frustrating, drawn-out, divisive war in Vietnam. As of this writing, it is assumed to cost the United States about $30 billion per year. If it can be brought to an end, and if military spending for other purposes can be kept in hand, the resultant peace dividend—modest for the first year or two but rising more rapidly thereafter—can provide funds for the relief of other festering sores on the body politic at home and abroad.[1]

Although the sense of international community is not particularly potent at the moment and nationalism is everywhere evident, there is a growing consciousness of the interdependence of nations and peoples, a gradual erosion of the traditional perquisites of sovereignty, and an erratic but observable expansion in the roles of international institutions, regional and global.

The Economic Environment

The economic situation of the world, not surprisingly, has changed as drastically as the political and military situation. The U.S. share in the gross national product of the world is still enormous—it accounts for more than a third of the GNP of the world as a whole and

1. See Kermit Gordon (ed.), *Agenda for the Nation* (Brookings Institution, 1968), especially the essay by Charles L. Schultze, "Budget Alternatives after Vietnam."

more than half that of the developed, noncommunist countries. The U.S. share is slowly decreasing, however, as a better-balanced pattern of world production emerges, particularly within the developed world. The GNP of the United States, which amounted to $285 billion in 1950, reached $861 billion in 1968 and should approach $1 trillion in 1970. Per capita GNP, running at about $1,875 in 1950, reached nearly $4,300 in 1968 and may be expected to approximate $7,000 by 1975.[2]

Growth in Western Europe and Japan during the 1950s, and in Japan during the 1960s as well, has been even more rapid than growth in the United States.[3] International trade among industrialized countries has skyrocketed. Tariffs have been reduced substantially in successive rounds of cautious but productive negotiations, with virtually none of the harmful effects that high-tariff advocates of the 1920s feared and with benefits to all from the increased volume of world trade. Private foreign investment has also increased, been unevenly distributed, and remained a source of controversy.

During the cold war era, severe restrictions on East-West trade were introduced under the leadership of the United States. This nation was much more successful, however, in persuading itself of the dangers and evils of trade with communist countries than it was in persuading others. Allies objected to the wide range of goods that the United States considered of strategic importance and began building up peaceful trade as soon as they detected the slightest thaw in the cold war, if not as an inducement to a thaw. The U.S. Congress has been reluctant to see the restrictions eased and eager to punish those engaged in trade with "the enemy." It has regularly used foreign aid legislation for this purpose. Trade between the communist and noncommunist world has nevertheless increased, and

2. In constant prices, the rise would of course be less spectacular. At 1958 prices, the GNP of the United States doubled rather than tripled between 1950 and 1968, rising from $355 billion to $707 billion. *Economic Report of the President Transmitted to the Congress January 1969, Together with the Annual Report of the Council of Economic Advisers* (1969), p. 228.

3. For an explanation, see Edward F. Denison, assisted by Jean-Pierre Poullier, *Why Growth Rates Differ: Postwar Experience in Nine Western Countries* (Brookings Institution, 1967).

the United States has failed, for what it has heretofore regarded as good and sufficient reasons, to share proportionately in the increase.

The United States, once thought to be suffering from a persistent tendency toward balance-of-payments surpluses, with resultant dollar shortages in the rest of the world, has been suffering instead from persistent balance-of-payments deficits. The deficits are widely felt to be a manifestation of a basic disequilibrium which requires correction. Certain situations that would be regarded as disequilibriums calling for adjustment among separate countries, however, are not so regarded when they occur among regions within a large country. A new view is gaining ground among analysts of international capital markets. As reported by a pioneering economist in this field:

> If the intermediary services which the United States has provided to the rest of the world are an important ingredient of the rest of the world's economic growth, then continuation of the liquidity deficit of the United States is important to sustain that growth. Continuation of that deficit, however, is inconsistent with the combination of (a) the present international monetary system, and (b) the present notions of monetary authorities and most economists about what constitutes "equilibrium" in international payments.[4]

Wider recognition of the role the United States plays as a world financial intermediary would greatly reduce fears about the liquidity deficit in the U.S. balance of payments and might weaken one of the inhibitions on foreign aid.

Awareness that the international monetary system, like so many other national and international mechanisms, is inadequate for the world of today has been slow to bear fruit in terms of reform of the system. After four years of intensive negotiations, a new facility, based on special drawing rights (SDRs) in the International Monetary Fund, has been created without, however, the connecting link

---

4. Walter S. Salant, "Capital Markets and the Balance of Payments of a Financial Center," in William Fellner, Fritz Machlup, Robert Triffin, and others, *Maintaining and Restoring Balance in International Payments* (Princeton University Press, 1966), p. 192. Salant defines financial intermediaries as those who "not only perform the brokerage function of bringing the savers and capital-formers together but are also willing to provide cash or other short-term claims to savers and to buy (and hold) the securities which capital-formers are willing to issue" (p. 179).

between reserve creation and development assistance that could have been forged. To supplement existing reserve assets, $9.5 billion worth of SDRs will be activated during the three-year period beginning January 1, 1970.[5]

The growth of multinational enterprises, a phenomenon of foreign investment among industrialized countries, is making it harder and harder to identify the national origins of goods, funds, and services. When a company is incorporated in one country, gets its finance from another, uses the money to build capital equipment in a third country, imports raw materials from a fourth, and sells substantial portions of the product in various countries, including the one in which it is incorporated, it becomes difficult—and irrelevant to anything that is economically rational—to allocate the various parts of its operations to the national accounts and balances of payments of individual countries.[6] Traditional concern about these matters, in the industrialized countries at least, is therefore being superseded by interest in international control of enterprises that appear to escape national control.

In the United States, commercial policy, monetary and investment policy, and foreign aid policy have tended to be the provinces of different U.S. government officials, operating under different mandates, through different agencies. (The United States in this respect is not alone.) Aid, in a sense, has been the "soft option," necessary in part because of reluctance to make fundamental changes in other areas of policy. As congressional resistance to aid appropriations has mounted, the soft option has become hard. The hard options, however, have not become noticeably softer.

Until the mid-1960s, the United States, thanks to its phenomenally productive agricultural sector, was well equipped to meet many aid requirements with a form of assistance—food aid—politically popular in the United States. Agricultural development lagged ominously in the low-income countries, but by 1968 the beginnings of an agricultural breakthrough were detectable in some of the key less developed areas. The probable result will be diminishing requirements

5. See also Chapter 9.
6. Paraphrased from a memorandum to the author by Walter S. Salant.

for food aid but sharply increased requirements for fertilizers, tractors, and other items politically less appealing to the Congress and the public as aid than food for the hungry.[7]

The United States, which was a trailblazer in the foreign aid field, is now only one of some two dozen nations in the foreign aid business. All of the rich and most of the middle-income noncommunist countries now have foreign aid programs. So do Russia, China, and other communist countries, as well as a number of the less developed countries themselves. The various bilateral programs began with quite different and mutually inconsistent rationales: maintaining historic ties with colonies and associated areas that had gained their independence, achieving international respectability, extending political influence, winning new markets, paving the way for private investment, or helping the needy.

Although national objectives continue to differ and different groups within each nation at different times justify foreign aid on different grounds, a growing convergence in the long-range objectives of the principal free-world donors is detectable. In virtually all the aid-giving countries, foreign aid has been institutionalized through the establishment of a department or ministry in the central government. A public responsibility has been accepted and the ministries are manned by a new brand of professionals. These professionals, and others as well, have found glaring weaknesses in some of the earlier rationales for their work.

In the World Bank, the UN Development Program, the Development Assistance Committee of the Organisation for European Cooperation and Development, and at other gatherings at which the professional corps and their political chieftains meet, they find themselves under pressure to harmonize their views. Development, economic, social, and civic, of low-income countries that are seriously interested in modernization is becoming the agreed objective of national and international efforts. Because the convergence on this objective results in part from the elimination through trial and error of other aid objectives, the political force of the current international consensus is in certain respects weaker than that of the national con

7. See also Chapter 3.

sensus behind earlier efforts. Nevertheless, nations like to live up to their rhetoric, and their rhetoric gradually influences their performance. Professions of devotion to the cause of development help promote the cause.[8]

Less than half, perhaps not more than 40 percent, of the $130 billion in overseas grants and loans made by the U.S. government since the close of World War II has been devoted to development. American aid has contributed to the substantial, indeed remarkable, economic improvement that has taken place in the less developed world since 1950.[9] Despite the progress made, there is widespread dissatisfaction. Rapid population growth has reduced the rate of improvement in per capita income and welfare to modest proportions. Defense is almost everywhere an increasingly greedy competitor for available resources. Ministates, ill equipped to survive as nations, raise the flag of independence and join the queue for foreign aid. Larger sums are needed to pay interest and amortization charges on previously received loans. Aspirations continue to escalate and run dangerously ahead of achievements.

The communications revolution both facilitates and handicaps the development drive. Communication satellites, television, motion pictures, jet flights to and from international conferences on every conceivable subject, and above all the transistor radio mean that anything dramatic or important that takes place anywhere in the world is known instantly everywhere in the world. Modernization can be, and is being, accelerated, but so is frustration.

The American Domestic Scene: Poverty at Home Becomes a Major Issue

The speedy reconversion of the American economy without major unemployment after World War II confounded hostile critics of the country. The United States appeared to be a model of economic efficiency and political stability—gradually integrating the diverse ele-

8. See also Chapter 2 and Robert E. Asher, "How to Succeed in Foreign Aid Without Really Trying," in John D. Montgomery and Arthur Smithies (eds.), *Public Policy*, Vol. 13 (Harvard University Press, 1964).

9. See Chapter 4.

ments in its population, capable of providing jobs for all and thereby eliminating poverty at home, united about its mission abroad.

The pockets of poverty that remained were thought of (by those who thought of them at all) as subject to elimination through the continuation and expansion of welfare programs begun in the 1930s. The pockets swelled as a result of the mechanization of agriculture and a massive migration of displaced blacks and whites from rural to urban areas. A simultaneous movement of middle- and upper-income whites from the cities to the suburbs resulted in black ghettos in all the larger cities. The optimism of the 1950s evaporated and poverty at home became a political issue during the 1960s.

In the inflationary terminology of the day, the United States envisaged itself as engaged in a two-front "war on poverty," which it was fighting at home and abroad, with a rising priority demanded for the domestic front and remarkably little effort being made to apply the lessons learned on one front to the other. Compared to the efficiency and ingenuity with which this country mobilizes its resources for military purposes, its attacks on the poverty problem are puny affairs, long on rhetoric and short on performance. My purpose in the ensuing relevant digression, however, is not to draw the easy invidious comparison between massive military and modest nonmilitary efforts. It is rather to draw attention to the domestic and international sides of the nonmilitary campaigns and to ask whether the divergence between them should be as broad as it appears to be.

The mountains of literature on economic development and foreign aid are replete with references to remedies of the past—to agricultural extension services, vocational education, cooperatives, hybrid corn, and the like. They are, however, singularly devoid of references to what we have learned, and are learning today, from the civil rights struggle and the domestic war on poverty which might be applicable in the international arena, and vice versa.

The promotion of economic growth and social change abroad has been the province of foreign policy specialists, development economists, and a heterogeneous crew of technicians in the Agency for International Development and predecessor agencies, the State Department, and the international divisions of certain other agencies.

The federal agencies most directly involved in the war on poverty at home have been the Office of Economic Opportunity (OEO), the Departments of Health, Education, and Welfare, Housing and Urban Development, Labor, and Agriculture. Although Sargent Shriver, former director of the Peace Corps, served as the first head of the OEO, on the whole the people concerned with the problems of Detroit, Newark, Harlem, Watts, and rural Mississippi communicate but little with the people concerned with the Alliance for Progress or with development assistance for India, Pakistan, and Nigeria.[10]

Parallels between the revolutions of rising expectations or frustrations at home and abroad can be overdrawn. Yet the antipoverty, civil rights, black-power movement in the United States and the struggle of the less developed countries for a place in the international firmament have enough in common to warrant calling attention to certain similarities and differences.

At home, black leadership, at least until recently, has sought integration into the American community. The less developed countries have sought integration into a nascent international community. Both ask an end to second-class citizenship, a better chance to earn a livelihood and educate their children, to acquire dignity and status, to own more of the means of production, to speak up and be heard. Both think of themselves as condemned by persons of another, paler hue to live in a world they never made, under arrangements that perpetuate their subordinate status. Gunnar Myrdal, however, has argued that neither the blacks in the United States nor the less developed countries of Asia, Africa, and Latin America are being exploited so much as they are being bypassed. With modern technology and its sharply decreasing demands for unskilled and semiskilled labor and for illiterate or semiliterate personnel, a superfluous "underclass" is being created.[11]

The underdeveloped at home and abroad also suffer because of a

10. The OEO's Job Corps is to some extent modeled on the Peace Corps. An Associated Press dispatch of Dec. 1, 1967, mentions an experiment in which six former members of the Job Corps had been sent overseas as Peace Corps volunteers. Officials of the Peace Corps described the program as "successful even beyond our original hopes" (*New York Times*, Dec. 3, 1967).

11. Gunnar Myrdal, *Challenge to Affluence* (Pantheon, 1963), pp. 34–39.

widespread tendency among more fortunate people to confuse the past with the present and the exceptional with the average. Critics of the domestic poverty program sometimes argue that, because the Irish or the Jews or the Poles or some other immigrant group managed to overcome its initial handicaps without federal and state assistance, the underprivileged of today could do the same if they worked harder, studied more, spent less, and had fewer babies. Like-minded critics of foreign aid point to Canada, Sweden, and other countries that have achieved high standards of living without foreign aid.

Critics with less interest in historical analogy assert that, because particular individuals with slum backgrounds have attained well-deserved eminence in contemporary America without the benefit of comprehensive welfare legislation, others could too, if they were so inclined. The parallel argument in foreign aid is that, because Malaysia or Mexico or some other country on one of the less developed continents is doing better with almost no aid than nearby nations that have received generous amounts, aid is unnecessary and can be ended. With millions of slum dwellers in the United States and with ninety or so less developed countries in Asia, Africa, and Latin America, there are bound to be exceptions in both groups; they prove very little about the policies appropriate in the average case.

By historical standards, both the black minority at home and the less developed countries abroad have in fact made remarkable progress in recent years. But man does not live by historical standards alone. Dissatisfaction, disenchantment, and xenophobia are rampant.

Time is a critical factor. Feelings of frustration can cause the frustrated to abandon integration as a goal and nonviolence as a technique. As Americans should have learned by now, programs that would have been acclaimed at one moment in history will be attacked as inadequate, ineffective, and insulting a few years later—if the psychological moment for adopting them has been allowed to pass.

Token efforts will not eradicate poverty; comprehensive, multifaceted programs are needed to foster appreciable improvements in the situation. Instant development is impossible, but a century of gradualism will be unacceptable. No single nostrum, whether better schools, decent housing, vocational education, birth control, work relief, locally owned business enterprises, or armed revolt, will do the trick. The difficulties of functioning at home through state and local governments that are out of touch with slum dwellers and hostile to reform have their analogue in the difficulties of working through unrepresentative national and local power structures abroad. How to bridge the communications gap, how to evoke popular participation in constructive development efforts, how to get through "to the people," are problems everywhere.

Some of the progress that has been achieved has exacerbated tensions. At home, part of the black community has profited dramatically from two decades of civil rights legislation and has entered the mainstream of American life. In the process, it has widened the gap separating the successful part of the community from the masses who feel untouched by the measures thus far adopted and increasingly ambivalent toward integration as a goal. Similarly, in many less developed countries, a new elite corps is becoming increasingly isolated from the local population it purports to lead, an elite comprised of political leaders who have acquired power and influence at home and attend international conferences abroad, of upper-level bureaucrats who deal chiefly with foreigners, of generals who were corporals a few years ago, and of entrepreneurs who have struck it rich.

Unlike the poverty-stricken at home, the poverty-stricken abroad are not a minority group. They constitute the overwhelming majority of mankind. This, in my view, underscores the peril of ignoring their needs. Some analysts may conclude that, so long as the disinherited remain poor and weak, numbers are irrelevant and the peril is virtually nonexistent. Others, like me, shudder at the prospect of a world in which most nations and most people, disregarded by what they think of as the power structure, become alienated and hostile. A valid question in either event is how much the United States, with 6 percent of the world's population and something over one-third of its GNP, can reasonably be expected to do.

The less developed countries cannot readily be accommodated through established political processes. The United States government exists, world government does not. The responsibility of the richest country in the world for warring on poverty at home is self-evident and confirmed in numerous laws and regulations. Its responsibility for coming to the aid of a multitude of poor countries is by no means equally self-evident and accordingly lacks legal buttressing.

Building a great society at home will pose a heavy claim on available resources and inevitably complicate the task of providing the wherewithal for promoting development abroad. Nevertheless, the direction of domestic progress can provide important clues for new directions in foreign aid. At home, society has been moving away from the harsh spirit of the Elizabethan poor laws, away from detailed surveillance of the recipients' private lives, away from distinctions between "worthy" and "unworthy" eligibles based on highly subjective judgments, and away from relief in kind rather than in cash. It has been moving toward fresh opportunities for paid employment, toward broader participation in drawing up the ground rules under which both assistance and employment are provided, toward uniform national standards in place of sharply varying local standards, and toward income maintenance via social security payments, negative income taxes, guaranteed annual incomes, and so forth. Are parallel new directions in foreign aid imperative, desirable, or fraught with danger?

CHAPTER TWO

Rationale for Development Assistance

THE FUNDAMENTALLY CHANGED domestic and international environment means that virtually all the familiar geopolitical moorings of U.S. foreign policy have become unhitched. What for years seemed axiomatic now seems dubious, if not false. John F. Kennedy may be the last President who could, without creating a credibility gap, maintain that "we in this country ... are—by destiny rather than choice—the watchmen on the walls of world freedom."[1]

The interventionist policy articulated in the Truman Doctrine in 1947 and widely supported within the United States for two decades thereafter found what appears to be its final fateful expression in Vietnam. At the deepest point of its involvement in the less developed world, the United States began to question most seriously the rationale for any real involvement. The arguments that for twenty years gave the greatest immediacy and urgency to the case for foreign aid—the communist threat, the essentiality of friends and allies, the need for continued access to vital raw materials, the economic benefits obtainable through increased trade, and the political dividends to be

1. *Public Papers of the Presidents of the United States, John F. Kennedy ... 1963,* remarks prepared for delivery at the Trade Mart in Dallas, Nov. 22, 1963 (1964), p. 894.

reaped in terms of peace and democracy—have lost much of their force.

Communism now seems a less contagious disease than when, according to the domino theory, its presence on one side of a frontier was believed deadly also to the population on the other side of that frontier. Forward military bases have become less valuable to the United States. Military pacts that harness a mouse to an elephant do not add noticeably to the stability, strength, and security of the elephant. Nor is the proximity of the elephant always reassuring to the mouse; the willingness and capacity of outside powers to safeguard the security of their underdeveloped allies and exert a sustained, beneficent influence on their evolution are doubted. The exhaustion of domestic resources that would make the United States heavily dependent on distant sources of supply appears less imminent today, in the age of atomic energy, plastics, synthetic fibers, and other substitutes for internationally traded raw materials, than it did only yesterday. Mounting evidence of hunger, malnutrition, poverty, and widespread discontent within the United States has changed America's image of itself and raised fresh doubts about the propriety of mitigating poverty abroad when so much remains to be done at home.[2]

While some of the earlier arguments have lost force, others have gained adherents, with the result that a program of sorts—battered, barnacle-encrusted, and truncated—remains in being. Let us review then some of the argumentation that has been employed, concentrating primarily on the rationale most applicable to the world of the 1970s and bearing in mind the pluralism of contemporary society and the relevance of value systems in determining priorities.

In a pluralistic society, different people will support or oppose a policy at different times for different reasons or combinations of reasons. While the intensity with which views are held and the positions of the holders in the policy-making process are extremely germane, a broad measure of popular support is usually needed to sustain a policy. At the same time, agreement on the details of a rationale is not essential and is probably unobtainable. The legislator may feel

2. I am indebted to my friend and former Brookings colleague, Robert H. Johnson, for much of the three foregoing paragraphs.

obliged to look at foreign aid in traditional what's-in-it-for-us terms. On the other hand, the political, economic, and strategic considerations that seem extremely important to the legislator may be less persuasive than simple humanitarianism to the average citizen. He may favor helping the poor because they are hungry and needy but have considerable difficulty understanding that, in order to serve the national interest, helping them should help us as much as, if not more than, it helps them.

As John Pincus has said:

> The quest for a valid rationale for aid or concessions is ultimately insoluble when we limit our analysis to "objective" considerations, and forgo any resort to questions of values. . . . Ethical considerations, uncomfortable though they may be in a power-centered world, are underlying elements of North-South economic relations. . . . They are as real as any other factor in world politics, although more erratic in their influence on events. We cannot and should not rewrite economic analysis as a theory of social justice. But views of justice permeate and shape economic and political systems. Once the analysis is done, stubborn issues of equity remain.[3]

My own contribution to the quest for a rationale is embodied principally in a pamphlet I wrote in 1966 for the National Planning Association. In it I discussed at some length the considerations which led me to conclude that more rapid development of the low-income world would affirmatively serve the long-term interest, or interests, of the United States. Writing today, I want not only to draw on my earlier discussion but also to take advantage of the contributions to the formulation of a rationale made by others in more recent writings.[4]

---

3. John Pincus, *Trade, Aid and Development: The Rich and Poor Nations* (McGraw-Hill, 1967), pp. 13–14.

4. See Robert E. Asher, *International Development and the U.S. National Interest*, National Planning Association, Planning Pamphlet 124 (1967); Pincus, *Trade, Aid and Development*, especially pp. 7–40; Ronald Steel, *Pax Americana* (Viking, 1967), especially pp. 253–70; Theodore Geiger, "Why Have a U.S. Foreign Aid Effort?" in *Looking Ahead*, Vol. 16 (January 1969); Max F. Millikan, "The United States and Low-Income Countries," in Kermit Gordon (ed.), *Agenda for the Nation* (Brookings Institution, 1968), pp. 509–48; Roy J. Bullock, *Staff Memorandum on What to Do About Foreign Aid*, House Committee on Foreign Affairs, 91 Cong. 2 sess. (1969); and Patricia W. Blair, "The Dimension of Poverty," in *International Organization*, Vol. 23 (Summer 1969).

Security as a Rationale

During the 1950s, as noted in Chapter 1, foreign aid was provided principally under the Mutual Security Act of 1951 as amended, and justified primarily as a national security measure needed to strengthen allies and to build up low-income countries so that they would be less vulnerable to communist invasion or takeover. During the 1960s, the long-term security argument remained a basic staple of the official rationale, but the definition of security changed with new perceptions of the nature of the East-West conflict, the U.S. role in world affairs, and the ambitions of the less developed countries for sophisticated weaponry, and with the accumulation of experience concerning the behavior of less developed countries. Security arguments will doubtless play a role also in the 1970s but will probably shade off still further from their strictly military connotations toward broadly political reasons.

Initially, economic aid was often the down payment on a military alliance with a less developed country. America wanted allies. The less developed country presumably wanted the protection and assistance of the United States, though not necessarily for the same reasons that the United States wanted it as an ally. Through its network of alliances, the United States did secure foreign bases in far-off lands, which could be used as points of concentration for U.S. military forces and for intelligence gathering. It also secured some additional combat troops of other nationalities to fight in Korea and Vietnam.

The case for military bases in less developed countries, whatever strength it may once have had, is clearly less convincing in an age of intercontinental ballistic missiles, Polaris submarines, and spy satellites than it was before their invention. Although the United States may still want and need allies, its own military security can no longer be said to depend heavily on formal alliances with preindustrial societies.

A corollary security argument of the 1950s was the falling dominoes analogy. The Soviet threat was viewed by the United States as worldwide in scope but greatest to nations on the periphery of the Soviet empire and mainland China. Each weak country in the region, it was argued, must be aided economically and militarily, "because the fall of that country would make it easier for Communism to triumph somewhere else, and each country would be more costly for the West to defend."[5]

Others questioned whether, from the point of view of the military security of the West itself, the front line needed to be drawn at such a distant point and any breach thereof considered militarily so significant. "If the communizing of a half-dozen countries is of little importance to Western military defense, then the military security arguments for opposing the fall of dominoes are unlikely to be impressive. On the other hand, the political arguments for bracing the dominoes may be persuasive and ultimately dominant."[6]

The potency of nationalism in less developed countries, the persistence of their quest for an independent niche in the world, and other well-known factors combined to discredit the falling dominoes argument. Although the dominoes are less of a pushover than was anticipated, it is not equally clear that there is no communist threat or that the Soviet Union and mainland China have no interest in picking up bits of real estate at bargain prices.

Another series of security arguments (or political arguments) is based on the risk to the United States of being an island of prosperity in a tidal wave of misery. For a while, as Arnold Toynbee has said, the chief penalty may be the moral isolation that this type of prosperity brings. But engulfment is also a risk. In an age of instant communication, substantial disparities in income and status can be politically tolerable so long as those at the lower end of the spectrum have before them a reasonable prospect of improvement. If they can expect some alleviation of their own lot and more dramatic improvement in the next generation—so that their children will be better fed, better housed, better clad, and better educated than they—they may not become unduly excited about the level of living in the United States. But (according to one line of argument) if the hopes and

5. Pincus, *Trade, Aid and Development*, p. 9.
6. *Ibid.*

dreams of people in poor countries appear doomed to frustration while people in rich countries grow steadily richer, the prospects for peace will be threatened.

If the dividing line between rich and poor countries is also a color line separating the white-skinned minority from those of other hues, the threat will be increased. If it explodes, the poor will enter the fray with inferior equipment, more primitive technology, and fewer resources, but with little to lose except their lives. They may not win, but they might succeed in pulling the house down around their ears.

Since neither the more developed nor the less developed world is monolithic, Armageddon, in the opinion of most prophets, is unlikely to arrive in quite this way. Less developed countries, with different resource endowments, different leadership, and different aspirations, will not simultaneously reach the boiling point. When in a given area the peace is shattered, the violence is as likely to be directed against domestic leadership or neighboring countries as it is against the United States.

Not even the largest of the less developed countries now has the resources to threaten directly the security of the United States. Several of them, however, have the capacity to acquire significant nuclear capabilities before long. Some authorities, therefore, argue that the security interests of the United States require not only an effective nonproliferation treaty but also positive programs to prevent nations that might acquire nuclear capabilities from feeling beleaguered or alienated. Development assistance, sensitively administered, can serve this purpose.[7]

Well before nuclear weapons in the arsenals of less developed countries became a practical possibility, and before the term "alienation" was widely enough understood to be employed in general literature, a parallel argument for development assistance as a peace-producing measure was advanced. Rather small-scale local conflicts in the less developed world, it was said, could draw additional parties into the conflict. The struggle would escalate and might lead to general conflagration. Efforts to build national consensus around

7. Millikan, "The United States and Low-Income Countries," pp. 513–14.

constructive programs for economic and social development were recommended as an important long-run protection, though not a guarantee, against violence born of frustration with the slow pace of development, violence containing within it the seeds of a major war.[8]

Awareness of the risks of escalation, however, serves as a restraining influence at least on the major powers, particularly since they have also learned that not every square mile of underdeveloped territory that shifts its international allegiance is a damaging loss to the side from which it shifts. This decreases the possibility that local conflicts will trigger a global holocaust. The decreased possibility, in turn, weakens the case for development assistance on military security grounds and encourages a more critical look at the nature of the links between poverty and war, or absence of poverty and presence of peace.

Harking back to Tocqueville's study of the French Revolution, Theodore Geiger reminds his readers that

the likelihood of violent social upheavals is greatest not when exploitation and repression are greatest but when, following such a period, the condition of the subordinate groups begins to improve. The gains already achieved heighten the sense of frustration and impatience at the slowness and difficulty of further progress. At the same time, the reforms already conceded, voluntarily or perforce, by the ruling élite weaken its privileged position, political power and self confidence.[9]

He goes on to suggest that the circumstances in which a country will engage in aggression depend

not simply upon the extent of its economic progress but more importantly on the character of its institutions and values, particularly the motivations of its leadership groups, upon its internal problems and pressures, and upon the relationships and opportunities in the world political situation.

For these reasons, although a correlation does exist between economic growth and peaceful and constructive international behavior, it is low, tenuous and very long term. . . . Influence designed directly to affect the character of institutions and values is, by its nature, potentially much

8. Max F. Millikan, "Why Not Foreign Aid?" *Sun-Times* (Chicago), Dec. 23, 1962.

9. "Why Have a U.S. Foreign Aid Effort?" p. 3.

more important than [influence designed only to step up the rate of economic growth]....For, what is decisive for the outcome of socio-cultural change in Asia, Africa and Latin America is not economic growth *per se* but the kinds of institutions, values, attitudes, and behavioral norms that evolve in those regions.[10]

Thus the case for development promotion, to the extent that it rests on security grounds, should take into consideration the capacity of the United States and other sources of aid to influence the character of institutions and values as well as their capacity to raise gross national product in low-income areas. It need no longer be based heavily on the fear of imminent communist takeover in particular low-income areas, the necessity of maintaining foreign bases, or the assumption that the outcome of a particular local dispute is in itself of transcendent importance to the United States. This change should make it easier to reconcile security considerations, which during the 1950s seemed overriding, with longer-term economic, social, and political objectives.[11] Autocratic regimes, uninterested in a decent sharing of the fruits of productivity increases, a functioning system of justice, and a voice for the voiceless in domestic decision making, need not be aided simply because they might otherwise leave the "free world" and fall forever into the hands of a monolithic enemy.

The security rationale for development assistance today would vary from country to country and, in an overall sense, would rest on the belief, the hope, and the faith that (1) the frustrations of poverty and the bitterness against the rich that such frustrations engender will ultimately be decreased rather than exacerbated by programs to reduce the poverty and the sense of injustice; (2) better living conditions—a growing stake in the world as it is—together with new attitudes and institutions, will gradually decrease racial tensions and provide a less fertile breeding ground for demagogues; (3) poor countries will at least in some instances be diverted from the foreign adventures, irredentist pursuits, and international posturing that the absence of domestic achievements might stimulate; and (4) develop-

10. *Ibid.* See also Theodore Geiger, *The Conflicted Relationship* (McGraw-Hill, 1967), pp. 225–26.
11. Millikan, "The United States and Low-Income Countries," p. 515.

ment, though it increases the overall capacities of low-income countries, including their capacity to intervene elsewhere, improves their power to protect themselves against assault from abroad and subversion at home, and should also enhance their long-term interest in machinery for the peaceful adjudication of international disputes.

Economic Rationale

The economic rationale for a U.S. commitment to the development of poor countries has been widely publicized. Basically, it is that development is good business. It widens the market for American exports. It provides new opportunities for productive private investments. It builds more promising, lower-cost sources of supply for imports.

Poor countries makes poor markets. Better markets will help the United States in two ways: directly, by buying more of its exports; and indirectly, by buying more in third countries which, in turn, may be able to take more American products. Insofar as imports are concerned, the United States can use a wide variety from many sources and would prefer the sources to be reasonably secure and stable. Poor countries tend to be unreliable sources for a very limited range of imports—typically one or two primary products that undergo sizable year-to-year fluctuations in price.

Numerous studies have been made to demonstrate that rich countries make better customers and better markets than poor ones. Unfortunately, one moral which can be drawn from this is that a given investment in expanding trade with countries that are already rich may pay off more rapidly and readily than the same sum invested in expanding trade with a country that is poor—and the investment in the first instance is more likely to be made voluntarily by nongovernmental sources.

Japan was not a rich country in 1950 and its foreign trade amounted to only $2 billion. By 1960, it was approaching $10 billion. By 1967, thanks to the spectacular growth of the Japanese economy (helped by $2.7 billion in American economic aid between 1945 and

1963), the level of Japanese foreign trade exceeded $20 billion, and Japan had become the largest overseas trading partner of the United States as well as the world's largest market for U.S. farm products.

In Taiwan, exports averaged about $110 million per year from 1951 to 1956, while annual imports were double this amount. The excess of imports over exports averaged $107 million per year, of which approximately 90 percent was covered by U.S. aid and less than 10 percent was offset by private investment. After 1956, Taiwan's exports spurted.[12] By 1965, they exceeded $500 million, and by 1967, $750 million. Taiwan's principal trading partner was Japan, and the United States ranked second.

The story in Korea is similar: only $79 million earned from exports of goods and services as recently as 1957 and $117 million in 1960, but $290 million in 1965 and $643 million in 1967.

The argument that increased international trade will be both a corollary and a consequence of economic development is almost unassailable. It will be noted, however, that although the rise in exports of Taiwan and Korea (and consequently of their capacity to import) is dramatic and over a long enough time period will substantially exceed the amount of aid received, this is not yet the case.

In a broad sense, increased international trade serves the national interests of the trading nations. Most nations unquestionably want to step up their earnings from exports and, though more ambivalent about imports, will benefit from increased imports of things they do not or cannot produce at home as cheaply as they can buy in world markets. The huge U.S. market is far more important to the less developed countries, however, than their national markets, individually, are to the United States.

If a higher level of trade with the less developed countries serves the American national interest, it is not because of its income effects in the United States, but primarily because various political and social crises to which the United States cannot remain indifferent may be somewhat more easily resolved in the context of a broadly shared expansion of the world economy. Furthermore, the additional busi-

12. Neil H. Jacoby, *U.S. Aid to Taiwan: A Study of Foreign Aid, Self-Help, and Development* (Praeger, 1966), pp. 97–99 and 292.

ness and jobs resulting from a higher level of U.S. exports may be extremely important to particular groups of exporters, workers, and farmers. (On the other hand, increased imports by the United States, however much they may be appreciated by American consumers, will threaten or appear to threaten the jobs or sources of income of some domestic interests and will therefore not be universally welcomed.)

Finally, a higher level of production and trade in the low-income world can enhance its interest in workable ground rules for the conduct of international trade and international financial transactions. Countries with weak, undiversified, inefficient economies make feeble, quixotic partners in the network of international institutions upon which, in this interdependent world, all nations, including the United States, rely increasingly.

With economic growth, less developed countries ought to become more responsible partners. The need to reconcile diverse domestic interests will make it harder for them to take extreme positions in international negotiations and they will have more to lose by disruptive tactics that jeopardize the flow of trade and investment.

According to Seymour Martin Lipset and others, more of the conditions favorable to democracy come into being as income increases and is more widely shared. A growing middle class "tempers conflict by rewarding moderate and democratic parties and penalizing extremist groups." An immense variety of organizations that serve as countervailing sources of power is spawned: labor unions, farm groups, chambers of commerce, trade associations, cooperatives, and professional societies.[13]

Samuel Huntington agrees that a large middle class, like widespread affluence, is a moderating force in politics, but believes that the creation of a middle class is often a highly destabilizing event.

Typically, the first middle-class elements to appear on the social scene are intellectuals with traditional roots but modern values. They are then

13. Seymour Martin Lipset, *Political Man: The Social Bases of Politics* (Doubleday, 1960), pp. 66–67. See also Gabriel A. Almond and James S. Coleman (eds.), *The Politics of Developing Areas* (Princeton University Press, 1960), especially Coleman's concluding chapter.

followed by the gradual proliferation of civil servants and army officers, teachers and lawyers, engineers and technicians, entrepreneurs and managers. The first elements of the middle class to appear are the most revolutionary; as the middle class becomes larger, it becomes more conservative.[14]

Thus there is no guarantee that economic improvement in the low-income countries will be accompanied by desirable social and political changes or, within a predictable time span, by economic benefits to the high-income countries commensurate with the cost of development assistance. Furthermore, it is by no means certain that self-sustaining, self-governing, increasingly prosperous peoples will be prepared to live harmoniously with themselves, their neighbors, or the United States. It does seem more likely than that frustrated, insecure, starving populations will do so.

Political Rationale

The idea that development assistance should have an early and obvious political payoff in winning friends for the United States is discredited but not dead.[15] More frequently put forward in recent years as the political justification for stimulating growth in the low-income world is the long-range "world order" argument: the improved international climate that should prevail in an expanding world economy and the stronger institutional underpinning that growth can provide for the peaceful conduct of world affairs. In this view, development assistance becomes a tool—one of several—for fashioning an international environment less likely to be divisive, polarized, and in other ways uncongenial to the United States. An environment in which the United States can calmly cultivate its own garden without having to worry about soil conditions, horticultural practices, or crop yields elsewhere has obvious attractions but must be dismissed as a nostalgic dream. The world is too much with us.

14. Samuel P. Huntington, *Political Order in Changing Societies* (Yale University Press, 1968), p. 289.
15. See, for example, Bullock, *Staff Memorandum on What to Do About Foreign Aid,* or almost any year's Senate or House hearings on foreign aid legislation.

Despite the power and persistence of nationalism, consciousness of the interdependence of nations and peoples is growing. Nevertheless, the institutional base for a better world order remains grossly inadequate.

If we can give substance to the fundamental idea that we are joined [with the new countries] in a constitutional endeavor to create a world order in which all peoples can find their separate identities, it should be possible for us to achieve that degree of integrity in our relations which will make it possible to avoid hypocrisy and to disagree at times without malice. Acculturation need no longer appear as a process in which some people take on the ways of others, but instead as one in which everyone is seeking to change and develop in order to build a better world community.[16]

Why give substance to this idea? "It is one thing to be in good physical or financial condition within an orderly and prosperous community, but quite another thing to be privileged by the wealth of one's possessions in surroundings of misery, ill-health, lack of public order, and widespread resentment."[17]

Counterarguments take two forms.

1. World community is a utopian goal, beautiful in the mind's eye, but as yet invisible even with a fairly powerful telescope. The role of development assistance in achieving it is tenuous at best. So long as we live in a world of sovereign states, the duty of the United States is to act in its own national interest, not in the interest of a nonexistent international community.

2. The world-order argument is usually linked with the idea of peaceful change, but what is needed in most less developed lands is revolutionary change. Revolutions are inherently disorderly affairs.

For the harsh facts we have yet to acknowledge are these: (1) in many countries of the underdeveloped world only revolutionary activity will rescue the populace from its unending misery, and (2) the United States has consistently opposed the kinds of revolutionary action that might

16. Lucian W. Pye, "The Foreign Aid Instrument: Search for Reality," in Roger Hilsman and Robert C. Good (eds.), *Foreign Policy in the Sixties* (Johns Hopkins Press, 1965), p. 112.

17. Arnold Wolfers, *Discord and Collaboration: Essays on International Politics* (Johns Hopkins Press, 1962), p. 75.

begin such a rescue operation. . . . What we call "economic development" is in truth little more than a holding action that has succeeded only in building up the dikes just enough to keep the mounting population from washing away everything, not a movement that has invested life with a new quality.[18]

The counterarguments in turn engender retorts such as: The case for the violent overthrow of authority was also good when Marx and Engels made it in 1848. It was defused in most of what is now the developed world by a series of reforms, individually modest and often almost imperceptible, but cumulatively successful in transforming the lives of virtually the whole of society. Development assistance can expedite a similar evolutionary process in the less developed countries. A policy of investment in a more peaceful, better-integrated world order as a long-range goal, moreover, is not fundamentally inconsistent with revolutions en route to that goal in countries unable to reach nonviolent accommodations with the forces of history.

A more immediate political rationale for development assistance than its effectiveness in promoting a new world order is simply the high priority given to development by most of the less developed world. Development is said to be the wave of the future and riding it is smarter than resisting it, letting it wash by, or commanding it to stand still. Despite formidable barriers to modernization, perceptible headway—enough to prevent aspirations from getting too far ahead of achievements—is supremely important to almost every one of the less developed countries.

Not only the United States but every other major power and many minor ones too now provide economic aid to low-income countries. Were it not for the prominent part the United States played in getting other high-income Western nations into—or deeper into—the development business, the continuation of these nations' programs would create a presumption that an American effort would serve the interests of the United States. As things stand, however, it may not quite be cricket first to have been instrumental in getting others into

---

18. Robert L. Heilbroner, "Making a Rational Foreign Policy Now," *Harper's Magazine* (September 1968), and *Congressional Record* (Sept. 18, 1968), pp. E8057–8060.

the development business and then to claim that, because they are there, the United States must also be there. Yet so long as other rich countries remain contributors to overseas development, they strengthen the belief that high-income countries have a political and moral obligation to help low-income countries.

Humanitarian Considerations

Closely related to the question of the type of world order the United States should seek among the divergent trends of recent years is the humanitarian argument for development assistance. Sometimes dismissed as soft-headed and irrelevant, it remains durable and potent. It involves justice and decency and the moral basis for leadership among nations.

The kind of inequality that exists between nations, the kind of grinding poverty that permeates so much of the world, are no longer tolerated within the borders of a modern, progressive nation-state. These torments are mitigated within a country like the United States, Great Britain, or Sweden by continuous transfers of wealth from the richer to the poorer citizens and from the richer areas to the poorer ones. Foreign aid is an extension of this process in a world that has become too small for fellow-feeling between man and man to stop at political frontiers.[19]

The rationale for attacking poverty is much the same at home and abroad, though better recognized domestically. The simple moral argument that the rich have an obligation to help the poor . . . is perhaps more compelling than it is fashionable to admit. And the connection between poverty and insecurity for the rich has been made frequently. While the urgency of attacking domestic poverty is easier for Americans to see— after all, *our* cities are burning—the argument on the international plane is still obvious enough. Basically, we must simply recognize that we are in the business of building a community, a sense of shared purpose and shared destiny, both at home and abroad. The central values of our civilization permit no less.[20]

19. "The Vienna Declaration on Cooperation for Development" (Vienna, Theodor Körner Foundation, July 1962; mimeographed), para. 2.
20. Blair, "The Dimension of Poverty," p. 683.

In a similar vein Barbara Ward has argued that "a sustained long-term economic strategy on the part of the West would have more than economic consequences. It would begin to institutionalize human solidarity and human compassion and underpin a world order with some claim to be called humane."[21]

Participation in international development programs is believed by many to be a necessary way of strengthening the moral claim of the United States to a position of world leadership, counteracting the isolation that tends to be the social and moral price of tremendous wealth, and helping the United States to live at peace with itself as well as with others. Given its traditions and ideals, the United States will find it hard to retain for itself the full fruits of its annual increases in output while the majority of mankind lives at the margin of subsistence.

The counterarguments are, in effect, that humanitarianism, admirable though it may be as a personal trait, has no permanent place in international relations, that compassion dwindles with distance, and that the less developed countries represent a bottomless pit into which the full resources of the United States could be poured with little visible effect other than the impoverishment of the United States. Roy Bullock says bluntly: "We should no longer endorse the position . . . that the developed countries have an obligation to share their resources with less fortunate nations."[22]

In its more elementary forms, the humanitarian appeal is simply a plea for the relief of suffering. A rationale based on the destitution of the recipients implies that aid is needed for consumption rather than investment. Only when it is conceded that relief is a palliative rather than a cure will the humanitarian appeal be transformed into an argument for the investments in agriculture, industry, and education that can help the receiving country overcome its poverty and move toward self-sustaining growth.

At this point, that fuzzy term "the national interest" comes more sharply into focus. So long as the problem is the sheer saving of the present generation of humanity, whether resident in Mexico or Albania, the national interest can be equated with a larger "international

21. "A Strategy for the Wealthy West," *SAIS Review* (Summer 1965), p. 9.
22. *Staff Memorandum on What to Do About Foreign Aid*, p. 7.

interest" that rises above geography, politics, or ideology. But with economic growth comes the economic, military, and political power that cannot be ignored in a rational assessment of either the national interest or the international interest. Economic growth in Mexico is certainly of higher priority to the United States in the short run, and probably in the long run, than economic growth in Albania or any other nation seemingly dedicated to the destruction of the United States or of the values it cherishes.

Humanitarians, however, recognize the resource limitation which makes it useless to spread assistance too thinly, and recognize also the obvious fact that no one feels equally well disposed toward the whole human race. Compassion moves in concentric circles. Empathy, the sense of community, and the compulsion to act are greatest for family and local community, strong for those living under the same flag, palpable for the inhabitants of nations that are not hostile, and feeble or nonexistent where hostile peoples are concerned. Such shadings in feeling are not inconsistent with a knowledge that the world is shrinking and that distinctions based on distance may blur with the passage of time.

Compassion, idealism, humanitarianism are more than personal traits. The collectivity of persons that constitutes a nation projects a national image which, as noted earlier in this chapter, is as "real" as any other factor in world politics. Though ideals are adopted for their own sake and not for their instrumental value, they can affect the distribution of world power. Throughout its history, the prestige and influence of the United States have depended on what the country stood for as well as on the strength of its economy and its military establishment. Its support for self-determination, for social justice, for political democracy, and for religious freedom has placed it in the mainstream of history and made it the lodestar of masses in the most faraway places.[23]

23. Power and prestige are far from synonymous. Prestige refers primarily to the attainment of a commanding position in men's minds and is a moral and intellectual achievement. Power implies some coercive authority and therefore depends more directly on armies, resources, technology, and the will to use them. As the exercise of power becomes more difficult and self-defeating, the maintenance of prestige and influence becomes more important. As Theodore Draper asked in *Encounter* in August 1968, "What is missing in the United States today? Is it power or influence?"

The national interest of the United States in a compatible and congenial world environment and its moral, humanitarian interest in the quality of life for the average man everywhere are said to come together in the growing American concern for the social and civic dimensions of the development process. The full potentials of human beings stand a better chance of realization in open societies in which all members have a voice in decision making and opportunity to advance without discrimination on account of caste, color, race, or creed. "Most Amercans share with many people abroad a faith that in the long run this multi-dimensional human development will greatly increase the prospects for a world environment of more open, more cooperative, and more liberated societies."[24]

The Whole versus the Parts

If on the home front one had to justify annually the whole concept of public investment in education, in agriculture, in social security, and in national defense, one would, I suspect, encounter grave difficulty in setting forth a fully convincing rationale. In matters of social policy, there appear to be no laws of physics: almost nothing is provable beyond doubt. Aid for less developed countries, examined de novo each year by the U.S. Congress, is a case in point.

Because so many of the propositions are not verifiable except over a very long period of time, agreement or disagreement with the various rationales is in part a matter of personal preference and individual value judgments. One of my friends has accordingly suggested that I conclude this chapter by saying quite simply that I favor aid basically because it pleases me to see poor people making economic gains in countries that I do not fear. It does please me, but I would like to suggest a further conclusion or two.

Only a lunatic would imply that propositions which are not provably true are probably false and should be abandoned. There are sizable kernels of truth in the security argument for development assistance—that widespread poverty and frustration represent a threat

24. Millikan, "The United States and Low-Income Countries," p. 519.

to the peace; in the economic argument—that development produces jobs, markets, trade, investment opportunities, and material benefits for virtually all concerned; in the political argument—that a broadly shared expansion of the world economy will contribute to a better-integrated political community with a greater stake in the peaceful resolution of conflict; and, above all, in the humanitarian argument—that aid is right and decent and that responsibility for the mitigation of poverty does not end at national shorelines.

Collectively, if not singly, these arguments may provide a more solid foundation for policy than the fact that it pleases me (and presumably others too) to see poor people make economic gains. The moral imperative is, I think, clearer than the U.S. national interest calculated in traditional, short-range terms. Fear, I suspect, has been overworked as a rationale.

While I much prefer the more positive approach, I am not repelled by the insurance salesman's argument that, though your house may never burn down, it is wise to take out fire insurance. The case for development assistance can be made analogously despite the impossibility of proving conclusively that outside aid is a sine qua non of development and that such development as may ensue will be worth the annual investment of 1 percent or some other fraction of the gross national product of the high-income countries. In other words, the risks involved in forcing the less developed countries to remain mired in poverty or to rise entirely by their bootstraps are real and difficult to reconcile with the sense of international community and decency the United States should (and I believe does) seek to foster. At the same time, the costs of providing assistance in the volume that can be used effectively are demonstrably bearable.

Aid, to be sure, is not the only way to prove the reality of America's long-term interest in the economic, social, and civic growth of the low-income world. It is an appropriate technique if (1) the resources that can be transferred via foreign aid are needed and can be put to effective use; (2) they can be supplied without denying other higher-priority claims on those same resources; (3) other techniques—for example, trade (with or without special concessions for low-income countries), private investment, cultural exchanges, or modifications of immigration and emigration policies—will not suffice or have been rejected; and (4) the aid technique does more than ease the consciences of the rich and make them feel more virtuous. It should stimulate the adoption of sensible policies in the aid-receiving nations and raise the level of available resources to a point more likely to provide a politically tolerable rate of development than would be provided in the absence of aid.

I believe these conditions are often enough fulfilled to justify the mounting of a sizable international development effort. Even the most convincing presentation of the general case for development assistance nevertheless begs the questions: How much? To whom? For how long? Some guidelines for responding to these questions will be brought out later in this study. Suffice it to say here that the program should be big enough to have some noticeable impact on the problem with which it purports to deal and suffice it to reiterate that nothing in this chapter is intended to imply that all poor countries are equally deserving or that their development will inevitably have beneficial and stabilizing effects at home or abroad. Development can provide the context in which a number of difficult problems become less difficult: the growing pie permits larger slices for everyone. But development is not a universal solvent for the ills of the world; some problems will almost certainly become more acute if and when power is more evenly distributed. Moreover, revolutions, counter-revolutions, hostility to erstwhile friends, folly in economic policy, inhumanity in social policy, and irrational acts as yet undreamed of will occur.

Yet I associate myself with Ronald Steel's conclusion:

The object of foreign aid is . . . to help alleviate human misery by aiding those who show a capacity to aid themselves, and by doing so to help create an international order where compassion will be joined to self-interest and where the poor may seek to join the rich rather than exterminate them. For those of us privileged to live in societies affluent beyond the imagination of most of mankind, foreign aid is not simply charity, but . . . as Oliver Wendell Holmes once said of taxes, our investment in civilization.[25]

25. *Pax Americana*, p. 270.

CHAPTER THREE

Aspects of the Development Process

FROM THE BEGINNING, informed people in the U.S. government were aware that development was a long-drawn-out, complex process which required thinking in terms of a generation or more rather than of a decade or an annual appropriation cycle. In their eagerness to contribute to speeding up the process and meeting other objectives of American foreign policy, there was an understandable tendency to overstate the gains that could be realized in the short term and to understate the uncertainties, the difficulties, and the setbacks being encountered. A series of panaceas in the form of "priorities" or "emphases" designed to overcome alleged "obstacles" and break particular "bottlenecks" was tried. Even when the new policies represented advances in dealing with current problems, the results were modest compared to what people had been led to expect. The progressive shattering of illusions contributed to the disenchantment that reached its peak—one fervently hopes—in the latter half of the 1960s.

Development Is More than Economic Growth

With due allowance for the primacy each professional accords to his profession as compared with all other professions, a slowly growing consensus about the nature of the revolution politely called "development" or "modernization" is detectable. Development is not a stage reached when per capita incomes attain some specified level, or after a particular list of obstacles has been overcome. It is a process—dynamic, pervasive, never ending, destructive as well as constructive. The essence of the process is the inculcation of new attitudes and ideas, of states of mind eager for progress, hospitable to change, capable of applying scientific approaches to an ever wider range of problems.

The rapidity with which the process unfolds depends far more on the will and capacity of the people of the underdeveloped country and the caliber of the economic, social, and political institutions they build than it does on natural resources or imported equipment and supplies. It depends on leaders who educate as well as agitate, and on followers who teach as well as learn. Communication between leaders and followers needs to be a two-way exchange, with a meaningful feedback from the people to their leaders. Popular participation in development programs appears to be essential to facilitate the learning process, to prevent unbridgeable urban-rural gaps, to enable inherited institutions to be transformed rather than replaced abruptly by unfamiliar, and therefore perhaps unworkable, transplanted institutions. As yet, the wish to develop is more widespread than the will, and not enough is known about how to translate the wish into the will.

Although gross national product (per capita as well as total), savings and investment rates, earnings from exports, and other economic indexes should move upward, modernization consists of more than maximizing these. A decent sharing of the increased wealth, the elimination of discrimination based on race, color, or creed, higher literacy rates, broader and better-informed participation in political life, and efficient and humane administration—these, too, are vitally important objectives of development.

Development can be studied as though it were distinct from other human processes, but

in the final analysis its goals are the goals of existence itself: to provide an opportunity for men to live fully human lives. . . . Definitions of development in terms of industrialization, urbanization, modernization, growth, maximization, or even of optimization are bad. It must be defined normatively. Lebret does this when he describes development as a coordinated series of changes, whether abrupt or gradual, from a phase of life perceived by a population and all of its components as being less human to a phase perceived as more human, generating various types of solidarity, both intranational and transnational, based not on homogeneity but on complementarity in the realms of culture and functions.[1]

Definitions such as this are in some respects troublesomely vague and raise numerous questions about whether life in certain societies usually classified as developed is any more "human" than it is in certain societies usually classified as less developed or underdeveloped. Just as in Chapter 2 the quest for a valid rationale for development assistance appeared to me futile without resort to questions of value, so here the quest for a definition of development must, in my view, embrace normative judgments and ethical considerations.

In any event, the term "economic development," popular during the first postwar decade, is gradually being superseded by the more generic term "development" (without any qualifying adjectives) or by the somewhat less satisfactory term "modernization," both understood to mean economic, social, and political growth. For countries in the very early stages of development—traditional societies where more than 70 percent of the people are still on the land, where fewer than 30 percent are literate, where the birth rate runs from 40 to 50 births per 1,000 inhabitants per year, where life is truly at the margin of subsistence and man is at the mercy of the elements—modernization involves a top-to-bottom transformation of society. It means fundamental changes in traditional values, motivations, institutions, and patterns of behavior. It is a long-term job. At best, it will be an erratic, two-steps-forward, one-step-backward, one-step-sideways movement.

Nevertheless, the journey toward that El Dorado of less developed countries, self-sustaining growth, need not be as drawn out and costly in human terms as was the comparable journey for the now high-income, better-integrated nations of Western Europe and North America. Their experience, some of their resources, and other

1. Denis Goulet, "That Third World," *The Center Magazine*, Vol. 1 (Santa Barbara: Center for the Study of Democratic Institutions, September 1968), p. 55.

more recent experience can be drawn on to shorten the time span. On the other hand, higher rates of population increase, greater difficulty in favoring investment over consumption, rising aspirations, and better-equipped competitors make the job more difficult than it was a century ago. Political exigencies demand speed, but how rapid the modernization process can become without destroying its organic nature and internal balance remains unknown. It will differ from area to area.

In addition to the increased consensus regarding the general nature of the modernization process, there is greater understanding than there was in 1950 of the vast differences among the ninety or more low-income countries. Each nation is to an important extent in a class by itself, wending its own way toward the satisfaction of its material and psychic requirements, and dubiously aided by broad-brush policy prescriptions designed to cover simultaneously Brazil and Burundi, Costa Rica and Nepal, Zambia and India.

From the point of view of foreign aid, the critical period in the development process has been assumed to be a relatively short span of years during which, with outside help, the country will move from a period of virtual stagnation in per capita levels of living to a period of modest but sustainable increases. In the earliest portion of this phase, the primary requirement, insofar as foreign aid is concerned, is believed to be technical assistance. Though capital assistance may also be required, technical assistance will be vital if skills are to be improved, attitudes modified, and institutions transformed or established. As the country acquires the skills and institutions that enable it to help itself, its capacity to invest is likely to grow more quickly than its ability to save. Moreover, it will have to obtain from abroad the great bulk of the manufactured and semimanufactured goods it uses in establishing new industries and raising incomes. Consequently, its requirements for imports will rise rapidly and in advance of any corresponding increases in exports. In other words, the pressure on the balance of payments of a developing country tends to swell before it falls.

India is a prime example of this stage of development. It is strategically located. It has the largest population in the noncommunist world. It is committed to development. It is making measurable progress without abandoning its democratic institutions (though subjecting them to severe strain). Until 1968, it had not achieved any dramatic increase in export earnings. It has therefore been seriously strapped for foreign exchange. It bears an almost intolerable debt-servicing burden and remains the most poignant reminder of the less developed world's need for financial and commodity assistance from abroad.

As agriculture becomes more productive, however, and new industries are established and foreign tourists are attracted, less developed countries begin to earn more foreign exchange. Import requirements will not necessarily shrink; indeed they will in all probability continue to grow in volume and variety. As the country becomes better able to pay for the imports it needs, however, its balance-of-payments deficit should be reduced—provided, of course, that it maintains a realistic exchange rate and generally manages its resources prudently.

As soon as the country has demonstrated that it can grow at an overall rate of 5 to 6 percent per year while closing its balance-of-payments deficit, it is graduated from American foreign aid and welcomed into the alumni club. It obviously has reached some kind of milestone. But whether it makes sense to cut off American aid at this point is another question.

Some Implications for Foreign Aid Policy

A national product that is growing at the rate of 5 to 6 percent per year in real terms without exerting excessive pressure on the balance of payments can be reached (1) while the country is still at an appallingly low level of per capita income; (2) while the rate of increase in per capita income—roughly, the overall rate of increase in the national product minus the rate of population increase—is also very modest; (3) long before self-sufficiency in skills has been attained; and (4) when the country is still at a rudimentary stage in terms of social and civic development.

Taiwan and Iran are already members of the alumni club. Turkey,

Korea, and Pakistan are said to be within hailing distance of membership. Yet per capita income in Taiwan in 1965, the year it was graduated, was only $190. In Iran, it was $210. In Korea and Pakistan in 1965, it was estimated to be $120 and $90 respectively. As the conscience of the world is increasingly awakened and the interdependence of nations becomes clearer, will people be satisfied with policies that bring aid to an end before the recipient has crossed some kind of agreed poverty line? [2] Meanwhile, there seems unsustainable irony in cutting a Taiwan adrift while continuing a subsidy to Latin American nations with per capita incomes twice as great as Taiwan's. [3]

Moreover, a major current objective of development assistance, according to the executive branch, is to contribute to the creation of an international community of better-integrated, self-governing, self-supporting nations, respectful of human rights and fundamental freedoms. The integration of society in a nation comes late in the modernization process.

2. The per capita income figures are from the *World Bank Atlas of Per Capita Product and Population* (Washington: International Bank for Reconstruction and Development, 1966). I am well aware of the booby traps in international comparisons of per capita incomes but do not believe my basic point is invalidated: virtue, as exhibited through efficient use of available aid, should not be punished, and gross disparities in income will be politically tolerable only if the minimum levels permit what might be called a twentieth-century level of life. Even within a single country, a time series showing rising per capita incomes can be misleading. Derived by dividing national income or product by population, it tells nothing about the actual distribution of the fruits of increased productivity. Rises may in reality be confined to small minorities.

3. The cutoff of aid is at times achieved by something resembling sleight of hand. In the case of Iran, for example, the occasion was commemorated by a well-publicized Department of State luncheon in November 1967, at which Iran was represented by Ambassador Hushan Ansary and the United States by Secretary of State Dean Rusk. A message from President Johnson celebrating Iran's graduation after fifteen years of economic aid was read, and Secretary Rusk said, "Tomorrow ...direct economic aid to Iran under our Foreign Assistance Act will end." This meant, however, that Iran could continue (and has continued) to receive agricultural commodities under the Food-for-Freedom program. Similarly, the military assistance program has not been brought to an end and the loan program of the Export-Import Bank in Iran remains unaffected. (Although many development specialists believe that the terms of loans from the Export-Import Bank and similar institutions in other countries are too "hard" to qualify such loans as development assistance, the "long-term loans" of the Export-Import Bank are included as "official contributions" in international comparisons of aid efforts.)

Integrated societies differ from those in the preceding phase of economic and social transformation in their structure of political power. Personal power tends to become institutionalized through bureaucratization, and the exercise of power is divided into many specialties and shared by many people. This corresponds in considerable measure to trends in social stratification, according to which those concerned with the direct exercise of political power are recruited to an increasing extent through university education and are much more numerous than in earlier phases. At the same time that the ruling groups are being enlarged, and come to depend more on merit than on privilege, the number of those at the opposite end of the social scale is reduced.

As societies become more productive, wealth tends to be more evenly distributed and the standard of living of urban and rural workers tends to approximate that of salaried employees.[4]

Clearly, Taiwan, Iran, Pakistan, and Korea are not yet integrated societies. Certain objectives of American assistance policy—rising levels of income, investment, savings, and exports—are on the road to realization, but achievement of other objectives, equally important in creating a collectivity of nations respectful of basic human rights and fairly firmly anchored to the value system implicit in the UN Charter, remains in the future. If aid is terminated before a country has made real progress toward social and civic as well as economic modernization, the ultimate objective of the aid effort will remain in limbo, and a relationship that has been mutually beneficial may be ended prematurely. Whereas heavy capital investment can normally be relied on to produce significant increases in GNP within a short span of time, the stimulation of significant social and political progress appears to require both longer time horizons and more subtle efforts.

Economic growth and diversification do tend to produce interest groups and train participants in essential political skills. Economically oriented development assistance also tends to provide an acceptable opening wedge for a dialogue between the United States and the receiving country on matters that extend far beyond the specifications for the generators, tractors, trucks, or fertilizers to be imported under aid programs. Where aid is substantial, discussions of patterns

4. C. E. Black, *The Dynamics of Modernization: A Study in Comparative History* (Harper and Row, 1966), p. 83.

of land ownership and use, wages, prices, taxes and exchange rates, import and export policies, and other arrangements that stimulate or retard economic growth are normal parts of the aid process. Such discussions clearly have more than economic implications.

However, just as the rather unsophisticated anticommunism of the U.S. government distorted the allocation of U.S. aid before, after, and especially during the 1950s, and in other ways encumbered the aid program with a burdensome legacy, so too some of the emphasis on development as primarily an economic phenomenon has masked the need for better criteria and more sensitive judgments concerning social progress and social justice in less developed countries. The questions are: Which noneconomic criteria are sufficiently reliable, even in a single country, to warrant introducing them into the aid-allocation and decision-making process? If none exist, how derive them? If and when they have been derived, how prevent their introduction from appearing to be a particularly obnoxious form of intervention in an aid-receiving country's internal affairs, thus adding fresh strain to the already delicate rich-donor–poor-recipient relationship?

The Punta del Este Charter developed by the United States and Latin America in 1961 represented an important milestone in the effort to formulate feasible social as well as economic goals, but it cannot be said that adequate techniques for incorporating those goals into the decision-making process have yet been devised. Presumably, the annual country reviews of the Inter-American Committee on the Alliance for Progress (CIAP) could be built up to include greater specificity about desirable social and institutional measures in participating countries. Indeed, the Foreign Assistance Acts of 1966 and thereafter include a provision that requires U.S. loan assistance to Latin American countries to be consistent with CIAP's conclusions and recommendations. No comparable guidelines are insisted upon for aid to Asia and Africa, partly because CIAP has no analogue in these regions.

Increased attention to the political as well as the social dimensions of development was the objective of those who added Title IX, Utilization of Democratic Institutions in Development, to the Foreign

Assistance Act in 1966. Just as a nation may need both military and economic assistance, or economic and social assistance, it may also need political assistance. Theoretically, one could design a program of direct political assistance in the form of projects that strengthen various underpinnings of democracy—widespread participation in the political process, effective parliaments, competent political parties, qualified leadership, independent judiciaries, a free press, and so forth. Such a program would hardly be acceptable if offered by the U.S. government in lieu of assistance for economic and social development, but some of it can be brought in acceptably under nongovernmental auspices and more of it may become acceptable when both the strengths and the limitations of purely economic aid have been demonstrated.

Experience during the postwar period—admittedly a brief span from which to draw firm conclusions about economic and social policy—encourages greater optimism about the rates of economic growth sustainable by developing countries for considerable periods of time. Until 1950 or so, the conventional wisdom was that an overall growth rate of about 4 percent per year and a per capita rate of 2 percent per year were the best one could hope for. Because population in most of the developing countries is expanding at a rate of 2.5–3.5 percent per year, a 4 percent increase in overall growth boils down to a 0.5–1.5 percent improvement in per capita income.

Since 1950, a number of countries at different stages of development and with different combinations of public and private sectors have been growing at overall rates well in excess of 4 percent per year, and the low-income nations as a group have grown somewhat more rapidly than the high-income nations. By the mid-1970s, or shortly thereafter, a nation seriously interested in development, which has established an effective nationwide family planning program, should be able to combine a 6–7 percent rate of overall growth with a 2.0–2.5 percent population increase for a 3.5–5.0 percent improvement per capita per year. A 4 percent improvement per person per year means a doubling of living standards in less than eighteen years, as compared with every thirty-five years at 2 percent.[5]

5. See also Chapter 4 below.

The purpose of this discussion is not to advocate a cradle-to-grave aid program that will operate until the receiving nation is a fully integrated society in the sense that Sweden is today. It is rather to cast doubt on the comfortable assumption that either the American national interest or the interest of the world as a whole has been adequately served, insofar as aid is concerned, as soon as a developing country is able to pay for necessary imports of goods and services from a rising level of export earnings, regardless of the absolute level of its per capita income, the rate of increase in that income, the degree of social cohesion within the body politic, and the sense of national identity and purpose which characterizes the area.

Termination of financial assistance before the country has reached a level of income per person per year of, say, $500–$600 and is increasing it at about 4 percent per annum may be dubious wisdom because it will prolong unnecessarily the period of widening income gaps between rich and poor countries.[6] In a strictly economic sense, aid works, and full advantage ought to be taken of this important lesson of the postwar era. Greater attention to the social and political components of the type of development considered conducive to a decent world order is also highly desirable, if not imperative, for the 1970s. The objective of the exercise should be to achieve, before the development relationship is terminated, the best possible prospects for balanced economic, social, and civic growth. The probability is that technical assistance in the form of expertise on concessional terms will be needed for more years than commodity assistance on concessional terms.

Technical assistance is not only the first requirement in the foreign aid field, but also the last. Partly because of the long lead time required for the production of skills as compared with that required

6. It can also be argued that the countries best prepared to carry out difficult sociopolitical reforms may be intermediate-income countries such as Chile, which are likely to be excluded from aid by the fixing of arbitrary cutoff points based on per capita income levels. On the other hand, graduation from aid increases the self-respect of the graduate. This, in turn, strengthens the argument for early graduation. It need not, however, preclude a postgraduate relationship that stresses technical assistance for agreed educational, scientific, and sociocivic ends more than economic assistance.

for the production for commodities, self-sustaining growth in skills may not be attained until long after what has been described as "the trade limit on growth" has been overcome.[7] Were there an international market in skills comparable to that in commodities, this would be no cause for alarm. The less developed countries could purchase the skills they needed and be at no great disadvantage as compared with the more developed nations. Commodities can be ordered from a catalog or from an agent at fixed prices. For imported experts, however, the price may well be 50 percent higher than it is in the home market, there is no catalog to consult, and no convenient system for importing them. Indeed, a number of factors, including a worldwide shortage of adequately trained specialists, conspire to produce a brain drain instead of a "brain gain" for the less developed countries.

Consequently, the case would appear to be strong for expanding fairly rapidly technical assistance of assured quality that can be paid for, or partially paid for, by the receiver after his need for capital assistance has tapered off. Some specific recommendations to this end are included in Chapter 6.

Further Implications of Postwar Experience

There are many further lessons from the experience of the last twenty years that should be recalled in formulating a development assistance program for the 1970s. Some of them have attained the status of clichés, even though they do not yet govern policy. The following are particularly relevant in designing an overall program, though not necessarily equally helpful in determining the size, scope, or direction of the program in any given aid-receiving nation.

1. The purpose to be served by the assistance must command sig-

7. "An important area of research is that of devising a reliable set of indicators of progress in social and economic sectors which are of particular interest from the technical assistance viewpoint. A strategy of technical assistance must be geared to longer-term results—not necessarily reflected in current overall growth rates—and must be adapted to a great variety of country situations." Organisation for Economic Co-operation and Development, *Technical Assistance and the Needs of Developing Countries* (OECD, 1968), para. 18.

nificant support at the receiving end. Modernization tends to be this kind of purpose, and the availability of external assistance helps to make it a more feasible goal in the less developed countries. Aid is not useless as a device for cementing alliances, winning friends, prolonging historic ties, extracting short-run political advantages, heading off offerings of rival powers, and promoting the exports of, or paving the way for private investment from, the aid-giving country. In theory, these desires on the part of donors can readily be reconciled with the development interests of the receiver. Surplus agricultural commodities can provide partial payment for employees on public works projects. The compensation for an air base can finance some high priority investment projects. The fact that fast footwork by the United States results in American underwriting for an enterprise that might otherwise have been financed by Communist China does not make the enterprise any less valuable from an economic point of view. Nevertheless, the multiple motives of donor countries tend not only to invite conflict among agencies and interests within those countries, but also to be divisive and corrosive at the receiving end by comparison with the unambiguous commitment to development that characterizes most of the multilateral sources of aid.

2. Development, as has been said ad nauseam, is a long-term process involving a serious attempt to mobilize energies and resources, to plan ahead, and to invest in the future. Flexibility is necessary and slavish adherence to a predetermined course is foolish. That the United States should want to make its assistance conditional on good performance and be free to turn the spigot on and off is understandable. Frequently, however, keeping the receiving nation on a short leash is a disincentive to orderly planning on its part. Performance can and should be reviewed continually, but the idea that supplies should be withheld unless certain actions are taken within a specified time limit, or that program loans must be subject to quarterly review and variation in order to guarantee pari passu fulfillment of the receiving country's commitments, is often illusory.

In connection with assistance for specific projects, such obvious technical quid pro quos as an appropriate site for the project, a feasibility study, allocation of necessary local currency, availability of personnel and materials, assurance of qualified management, and continuation of the activity after the subsidy ends can appropriately be sought. Reforms unrelated to the specific project or only indirectly related—introduction of an effective income tax system in return for help in building an electric power plant—cannot plausibly be requested, however important they may be. Requirements such as a revised rate structure in return for help in modernizing a railroad, or the more elaborate quid pro quos exacted by the AID a few years ago in connection with its loan to the Bolivian Mining Bank, will probably be recognized as relevant but may nevertheless be resented to the point of becoming counterproductive.[8]

Land reform, tax reform, import liberalization, devaluation of the currency, revisions of wage and price policies, and other macro policies may appropriately be sought in return for program aid—assistance that finances a variety of imports required for the economy as a whole (for example, repair and maintenance supplies) rather than items destined for a specific project site. "Typically, program loans are now [1967] disbursed in quarterly installments contingent on review of self-help progress."[9] But the timing of major changes in economic and social policy is a matter of great delicacy. The changes will be hard to introduce on schedule even though they have long been needed and commitments to initiate them have been made. The leverage afforded by the U.S. aid program is more limited than it is popularly thought to be, and the more bluntly the aid instrument is used the less effective it becomes.

The point at issue in the foregoing paragraphs is not project versus program assistance but the use of program loans to establish and main-

8. According to the AID's Summary Presentation to the Congress, *Proposed Foreign Aid Program FY 1968* (May 1967), "A loan to the Bolivian Mining Bank to finance expansion and modernization of the private mining industry was not agreed to until the Bolivian Government undertook a major reform of the country's mining code, a reorganization of the bank, and the passage and enforcement of new mineral export tax laws to encourage mining investment; the new code is in effect, the new tax law has been passed, and the required reorganization is being carried out" (p. 16). But will the people in Bolivia be as satisfied with the bargain struck as the AID is? Will the suspicion that they bowed to superior power encourage them to compensate by rising up and kicking the United States in the teeth at the next opportunity?

9. *Ibid.*, p. 17.

tain tight time schedules. Agreement concerning policy directions during the medium-term future (two to five years), with provision for annual reviews of progress made, will probably be more effective than policing on a quarterly basis. Neither the appropriation process in the United States nor the operating policies of American aid agencies are as yet properly geared to the long-term nature of the development process. Repeated attempts to secure longer-term authorizations from the Congress have been rebuffed or the authorizations withdrawn after having been granted. Because the legislative branch is determined to give the executive branch little freedom, the tendency is for the executive branch to give the aid-receiving nations even less freedom and to demand better behavior of them than will be forthcoming.

The two-to-five-year commitment may succeed in inducing better *initial* planning for the next several years on the part of an aid receiver, but without at least an annual review this advantage—if AID experience is a trustworthy guide—may be more than offset by the effect of the commitment in reducing *continuing* outside influence on policy decisions *during* the period.[10]

3. In accelerating development, sensible economic and social policies on the part of the less developed country are more important than injections of foreign funds or commodities. Aid on the average has been accounting for only about 20 percent of the investment resources of the less developed countries. A vital question, therefore, is not just how efficiently the 20 percent, in and of itself, is used, but how effective it can be in building institutions and promoting policies that improve the overall use of a nation's resources. This means that channels of communication should be kept open and expert advice made available whenever policies are being formulated or reassessed. The supreme importance of sensible policies in the developing country is reflected in a recent addition to the conventional wisdom

10. Joan M. Nelson, *Aid, Influence, and Foreign Policy* (Macmillan, 1968), p. 81. Preceding this conclusion of hers is an informative discussion of AID experiments with two- and three-year commitments during the early 1960s in response to the recommendations of President Kennedy's Task Force on Foreign Economic Assistance. The experiments resulted in about as much disenchantment in official circles with a firm three-year commitment as I feel about a commitment good for only three months.

according to which "the quality of our aid is as important as the quantity," or in the jargonese version, "aid's influence potential is much more important than its resource contribution." Although perfectly true, the statement seems to imply that money does not really matter. Yet virtually all the success stories in foreign aid—success in the limited, previously discussed sense of rising per capita incomes and improved capacity to import—are stories of generous amounts of assistance.

Aid on a generous scale is required because development is expensive, because mistakes will be made, and because the shift to growth-promoting policies often involves political and economic risks which will not be incurred unless the period of maximum risk is, to some extent, underwritten in advance. Material assistance can be both incentive and insurance. Money, in summary, does matter even though it is never the full story.[11]

4. The aspect that matters most about the inflow of financial resources is not necessarily the immediate use to which funds are put, but the way in which increments to the national income resulting from the initial investment are used over time.

Even if the short-run productivity is high, the economy may continue to be dependent on external assistance indefinitely unless the additional output is allocated so as to increase saving and reduce the trade gap.... The initial elements in the [economic] development sequence are getting the initial increase in the rate of growth, channeling the increments in income into increased saving, and allocating investment so as to avoid balance-of-payments bottlenecks....[12]

Chenery and Strout go on to argue that the long-run effectiveness of aid will be increased by supporting, not just a tolerable growth rate, but as high a rate as the economy of the receiving country can

11. See Chapter 4 below. The relationship of large-scale economic aid to rapid economic growth need not be one of cause and effect. Yet it seems to me, and to almost everyone else who has studied the problem, plausible to conclude that the substantial inflows of assistance to Greece, Israel, southern Italy, Jordan, Korea, Pakistan, Taiwan, and so forth, have been instrumental in sparking the economic improvements registered there. Comparable per capita levels of assistance for all less developed countries equally capable of using it, however, would require considerably more assistance than is likely to be forthcoming in the early 1970s. This underscores the need also for more efficient use of available assistance.

12. Hollis B. Chenery and Alan M. Strout, "Foreign Assistance and Economic Development," *American Economic Review*, Vol. 56, no. 4, pt. 1 (1966), p. 724.

achieve "without a substantial deterioration in the efficiency of use of capital." The higher the rate, the smaller will be the proportion of the increase in GNP offset by population growth. More aid in the short run may mean smaller aid requirements in the long run. When GNP is growing rapidly rather than just tolerably, it should also be easier to raise marginal saving rates, to expand exports, and to attract foreign private investment.[13] Furthermore, an economy that is growing at 6 or 7 percent per year and increasing its export earnings at about that rate will be in a strong position to service foreign loans—a vital attribute in an era of antipathy to grant aid.

5. The correlation between volume of aid and amount of economic growth is probably greater and certainly more demonstrable than the correlation between volume of assistance and amount of influence acquired by the donor. The "influence potential" of foreign aid is to some extent correlated with the amount of aid provided. Up to some point, it rises with increasing amounts of aid and, from that point, tends to decline with declining amounts. In the process of rising, however, it encourages arrogance on the part of the donors and stimulates fears and resistance among receivers. Consequently, the peak is never very high and hopes of obtaining or maintaining vast amounts of leverage through foreign aid are unlikely to be realized. In view of the limited knowledge aid donors have about the real needs of less developed countries and the frequent desire of donors to use their leverage for questionable purposes, this may be a blessing.[14]

In discussing aid and influence, Joan Nelson draws a distinction between the difficult problem of using aid to improve development policies and stimulate self-help in a low-income country and the still more difficult and controversial problem of using aid for short-run

13. *Ibid.*, pp. 724–25.

14. The less reason the receiver has to suspect the motives of the foreign adviser, the more likely it is that the advice will be judged on its merits. The contribution of the Harvard Advisory Group to policy formulation in Pakistan, for example, has been enormous and indicates the desirability of more extensive use of this type of high-caliber advisory mission of persons who are not emissaries of governmental or intergovernmental agencies. The limiting factor appears to be the small number of truly top-notch personnel available to manage this kind of enterprise or be assigned to its country missions.

political purposes. With respect to the former, the first problem is to understand the country well enough to identify the most important self-help measures needed. The second problem is to employ the techniques most suitable for encouraging the adoption of these measures.

Potentially, all forms of aid can be used to exercise influence. Some forms of aid are better suited to influencing macro-economic policies; others relate more readily to sector or subsector policies. Moreover, some forms lend themselves not only to the exercise of influence, but also to the narrower concept of leverage ... actions that go beyond influence and persuasion to condition aid, explicitly or implicitly, on specified host country measures. Leverage may be negative or positive: aid may be withheld unless certain conditions are satisfied, or additional aid may be made available if host country performance achieves specified standards. Positive leverage is sometimes called "incentive programming."[15]

Because of the commendable reluctance of the United States to let people starve, food aid which is really for the relief of the hungry will be discontinued only under the most extreme provocation. Individual technical assistants can exert enormous influence, but the very limited leverage inherent in a technical assistance program is now so generally recognized that technical assistance is often continued when capital assistance programs are suspended for disciplinary reasons. Capital assistance in substantial volume does carry leverage. The constraint in this case is that, if such assistance is limited to specific projects which have long been in gestation and finally been launched, donors will be as reluctant as receivers to leave the landscape dotted with monuments half-finished due to ruptured aid relationships.

Loans for commodity imports, which are almost always larger in volume than loans for specific projects, represent the most powerful and flexible means of influencing macroeconomic policies in the countries that receive such loans.[16] The truth is, however, that regardless of the amount or type of assistance the ceiling on external influence is lower than is commonly realized. Donors do not know enough about the development process or about the manner in which

15. *Aid, Influence, and Foreign Policy*, p. 75.
16. Joan Nelson gives reasons for this. *Ibid.*, pp. 77–78.

it will unfold in a given nation to prescribe with complete confidence. Even if the prescription is good, the patient may be unready or unable to take it. Additional pressure may backfire on the donors or cause the downfall of a decent government at the receiving end. Adequate underwriting of the risks to the receiver, feasible in a period of rising aid levels, may be impossible when aid is shrinking.

6. The project approach—the use of aid to finance specific, identifiable undertakings that could serve as visible monuments to the program—reigned supreme during the early years of foreign aid but placed excessive emphasis on the initial use of the aid funds. Although it has long been known that foreign financing of "good" projects might only ease the diversion of domestic resources to "bad" projects, the shift from the project approach to the program approach or to a reasonable meld of the two approaches has been slow. Since project financing should continue to be an element in the aid program, it would be unwise to oversell the program approach, which provides imported resources needed by the economy as a whole, or by a particular sector such as agriculture, rather than the equipment and supplies needed at a particular project site.

The designers of the project approach wanted to avoid the kind of unproductive international loans for ill-defined purposes that had been made during the 1920s and followed by wholesale defaults. If aid were tied to specific productive enterprises and activities, there would be a better opportunity to judge the amounts needed, the goods and services for which the funds would be expended, and the prospects of repayment (or, in the case of grant aid, the productivity of the enterprise). Like every shift of public policy, the new line proved to be an overcompensation for the alleged shortcomings of the earlier policy and to have unforeseen defects of its own.

The project approach tends to limit involvement in ways acceptable to both parties. In due course, one party requests commodities, equipment, or experts for a stated, well-defined purpose; the other makes them available for that purpose, thereby identifying itself with a particular undertaking. As previously indicated, aid can be made conditional on the completion of prior engineering or market surveys, the allocation of domestic resources in specified amounts, the employment of qualified management, and other actions expected to help guarantee competent supervision and execution of the project. Under the project approach, technical assistance can more readily be integrated with capital assistance. The odds that at least the project in question will receive the supplies and the attention it needs will improve. For economic growth to occur, growing points must be established. Successful projects provide, at local levels, both growing points and visible evidence of international cooperation.

The tying of foreign aid to specific projects encourages the kind of detailed discussion that can spell the difference between success and failure of those projects while avoiding the political impasses implicit in broader discussions of national policy.

Because the project approach historically has meant, not the financing of entire projects or an agreed fraction of the full costs, but rather financing the foreign exchange costs, the less developed countries have been given an incentive for the prosecution of projects having a relatively high foreign exchange content: for industrial undertakings in preference to schools, for railways instead of roads, for processes that are capital intensive rather than labor intensive. Foreign aid, particularly in the earlier years of development assistance, tended to become the sum of the foreign exchange requirements of those projects, a sum likely to fall considerably short of the amount that could be invested productively by the aid receiver.

All the major lending agencies combined can process only a few hundred loan applications per year. The project system consequently contains incentives to both donors and receivers "to select large projects with a high import content in order to minimize administrative efforts and maximize the aid received."[17]

When critics of the project approach contrast it with the program approach, or vice versa, the comparison is frequently between stereotypes that do not conform to current reality. The project approach is depicted as the provision of assistance for a narrowly defined undertaking like the construction of a fertilizer plant at a specific

17. Hollis B. Chenery, "Foreign Assistance and Economic Development," in John H. Adler (ed.), *Capital Movements and Economic Development* (St. Martin's Press, 1967), p. 280.

location, and the program approach as a general line of credit open to the aid-receiving country either after agreement on a comprehensive development program or in the expectation that a periodic or continuing review of development progress within the country will indicate whether its resources, domestic as well as foreign, are being used effectively and whether aid should be continued. Projects, however, can be both broadly and narrowly defined, and programs can be drawn up for sectors of the economy, for areas of the country, or for categories of the population as well as for the nation as a whole. The theoretical differences between the two approaches have been blurred in practice, though they remain real enough to constitute a live issue in the never-ending debate on foreign aid.

Under the Marshall Plan, the issue was not a controversial one. In the reconstruction of Europe, the most important missing ingredient was obviously foreign exchange, or rather the equipment and supplies available for dollars from North America. The European countries had a balance-of-payments problem, a shortage of dollars. The United States provided balance-of-payments support; the Europeans imported a variety of agricultural and industrial supplies, allocated them efficiently, and were soon independent of the need for economic aid.

The problems of the less developed countries were far more complex, and it probably would have been folly to try to meet the balance-of-payments deficits they could so easily generate. The project approach, as indicated, was a logical alternative. The current popularity of the program approach can be attributed both to a clarification of the purpose of aid—to promote long-term growth in an orderly way—and to a realization that growth promotion is to a greater extent a function of the overall policies pursued by the less developed country than of any given handful of projects.

The main argument in favor of the program approach is the ability to relate the amount and form of aid to the objectives and performance of the receiving country. Furthermore, it can be administered to provide incentives to improved performance.[18] It can more quickly

18. *Ibid.*, pp. 280–81.

galvanize the whole economy, including the private sector. In designing an aid program for the 1970s, therefore, assurance of proper scope for the program approach is important.

For countries in the earliest stages of development, that is, with the least capacity to prepare and carry out a comprehensive development program, most of the outside aid should probably take the form of project assistance, thereby concentrating effort on the establishment of a few, well-managed enterprises. For countries farther along the road to development, advanced enough to have good country development programs or good sector programs and some competence in translating them into action, most of the outside aid should take the form of program assistance. To regard project and program assistance as mutually exclusive techniques, however, is no longer necessary. The term "project" has gradually been broadened to the point where it can embrace investment in a whole sector of the economy or region of the country, while the term "program" is often narrowed so that it, too, refers to a sector, or a region, or a program for the use of a single commodity such as fertilizer.

7. With the advent of the Kennedy administration and the launching of the Alliance for Progress, the preparation of overall country development programs was given considerable impetus. The initial swing of the pendulum probably overemphasized the value of preparing an impressive, internally consistent five-year plan, based all too frequently on statistical data of doubtful validity and in any event unlikely to be carried out because of the absence of machinery and procedures linking the plan to the actual investment decisions of the government and the private sector. Although fifty or more countries now have partial or comprehensive national development plans and development planning, like development lending, has become respectable, in only a few countries has the planning exercise sparked the actions that ought to follow from it.

Consequently, more attention is currently being given to sector programming in agriculture, education, transportation, and other fields and to the readying of priority sectors for both program *and* project assistance. More attention is also being given to the formulation of integrated area development schemes that seek to direct toward a single manageable geographic region within a developing country all the necessary developmental inputs, simultaneously and in such fashion as to reinforce each other. Thus, areas such as northeast Thailand, Brazil's Northeast, Turkey's wheat-growing lands, and Iran's Ghazvin region can be given an opportunity to make a real forward leap.

Overall programming, sector programming, and area programming all tend to lengthen the time horizons of the programmers and to bring out the need for broader, longer-term aid involvements than are typically afforded by the project approach.

8. The limit on the number of objectives a government can simultaneously pursue with any vigor is depressingly low, even in large, diversified, advanced nations. In less developed countries, a systems approach to a few high priority goals may be more effective than either the project or the program approach and can to some extent serve as an alternative to more elaborate country planning. According to James P. Grant and other experienced aid administrators, concentration of substantial aid resources and management on a limited number of important goals can produce several times the benefits that would be obtained if the same financial and management resources were spread over many projects. The essence of the systems approach is the identification of a few realizable targets, a thoroughgoing commitment to achieve them within a specified time, the elaboration of a plan for providing all the required inputs and disposing appropriately of the resultant outputs, and building into that plan feedback arrangements that identify difficulties as they arise and assign responsibility for correcting them.

In other words, if the United States and, say, Turkey can agree in 1967 to give top priority to (1) self-sufficiency in wheat for Turkey by 1972, (2) a $200 million increase in earnings from lumber exports, and (3) a quadrupling of foreign exchange earnings by 1972, Turkey should be closer to graduation from U.S. aid than if it tries to progress in balanced fashion to a wider series of goals. Systems directors for the top priority objectives can be designated and authorized to cut across organizational and jurisdictional lines to get things moving. The prime minister himself can become the systems director for a truly important effort. Upon success, new goals, designed in part to correct recently created imbalances in the growth process, can be set.

9. More planning on a transnational basis is necessary to reconcile overall and sector programs of national governments; if all countries expect to increase their exports more rapidly than their imports, some are bound to be disappointed. Planning on a wider basis can also contribute to strengthening the sense of international community and achieving a more rational division of international labor.

Although the Food and Agriculture Organization of the United Nations is engaged in drawing up an Indicative World Plan for Agriculture, regional plans are more frequently mentioned in discussions of the future of foreign aid. The term "regionalism," however, is used in several quite different senses. These include (1) the use of regional institutions as allocating agencies for financial or technical assistance; (2) the development of telecommunications, highway systems, river basins, and power networks intended to facilitate trade, tourism, and communication within the region; and (3) the launching of common markets, currency unions, supranational authorities, or other devices to promote political and economic integration, particularly among the smaller and weaker sovereign entities of the low-income world.

Under the first of these arrangements—the allocation of assistance pursuant to the recommendations of regional agencies such as the regional economic commissions of the United Nations, or through regional institutions such as the Latin American or Asian development banks, in the management of which the countries of the region have a strong voice—the assistance itself may or may not foster regional integration. The process of reviewing the competing claims on available resources may build up esprit de corps within the region, but the resources themselves may be allocated entirely to national development projects and programs in ways that tend to promote national self-sufficiency rather than international integration. Alternatively, they can be used to finance Pan-American highways, Asian highways, and Mekong River development schemes, or regional or subregional common markets. Donor countries interested in more than the slow buildup of regional morale and habits of cooperation can allocate assistance to special funds administered by regional bodies; for example, the Pre-Investment Fund for Latin American Integration of the Inter-American Development Bank.

Whereas four countries—India, Pakistan, Indonesia, and Brazil—together contain more than half the population of the less developed noncommunist world, close to a hundred of the developing countries have populations under fifteen million and two-thirds of these have populations of less than five million. A nation of four million inhabitants with a per capita income of $125 per year represents a market comparable in economic importance (if one ignores income distribution) to an American city the size of Bridgeport, Connecticut, Corpus Christi, Texas, or Fort Wayne, Indiana. The best hope for such countries would seem in most cases to lie in regional integration schemes to enlarge markets, support more diversified economies, shake up stratified societies, and reduce the burdens of separate defense and diplomatic establishments.

So far, the most successful non-European effort at integration is the Central American Common Market. The East African Community (Kenya, Uganda, and Tanzania) has been making commendable progress, but the Latin American Free Trade Association is in the doldrums. The association of various African countries with the European Economic Community has brought important advantages to the associated nations and considerable uneasiness to developing countries in Asia and Latin America.

Countries that are economically inconsequential will have trouble surviving as sovereign entities. Nations with respectable economic potential can fail for other reasons—tribal or religious differences about which emotions run high, irreconcilable language difficulties, an unbridgeable urban-rural split, or incompetent leadership.

The merger of nonviable nations into something stronger and better integrated is essential, but the pathway is so strewn with political pitfalls that many seemingly sensible arrangements will come to naught. The wise course for the United States may be to support politically the principle of integration and support financially the regional development funds, banks, and other institutions that help promote common markets, free trade areas, river development schemes, and perhaps political unions within the region, but to avoid close identification with particular arrangements.

10. Americans have found it difficult to maintain a proper balance between optimism and skepticism or pessimism, particularly with respect to innovations and alleged breakthroughs in the field of development. During the decade 1955–65, predictions were regularly made that the 1980s would see famine in Asia and mass starvation on an unprecedented scale because of Asian inability to modernize agriculture in the face of the population explosion. When in the mid-1960s "the pill" and the intrauterine device (IUD) seemed to promise an early end to the population explosion, the gloom was briefly dispelled. It reappeared shortly thereafter with the realization that most of the people who would be eating in the 1980s were already with us and furthermore that the pill and the IUD had side effects and drawbacks that would slow down their acceptance.

In January 1967, President Johnson in his State of the Union message was pessimistic. "Next to the pursuit of peace, the really great challenge to the human family is the race between food supply and population increase. That race tonight is being lost."[19] The World Food Supply Panel of the President's Science Advisory Committee in its May 1967 report spoke of the "grim reality of the food shortage that will occur during the next 20 years ... before programs of family planning can be expected to bring about long-term amelioration of the problem by reducing world population growth."[20]

Nine months later the thoughtful and responsible administrator of the Department of Agriculture's International Development Service reported to the Second International Conference on the War on Hunger:

The good news is that we may be on the threshold of an agricultural revolution in many of the hungry, densely populated countries of the less developed world, particularly in Asia. Further, we are witnessing

19. *Congressional Record*, Vol. 113, no. 1, 90 Cong. 1 sess. (1967), p. H29.
20. *The World Food Problem*, Report of the President's Science Advisory Committee, Vol. 1 (May 1967), p. 14. This and the passage from the President's State of the Union message are both mentioned in *Resources*, no. 27 (Washington: Resources for the Future, January 1968), p. 3.

some advances in food technology which, if commercially feasible, can make quality diets available to millions at much lower costs.

Exciting new varieties of rice, wheat, grain sorghum, and corn are now available. In large part, they have been developed at the International Rice Institute in the Philippines and at what is now the International Maize and Wheat Improvement Center in Mexico. (The Institute was sponsored by the Rockefeller and Ford Foundations, the Center by Rockefeller.) The new varieties are much more responsive to fertilizer than traditional varieties. Under proper growing conditions, they outyield traditional varieties not by a mere 10, 20, or 30 percent but by a multiple of two or more. This is why they have caught the imagination of so many Asian farmers.

The new food grain varieties are far more than just another technological breakthrough—they may be to the agricultural revolution in Asia what the steam engine was to the industrial revolution in Europe.[21]

This theme was promptly taken up by the AID administrator in a series of speeches beginning with a talk to the Society for International Development entitled "The Green Revolution: Accomplishments and Apprehensions."

Record yields, harvests of unprecedented size and crops in the ground demonstrate that throughout much of the developing world—and particularly in Asia—we are on the verge of an agricultural revolution. . . . Pakistan has an excellent chance of achieving self-sufficiency in food grains in another year. . . . India will harvest more than 95 million tons in food grains this year—again a record crop. She hopes to achieve self-sufficiency in food grains in another three or four years. She has the capability to do so. . . . The Philippines are clearly about to achieve self-sufficiency in rice.[22]

The foreign aid program is desperately in need of new successes and may indeed be in the process of achieving one here that merits all the optimism currently being mustered on its behalf. Yet the long record of programs previously hailed as breakthroughs or keys to modernization at an early date should give us pause. The insecticide DDT promised to end malaria and permit the productive use of millions of man-days otherwise lost in debilitating illness. But DDT-

21. Lester R. Brown, speech of Feb. 20, 1968, to the Second International Conference on the War on Hunger, Washington, D.C. See also Mr. Brown's article, "The Agricultural Revolution in Asia," in *Foreign Affairs* (July 1968), pp. 688-98.

22. William S. Gaud, administrator, Agency for International Development. Address of March 8, 1968, to the Society for International Development, Washington, D.C.

resistant mosquitoes made it more prudent to talk about malaria control than malaria eradication, and the man-days gained through malaria control have made only modest contributions to GNP. Community development programs were far more promising under their early, inspired leadership than when the bureaucrats took them over. Atomic energy was hailed as a release from poverty and drudgery until the economics thereof was soberly analyzed. Transistor radios and educational TV were expected to solve the teacher shortage until it became clear that they are more effective as supplements to than as replacements for face-to-face encounters. The road to development is long and rocky and winding.

Miracle wheat and miracle rice may well take longer to transform deficits into surpluses than their proponents now believe. If not, they may give rise to the problems associated with falling prices and insufficient returns to producers. Nevertheless, they represent real triumphs for the persevering, long-range, high-quality, research approach most notably fostered by the Rockefeller Foundation and more or less foreclosed to American governmental agencies in the foreign aid business because of their short time horizons.

After mentioning six reasons for believing that the new agricultural technology will not in fact spread nearly as widely or rapidly as has been predicted, Clifton R. Wharton, Jr., illustrates vividly the way in which progress on one set of development problems tends to create a new, almost equally alarming set of problems on some other front:

From all this one may deduce that the "first" or "early" adopters of the new technology will be in regions which are already more advanced, literate, responsive and progressive and which have better soil, better water management, closer access to roads and markets—in sum, the wealthier, more modern farmers. For them it is easier to adopt the new higher-yield varieties since the financial risk is less and they already have better managerial skills. When they do adopt them, the doubling and trebling of yields means a corresponding increase in their incomes. One indication of this is the large number of new private farm-management consultant firms in the Philippines which are advising large landlords on the use of new seed varieties and making handsome profits out of their share of the increased output.

As a result of the different rates in the diffusion of the new technology, the richer farmers will become richer. In fact, it may be possible that the more progressive farmers will capture food markets previously served by the smaller semi-subsistence producer.... Such a development could well lead to a net reduction in the income of the smaller, poorer and less venturesome farmers. This raises massive problems of welfare and equity. If only a small fraction of the rural population moves into the modern century while the bulk remains behind, or perhaps even goes backward, the situation will be highly explosive.[23]

11. Musing on the problem of properly estimating costs and benefits of development ventures, including nonagricultural undertakings, Albert O. Hirschman has written a perceptive and entertaining introductory chapter to his book, *Development Projects Observed*.[24] Not only are obstacles usually underestimated, but resourcefulness in overcoming obstacles is likewise underestimated. An invisible hand, he suggests, beneficially hides difficulties from developers.

Since we necessarily underestimate our creativity, it is desirable that we underestimate to a roughly similar extent the difficulties of the tasks we face so as to be tricked by these two offsetting underestimates into undertaking tasks that we can, but otherwise would not dare, tackle [p. 13]. The Hiding Hand is essentially a mechanism that makes the risk-averter take risks and in the process turns him into less of a risk-averter. In this manner, it opens an escape from one of those formidable "prerequisites" or "preconditions" to development; it permits the so-called prerequisite to come into being *after* the event to which it is supposed to be the prerequisite. In our model, risk-taking behavior is engaged in actively (though involuntarily) prior to the arrival on the stage of the "risk-taking, achievement-oriented personality"; instead, it is this personality that is fashioned by risk-taking behavior [p. 26].

Professor Hirschman's insight is not readily translatable into an operational principle—he does not advocate initiating complex undertakings in the expectation that the Hiding Hand will inevitably come to the rescue. Yet his mastery of the paradoxes of development is worth directing attention to in this brief discussion of some of the lessons of experience during the postwar period.

12. One of the paradoxical and disappointing features of the re-

23. Clifton R. Wharton, Jr., "The Green Revolution: Cornucopia or Pandora's Box?" *Foreign Affairs* (April 1969), pp. 467–68. For additional second thoughts on the green revolution, see also Hubertus zu Lowenstein, "The Story of a Sophisticated Breed," *Ceres*, Vol. 2 (January–February 1969), pp. 44–46.

24. Brookings Institution, 1967.

markable economic progress made to date by the less developed countries has been the modest payoff in terms of new jobs, especially in industry. During the first postwar decade, rapid industrialization was almost invariably given top priority in the development strategies of low-income nations. Their affection for steel mills, atomic reactors, and capital-intensive undertakings has been the target of so many brickbats from commentators in high-income countries that this writer would be ashamed to add to the traffic.

The objective of rapid industrialization, if not the emphasis on capital-intensive projects, was certainly understandable. Where would the unemployed and the underemployed be absorbed and become productive if not in the industrial sector? Where else would value added per worker be so great that, even if no big dent were made in the ranks of the unemployed, GNP would be substantially increased? What else would provide better evidence of growing economic muscle and forward movement into the twentieth century, thereby fulfilling a pressing political need?

The dynamism of the industrial sector is substantiated by the record. In almost every country that has made a serious attempt to industrialize, manufacturing has been the most active sector.[25] Typically, however, industry has not provided enough new jobs to absorb the increase in the labor force; GNP is up, but unemployment is not down. This disappointing outcome of industrialization has kept alive the idea that the less developed countries have too slavishly adopted the production techniques of the advanced nations in which labor is the scarce resource and capital is relatively plentiful. The less developed countries, in other words, should concentrate on the development of labor-intensive techniques more in line with their own factor endowments and on types of industry known to be labor intensive.[26]

25. See Werner Baer and Michel E. A. Hervé, "Employment and Industrialization in Developing Countries," *Quarterly Journal of Economics*, Vol. 80 (February 1966), pp. 88-107.
26. As noted earlier in this chapter, however, the rich countries have encouraged the adoption of capital-intensive techniques in poor countries by providing so much of their aid in the form of project assistance limited to the foreign exchange costs of those projects. Where, in addition, the poor countries have allowed the cost of unskilled labor to rise unduly, the local entrepreneur who opts for capital-intensive technology is, within his lights, behaving rationally.

More can doubtless be done to develop efficient patterns of industrialization that provide more jobs per unit of investment than are currently being provided—real jobs, not the compulsory hiring of four men to do what one could do. Nevertheless, it seems clear that the job-creating potentialities of manufacturing are well below what less developed countries assumed them to be in the first half of the 1950s.

This has directed fresh attention to the trade and services sector and led economists such as Walter Galenson to conclude that

too little attention has been paid to those sectors of the economy in which the bulk of the new jobs are likely to be located, namely commerce and services. This does not mean that manufacturing is unimportant; on the contrary, it is, in my estimation, the key sector for economic growth. Under conditions of modern technology, however, its role is not likely to be that of a major source of new employment. Rather, it will tend to generate the effective demand leading to employment expansion in other sectors. This multiplier effect is apt to be much more significant than any direct contributions that the manufacturing sector can make to the alleviation of mass unemployment.[27]

13. In some senses, however, the service industries in less developed countries are merely the urban counterpart of agriculture—overcrowded with unskilled, underemployed personnel contributing little or nothing to GNP. Countless numbers try to survive by operating hole-in-the-wall shops, selling artificial flowers or lottery tickets in the streets, shining shoes, opening the doors of public buildings or standing respectfully but idly at attention when officials enter and depart.

The notion that service industries such as tourism can make a real contribution to development was slow to take root. There was nothing very glamorous about the prospect of more jobs for porters and chambermaids. Knowledgeable people spoke of the "low multiplier" in tourism and dismissed earnings from this source as being of little value in promoting development. But as each developing country encounters, almost inevitably, both employment and balance-of-

27. Walter Galenson, "Economic Development and the Sectoral Expansion of Employment," *International Labour Review*, Vol. 87 (June 1963), pp. 506–07; quoted in Baer and Hervé, p. 105.

payments crises, its respect grows for activities that create jobs and earn foreign exchange. Tourism is one such activity.

The experience of Switzerland (the classic case), Puerto Rico, Jamaica, Greece, Italy, Mexico, Spain, Portugal, Israel, Jordan, Tunisia, and Morocco has shown that tourists are worth courting and that earnings from tourism can be applied to development ends. Construction of everything from hotels to roads and electric power lines will be given a boost, and employment in the tourist sector can be a conveyor belt for persons in transition from the subsistence sector to the money economy. Not all the "demonstration effects" of tourism are pluses, but over time an expanding tourist industry can forge numerous links between less developed and more developed nations.

14. The trend toward longer-term thinking and planning, whether for sectors of national economies, for the economy of the nation-state as a whole, or for a group of nation-states, is evident. Even the most rudimentary kind of development planning will tend to bring out the relationships among aid, trade, and investment policies.

From the point of view of their self-respect, integration into the world economy, and long-run development, there is every reason to make it as easy as possible for developing nations to increase their earnings from international trade and to receive a larger inflow of private capital. Aid is not nobler than trade, and modifications in the trade policies of the United States and other high-income countries, which would permit the low-income countries to earn through trade more of the foreign exchange they need, are highly desirable even if the modifications tend to blur the conventional distinctions between trade and aid and even if the immediate benefits of trade liberalization accrue primarily to the most advanced of the developing countries. Although trade liberalization on the part of the United States would not require appropriations (except perhaps for adjustment assistance) or an annual Donnybrook with the Congress, substantial changes in trade policy are politically fully as difficult to obtain as aid appropriations.[28]

Finally, there is also much to be said in favor of increasing the flow

28. See Chapter 7.

of private investment to the less developed countries; the United States has been saying it for many years. Too much of its talk, however, has been devoted to the need for creating a "favorable climate" for foreign private investment and to the desirability of an investment code. Until the expansion during the 1960s of investment guarantee programs, not enough effort was devoted to ways of stimulating private investment in the absence of, or in advance of, a favorable investment climate.[29]

29. See Chapter 8.

CHAPTER FOUR

Entering the Seventies

ALTHOUGH MUCH HAS BEEN LEARNED about the development process and about the role of foreign aid in advancing it, much remains unknown. Development promotion is still more an art than a science and is likely to remain so for some time to come. The techniques for stimulating economic growth are better understood than the techniques for affecting constructively the psychological, sociological, and cultural dimensions of the nation-building process. Yet fifteen or twenty years ago, the former were hardly any better understood than the latter are today. In this sense, it can be said that the underlying quality of aid efforts in recent years has been improving and thus moving in an opposite direction from congressional support, which has been declining. The paradoxical position of the United States (and to a lesser extent of other industrialized nations) is that just as they are begining to know enough to participate effectively in DD II—the second decade of development—they are wondering whether the game is worth the candle.

The borderlines between trade, private investment, and aid are growing fuzzier, but the fundamental distinction remains clear. In aid, there is a substantial element of subsidy, an unrequited transfer of resources. Because of this, aid can be directed to purposes that are unprofitable in terms of the calculus applied to trade and investment transactions but are considered mutually beneficial by donor and receiver. Aid is a peculiarly flexible instrument. It can be turned to the solution of a particular problem, "in a particular place and at a particular time, in a specific and unique way."[1]

The definitional fuzziness results from the fact that some elements of subsidy (and hence aid) may enter into commodity agreements, trade preferences, sales of surplus foodstuffs, stockpile purchases, and investment guarantee schemes, that is, into transactions not normally considered aid. Properly speaking, contemporary economic relations between rich countries and poor countries should be envisaged as covering a spectrum of transactions shading off from those with a zero aid content to those with a 100 percent aid content. At the zero end would lie commercial trade and straight private investment. At the 100 percent end, one would find outright grants. In between would be transactions with a modest aid content (preferential trading arrangements, government guarantees for private investment) and transactions with a large aid content (long-term loans at nominal rates of interest or sales by rich countries of surplus commodities or other goods at prices well below those prevalent in world markets).

Changes in what are usually referred to as the trade and investment policies of rich countries can diminish the need of poor countries for the grants, loans, and technical assistance usually thought of as aid. More effective self-help efforts in the low-income world can further diminish the requirements for foreign aid. Nevertheless, a basic conclusion of most experts is that, although more can and should be done to reduce the need for aid, "requirements" (a flexible, somewhat subjective concept into which political and ethical judgments as well as economic considerations will enter) will not decrease in the foreseeable future.

The Trend of U.S. Aid during the 1960s

Decision makers in high-income countries who have to weigh the needs of low-income countries for foreign aid against other claims

1. Andrzej Krassowski, *The Aid Relationship* (London: Overseas Development Institute, 1968), p. 11.

on available resources do not as yet accord a very high priority to foreign aid. During the 1960s, the volume of American aid for development has been leveling off or declining while the cost of the experts and commodities and services financed by aid has been rising. The annual debates on the authorization and appropriation measures have become increasingly bitter and divisive. Arbitrary ceilings have been placed on the number of countries to which different types of assistance may be given. Numerous restrictions have been introduced to make particular countries ineligible for assistance. The ratio of grants to loans has been falling. The terms for loans have been hardening. The principle that aid-financed goods and services should be purchased from the lowest-cost source of supply, never very firmly rooted, has been sacrificed in favor of purchases in the U.S. market additional to what would be bought commercially by the aid receiver. The share of the available aid going to Vietnam, a special case affecting less than 1 percent of the total population of the less developed world, has risen sharply. The proportion of gross national product (GNP) devoted to foreign economic aid has dropped from 2.75 percent in 1949 to less than 0.5 percent in 1968.

The figures on U.S. economic aid vary substantially according to whether one cites authorizations, appropriations, gross or net obligations, or gross or net expenditures. They also vary according to whether one includes or excludes Food-for-Freedom, the Peace Corps, long-term loans of the Export-Import Bank, and related sources of assistance. Furthermore, it is important to know not only what proportion of the total is in grant form and what proportion is in loan form, but also what the terms of the loans are.

The general trend is evident from Table 1, which was compiled from data submitted to the Foreign Affairs Committee of the House of Representatives by the Agency for International Development (AID). The figures cover obligations and loan authorizations, not expenditures (which lag behind obligations and would therefore be slower to reflect a downturn in the availability of resources). Only the cumulative 1946–68 totals have been adjusted to take into account loan repayments and interest received by the United States.

According to the AID data, economic assistance to less developed countries, unadjusted for amortization and interest payments re-

TABLE I. *U.S. Gross National Product and Overseas Loans and Grants under Years, July 1, 1945–June 30, 1968[a]*

(In millions of dollars)

Item	Post-war relief period 1946–48 (1)	Marshall Plan period 1949–52 (2)	Mutual Security Act period 1953–61 (3)	1962 (4)
1. *Gross national product*	671,500	1,171,000	3,851,400	542,100
2. *Total economic assistance, all countries*	14,644	19,541	27,404	4,715
3. Loans	8,058	3,459	9,451	2,468
4. Grants	6,586	16,082	17,953	2,248
5. Grants as percent of total	45	82	66	48
6. *Total economic assistance, LDCs[c]*	3,052	4,601	23,991	4,540
7. Loans	760	1,246	8,506	2,338
8. Grants	2,292	3,355	15,485	2,202
9. Grants as percent of total	75	73	65	49
10. *AID and predecessor agencies, total to LDCs*	—	2,034	14,518	2,503
11. Loans	—	174	2,996	1,330
12. Grants	—	1,860	11,522	1,173
13. *AID and predecessor agencies, total to LDCs, exclusive of Vietnam*	—	2,034	13,053	2,392
14. Loans	—	174	2,906	1,330
15. Grants	—	1,860	10,147	1,062
16. *Food-for-Freedom, total to LDCs[d]*	—	53	5,542	1,353
17. *Title I, total[e]*	—	—	3,592	961
18. Payable in U.S. dollars, loans	—	—	—	19
19. Payable in foreign currency, for country use[f]	—	—	3,592	942
20. Economic development loans	—	—	2,050	470
21. Economic development grants	—	—	876	276
22. Common defense grants	—	—	423	148
23. Cooley loans to private industry	—	—	203	48
24. Other grants	—	—	—	—
25. Assistance from other country agreements	—	—	41	—
26. *Title II, total*	—	53	1,950	392
27. Emergency relief, economic development, and World Food Program	—	—	586	155
28. Voluntary relief agencies	—	53	1,364	237
29. *Export-Import Bank long-term loans*	271	843	3,204	224
30. *Other U.S. economic programs*	2,781	1,671	727	460
31. Contributions to international lending agencies	438	—	189	172
32. Peace Corps	—	—	[g]	30
33. Social Progress Trust Fund	—	—	—	226
34. Other	2,343	1,671	538	32
Memorandum				
35. Military assistance, LDCs	481	1,105	10,272	1,018
36. Military assistance, all countries	481	2,842	23,182	1,527
37. Economic and military assistance, LDCs[h]	3,533	5,706	34,263	5,558
38. Economic and military assistance, all countries[i]	15,125	22,383	50,586	6,242

For notes, see pp. 76–77.

Economic Programs, Net Obligations and Loan Authorizations, for Fiscal

Foreign Assistance Act period						Total 1962–68 (11)	Gross total 1946–68 (12)	Repayments and interest 1946–68 (13)	Net total 1946–68b (14)
1963 (5)	1964 (6)	1965 (7)	1966 (8)	1967 (9)	1968 (10)				
573,400	612,200	654,200	720,700	766,500	822,600	4,691,700	10,385,600	—	—
4,564	4,332	4,410	5,147	5,216	4,754	33,138	94,726	16,000	78,727
2,387	2,343	2,402	2,637	2,971	2,606	17,815	38,782	16,000	22,782
2,176	1,988	2,008	2,510	2,244	2,148	15,323	55,944	—	55,944
48	46	46	49	43	45	46	59	—	71
4,390	4,216	4,308	5,034	4,747	4,450	31,685	63,330	7,215	56,115
2,245	2,259	2,314	2,538	2,510	2,317	16,522	27,034	7,215	19,818
2,144	1,958	1,994	2,496	2,236	2,134	15,164	36,296	—	36,296
49	46	46	50	47	48	48	57	—	65
2,299	2,141	2,034	2,554	2,253	1,892	15,675	32,228	1,572	30,656
1,346	1,333	1,129	1,228	1,091	929	8,385	11,555	1,572	9,983
953	808	904	1,326	1,162	963	7,290	20,672	—	20,672
2,166	1,982	1,818	1,970	1,786	1,588	13,700	28,788	1,501	27,287
1,346	1,335	1,129	1,228	1,092	929	8,388	11,468	1,501	9,967
820	647	688	742	694	659	5,313	17,319	—	17,319
1,450	1,502	1,394	1,629	1,002	1,392	9,722	15,316	774	14,542
913	951	981	1,124	626	1,021	6,578	10,170	774	9,396
61	88	142	321	125	469	1,225	1,225	134	1,092
852	863	839	804	501	552	5,353	8,945	640	8,305
456	466	562	609	331	319	3,212	5,262	519	4,743
247	236	113	—	20	38	930	1,805	—	1,805
108	133	102	137	106	152	886	1,310	1	1,309
27	29	55	40	23	28	250	452	118	335
—	—	—	—	17	6	22	22	—	22
15	—	8	18	3	9	52	94	3	90
537	550	413	505	376	371	3,144	5,146	—	5,146
239	190	168	261	181	182	1,376	1,962	—	1,962
298	360	245	244	195	189	1,767	3,184	—	3,184
158	301	331	301	940	570	2,826	7,143	4,256	2,887
482	273	550	549	553	596	3,464	8,642	613	8,030
122	112	312	354	374	424	1,869	2,496	—	2,496
55	76	85	113	104	107	570	571	—	571
127	42	101	24	5	5	530	530	58	472
178	43	52	58	70	61	494	5,046	555	4,491
1,405	1,098	1,078	1,071	828	773	7,272	20,684	326	20,357
1,986	1,537	1,309	1,406	1,480	1,471	10,717	38,778	700	38,078
5,795	5,314	5,386	6,105	5,576	5,223	38,958	84,013	7,541	76,472
6,550	5,869	5,719	6,553	6,696	6,225	43,854	133,504	16,699	116,805

Notes to Table 1, pp. 74–75

Sources: *Agency for International Development, U.S. Overseas Loans and Grants and Assistance from International Organizations*, Obligations and Loan Authorizations, July 1, 1945–June 30, 1968, special report prepared for the House Committee on Foreign Affairs (AID, May 29, 1969), primarily pp. 6, 9, 63. The GNP figures on *line 1* are from *The Budget of the United States Government, Fiscal Years 1968 and 1970*.

a. The figures represent net obligations and loan authorizations, not disbursements. *Lines 2–5, 36, and 38* include assistance to all countries, developed and less developed; *lines 6–34, 35, and 37* exclude assistance to developed countries, i.e., Japan, Australia, New Zealand, Republic of South Africa, Canada, and all of Europe except Greece, Malta, Spain, Turkey, and Yugoslavia. Because of rounding, components may not add to totals.

Lines 10–14: Include such predecessor agencies as the International Cooperation Administration, the Foreign Operations Administration, the Mutual Security Agency, and the Economic Cooperation Administration. The figures include also U.S. contributions authorized under the Foreign Assistance Act and predecessor legislation to certain international programs, including the UN Development Program ($612 million), the UN Relief and Works Agency for Palestine Refugees, the UN Children's Fund, and the Indus Basin Development Fund.

Lines 13 and 15: Include prepartition economic aid in grant form to Indo-China in the amount of $47 million for FY 1949–52 and $778 million for FY 1953–61.

Lines 16–28: Data represent economic assistance to less developed countries from Public Law 480, the Agricultural Trade Development and Assistance Act of 1954 and amendments thereto. Title I of the current act provides for the sale of agricultural commodities either for foreign currency or for U.S. dollars on credit terms. Sales on credit terms directly to the foreign country are shown on *line 18*. The figures on *line 19* do not represent total sales agreements payable in foreign currencies, but the amounts after subtraction of the sums planned for U.S. uses. They do represent planned use for less developed countries. The various planned country uses are shown separately on *lines 20–25;* on *line 24,* Other grants are principally for maternal welfare and family planning. In some cases, countries have also received, on a grant or a loan basis, foreign currency generated by a sales agreement between the United States and a third country: such loans or grants are shown on *line 25*. For years prior to FY 1955, the data represent transfers authorized under Section 416 of the Agricultural Act of 1949 (P.L. 81–439). *Line 27* covers transfers of commodities held in stock by the Commodity Credit Corporation to help people in friendly countries meet famine or other urgent or extraordinary relief requirements or to promote economic development. Transfers to the World

Food Program are included in this part of Title II of P.L. 480. Data represent commodities authorized at CCC cost, plus ocean freight. *Line 28* covers donations of commodities to voluntary relief agencies such as CARE, National Catholic Welfare Conference, and so forth, for distribution to needy people abroad. The figures represent valuations at CCC cost.

Line 29: Includes authorizations for loans of five years' or more maturity.

Line 31: Includes capital subscriptions and contributions to the World Bank and its affiliates (adjusted to take into account support for developed countries), the Inter-American Development Bank, and the Asian Development Bank. It does not include capital subscriptions to the International Monetary Fund.

Line 33: Represents loans authorized by the Inter-American Development Bank from the $525 million Social Progress Trust Fund which the Bank administers for the United States. The data also include minor amounts of technical assistance from the Trust Fund.

Line 34: Includes some large early programs such as UNRRA, Greek-Turkish Aid, and Civilian Relief in Korea; also development assistance and support for trust territories, support for the Inter-American Highway, and certain other programs. (As noted above, however, U.S. contributions to the UN Development Program and certain other international programs are included in *lines 10–14,* not in *30–34.*)

Line 35: Consists primarily of military assistance charged to Foreign Assistance Act appropriations but includes also $1,299 million of other military assistance grants.

Line 36: Consists overwhelmingly of military assistance charged to Foreign Assistance Act appropriations, but includes $1,738 million of other military assistance grants and $1,415 million of Export-Import Bank military loans.

The annual data for FAA military assistance represent deliveries. The cumulative totals represent the total amounts programmed for each country for the period 1950–68; the difference between the sum of the fiscal years (*cols. 1, 2, 3, and 11, lines 35–38*) and the cumulative total (*col. 12, lines 35–38*) is the value of FAA military goods and services programmed but not yet delivered.

    b. Column $14 = 12 - 13$ (except lines 5, 9).

    c. Line $6 = 10 + 16 + 29 + 30$.

    d. Line $16 = 17 + 26$.

    e. Line $17 = 18 + 19$.

    f. Line 19 = sum of lines 20–25.

    g. Less than $500,000.

    h. Line $37 = 6 + 35$.

    i. Line $38 = 2 + 36$.

ceived by the United States, amounted to $5 billion in the fiscal year 1966, but by 1968 had fallen to $4.45 billion, or less than the 1962 figure. During the Marshall Plan period, more than 90 percent of the aid from the principal aid agency was on a grant basis, but during the Foreign Assistance Act period, less than 50 percent took the form of grants. And with Vietnam excluded, the proportion of AID assistance in grant form fell below 40 percent for the three most recent fiscal years (1966–68).

During the Mutual Security Act period (1953–61), well over half the assistance provided by the United States to less developed countries came directly from the Mutual Security Agency, the Foreign Operations Administration, or the International Cooperation Administration (lineal forebears of AID); Food-for-Freedom accounted for less than 25 percent of total economic aid. During the period 1962–68, AID's share fell below 50 percent of the total while that of Food-for-Freedom rose to more than 30 percent of the total.[2] Net of repayments and interest, the contribution of the Export-Import Bank has been modest—less than $3 billion in long-term loans to less developed countries during the twenty-two years covered in Table 1.

United States contributions to international agencies rose, absolutely as well as relatively, during the 1960s but in the banner year 1968 still represented only one-eighth of the total U.S. contribution. Although the AID and predecessor U.S. aid agencies for many years dwarfed all other sources of development assistance, by mid-1969 the World Bank Group was providing as large a volume of assistance as the principal U.S. agency.

Assistance provided by the AID has in recent years been concentrated on a small number of countries. Nearly 90 percent of AID's total country assistance in fiscal year 1968 was received by fifteen countries. The largest commitment was to Vietnam ($400 million), which was followed in order by India ($301 million), Brazil ($194 million), Pakistan ($132 million), Colombia ($77 million), Korea

---

2. The point of the above comparison is the decline in institutional predominance of the aid agency, not the volume of food shipments. During the Mutual Security Act period, some MSA funds were regularly expended on surplus foodstuffs of the types later financed almost wholly by the Food-for-Freedom program.

($75 million), Turkey ($72 million), Laos, Chile, Thailand, the Dominican Republic, Indonesia, Nicaragua, Nigeria, and Panama.

In absolute size, as can be seen from Table 2, no other bilateral development assistance program begins to approach that of the United States. The figures were compiled by the Organisation for Economic Co-operation and Development (OECD) in Paris and are on a disbursement basis. They show dollar flows, net of amortization payments but not of interest, and they relate to calendar years, not fiscal years. In these reports, the U.S. flow of resources under official development assistance programs rises from $2.7 billion in 1960 to $3.6 billion in 1963 and 1964, but drops back to $3.3 billion in 1968. The second largest program, that of France, never quite reaches the billion-dollar level. For purposes of comparison, Table 2 includes net flows from all members of the OECD Development Assistance Committee that disbursed more than $100 million per year in 1967 and 1968. Previous OECD reports and press releases did not make the distinction between "official flows" and flows under "official *development assistance* programs," which is spelled out in footnote *a* to Table 2. Accordingly, John Pincus could report in 1967:

The Development Assistance Committee ... in effect defines aid as consisting of grants, loans of whatever terms or duration, contributions in kind, reparations payments, and consolidation credits (loans that allow a debtor to refinance his debt under more favorable conditions). Under the more inclusive heading of "flow of financial resources," it includes direct private investment, purchase of World Bank bonds, and government-guaranteed private export credits.... This definition doesn't make much sense, because it lumps together incommensurate transactions.... From the donor's viewpoint, a foreign loan is not aid if its terms and conditions approximate those of the domestic capital market. Of course, the recipient may still look on it as aid because his alternative borrowing rates are higher. The aid element in a loan can therefore be computed, for donors, as the difference between the face value of the loan and the present value of future interest and amortization discounted at the lender's alternative lending rate.[3]

3. John Pincus, *Trade, Aid and Development: The Rich and Poor Nations* (McGraw-Hill, 1967), pp. 308–09. Pincus is one who has struggled manfully with the problems of definition and comparison in this field. See also his earlier book, *Economic Aid and International Cost Sharing* (Santa Monica: RAND Corporation, July 1965), Chaps. 3 and 5.

TABLE 2. *Net Flow of Resources under Official Development Assistance Programs from Selected Industrialized Countries to Less Developed Countries and Multilateral Agencies, 1960–68*[a]

(Disbursements in millions of U.S. dollars)

Country	Calendar year								
	1960	*1961*	*1962*	*1963*	*1964*	*1965*	*1966*	*1967*	*1968*
Australia	59	71	74	96	100	119	126	157	160
Canada	75	61	34	65	78	96	187	198	175
France	847	943	976	852	828	752	745	826	855
Germany	242	322	400	398	473	437	440	528	554
Italy	91	79	94	113	59	80	62	120	165
Japan	105	108	85	138	116	244	283	384	355
Netherlands	35	56	65	38	49	70	94	114	134
United Kingdom	407	457	421	414	493	481	526	498	428
United States	2,702	2,943	3,272	3,627	3,611	3,571	3,599	3,559	3,347

Source: Organisation for Economic Co-operation and Development, press release A(69)33 (July 11, 1969), Table 6.

a. "Official development assistance" covers aid flows that are intended primarily to promote the economic development and welfare of less developed countries and to be concessional in character. The "total net flow of official resources" is consequently normally larger than the net flow "under official development assistance programs." The "selected industrialized countries" are those members of the OECD Development Assistance Committee having net disbursements in excess of $100 million per year in 1967 and 1968. "Net disbursements" represent gross disbursements during the year in question, minus capital repayments received during the year (that is, minus amortization but not interest payments on earlier loans). Disbursement figures include wide variations in grant–loan proportions and in loan terms. Disbursements reflect earlier commitments, not current appropriations or allocations. "Less developed countries" in OECD statistics include Greece, Spain, Turkey, Yugoslavia, and certain other areas not included as less developed countries in United Nations compilations.

Pincus's analysis led him to the conclusion that for the members of the Development Assistance Committee (DAC) in 1961 and 1962 the real cost of aid, from the donors' viewpoint, was about 60 percent of the nominal cost as then reported. The 1967 and 1968 DAC reports include more recent data on the grant element in donors' assistance programs (calculated on the basis of a discount rate that makes the donors appear somewhat more generous than they are), along with numerous other improvements in statistical detail and its analysis. Genuine dehydration of donor figures and convincing international comparisons of effort are hampered not only by conceptual difficulties that are hard to resolve, but also by the desire of each donor to look good—that is, generous—on the record and to avoid invidious comparison of his record with that of other donors.[4]

According to DAC records, the United States in 1968 ranked eighth among sixteen member countries in terms of the percentage of its GNP represented by net flows of official development assistance, and twelfth in terms of official plus private flows.[5]

Growth in Less Developed Countries

By historical standards, the overall growth record of the less developed countries as a group has been excellent during the 1960s, even better than the rate during the 1950s. If the rapidly growing less developed countries of southern Europe are included, the record for 1960–67 has been good enough to realize the principal growth target of the less developed countries, a 5 percent per year increase in gross domestic product (GDP). Table 3 shows, however, how modest the per capita gains in Africa, Asia, and Latin America have been, except in the Middle East and the Far East.[6]

The averages, of course, conceal wide differences in country performance. Of the 76 non-European countries on which data were available to the OECD Secretariat, 10 (Hong Kong, Iran, Israel, Jordan, Nicaragua, Panama, South Korea, Syria, Taiwan, and Thailand) registered overall growth rates of 7 percent per year or better, 5 (El

4. For an up-to-date discussion of the problems of measuring the concessionary or grant element in loans, see *World Bank, International Development Association, Annual Report 1968* (WBIDA, 1968), pp. 38–39, and, on p. 64, references to the literature on this subject.

5. Organisation for Economic Co-operation and Development, press release A(69)33 (July 11, 1969), Table 8.

6. As noted in Table 2, OECD reports include four European countries, Greece, Spain, Turkey, and Yugoslavia, among the developing countries. Collectively (and individually, with the exception of Turkey), they performed better than the average developing country during the period 1960–67. Moreover, they had by far the lowest rates of population increase, with the result that their per capita gains were better than double the average in Asia, Africa, and Latin America. With the inclusion of the four European countries, not only does the 5 percent growth target appear to have been realized, but the per capita target of 2.5 percent per year has been missed by only 0.1 percent.

TABLE 3. *Average Annual Rates of Growth of Gross Domestic Product, Population, and Per Capita Product of Less Developed Countries, by Region, 1960–67*

	Average annual percentage increase, 1960–67		
Region	Gross domestic product	Population	Gross domestic product per person
Africa	3.1	2.3	0.9
North of Sahara	2.2	2.6	−0.3
South of Sahara	3.7	2.3	1.4
Asia	5.2	2.5	2.6
Middle East	7.2	2.8	4.4
South	4.1	2.4	1.6
Far East	5.9	2.7	3.1
Latin America	4.7	2.9	1.7
North and Central	6.0	3.2	2.7
South	4.0	2.7	1.3
Europe	7.1	1.4	5.6
Total	5.0	2.5	2.4

Source: Organisation for Economic Co-operation and Development, *Development Assistance, 1968 Review*, Table VI-1, p. 117.

Salvador, Iraq, Mexico, Peru, and Trinidad and Tobago) attained rates between 6 and 7 percent, 25 were in the 4–6 percent range, and 36 fell below 4 percent. The 36, it should be added, include Brazil, India, Indonesia, and Pakistan and account for about half the population of the less developed world.[7] The relatively good record of the Far East, as shown in Table 3, reflects the fact that the superior economic performances of Hong Kong, South Korea, Taiwan, and Thailand more than made up for the sorry record of Indonesia during the Sukarno era.

Some of the largest receivers of aid enjoyed some of the best growth records. Frequently, however, it was not their promising growth prospects that first attracted a generous inflow of American aid, but the fact that the United States thought the countries merited

7. Large countries are more like continents; their growth rates represent an amalgam of regional records that are good, bad, and indifferent. They often include nation-sized areas such as the Punjab, Madras, and Gujarat in India in which economic progress has been as spectacular as anywhere else.

assistance on security grounds. Greece, Israel, Jordan, Korea, Taiwan, and Turkey are examples and the outstanding characteristic of U.S. aid to those countries was sustained, large-scale commodity assistance. The assistance appears to have had pump-priming effects that could not clearly be foreseen at the time the aid programs were launched but, in the words of Joan Nelson, "almost surely served as a powerful catalyst for later rapid growth." In some of the other aid-receiving countries, she suggests, "U.S. insistence on rather tightly drawn economic criteria for aid" may have caused the United States to fall short of its development objectives. Her concluding hypothesis is that "more generous assistance, provided with less concern for precise justification of the level, might be more effective."[8]

The effectiveness of U.S. aid to Taiwan during the period 1951–65 has been the subject of a sophisticated book-length evaluation by Neil H. Jacoby. At one point in the book he describes the construction of a "No-Aid Growth Model" for Taiwan on the basis of assumptions that probably exaggerated Taiwan's ability to make progress without aid. The exercise led him to the conclusion that

aid more than doubled the annual rate of growth of Taiwan's GNP, quadrupled the annual growth rate of per capita GNP, and cut thirty years from the time needed to attain 1964 living standards. Without aid, it was calculated that the GNP would have grown only 3.5 percent a year until 1983. The GNP in 1964 would have been only about 58 percent of the actual amount. The actual GNP of 1964 would not have been attained until 1980. Actual per capita GNP of 1964 would not have been produced until 1995.[9]

Equally relevant to conclusions about the value of foreign aid is the careful analysis and comparison of the growth experience of Pakistan and India during the years 1950–65 by Edward S. Mason. During the 1950s, the performance of the Indian economy was substantially better than that of Pakistan. During the first half of the 1960s, the positions were reversed. Mason believes Pakistan did a better job in managing its foreign exchange resources, and the difference in aid levels—it received substantially more aid per capita than India—

8. Joan M. Nelson, *Aid, Influence, and Foreign Policy* (Macmillan, 1968), p. 41.
9. Neil H. Jacoby, *U.S. Aid to Taiwan: A Study of Foreign Aid, Self-Help, and Development* (Praeger, 1966), p. 152.

facilitated better foreign exchange management, and would have made industrial development in Pakistan a great deal easier than in India even without better foreign exchange management. After reviewing the recent course of economic development as a whole in the two countries, he reports that "the difference in aid levels explains much but not everything." [10]

Needless to add, there are also documented cases of aid efforts that have not been spectacularly successful. But it is difficult to escape the conclusion that aid receipts have been vital in enabling a number of countries to attain highly encouraging rates of increase in overall and per capita income, rates that are truly spectacular by pre-World War II standards.

Aid Requirements during the 1970s

Specialists (including many in more developed countries who accept with equanimity domestic indexes and targets that are no more meaningful than overall increases in gross domestic product in low-income countries) have gone to great pains to highlight the inadequacies of the rate of increase in GDP or GNP as a measure of progress. They are right to point out its shortcomings; it *is* a simplistic measure. Yet oversimplification, initially at least, is almost a necessary price for moving a problem from the agenda of academia into the political realm.

For all their shortcomings, percentage increases in national product, overall and per capita, represent the kinds of broad, easily understood targets that are more or less indispensable as galvanizers of national and international efforts during the 1970s. The questions are: What should the overall growth targets be? With what other targets, quantitative and qualitative, should they be combined? [11]

10. Edward S. Mason, *Economic Development in India and Pakistan* (Harvard University, Center for International Affairs, September 1966), p. 64.

11. For an effort to measure "growth performance" rather than growth, see the paper by Alan M. Strout and Paul G. Clark, "Aid, Performance, Self-Help, and Need," AID Discussion Paper 20, Office of Program and Policy Coordination (July 1969; processed). The authors suggest that growth performance involves: the mobilization of additional resources for growth and development; efficiency in the use of

For countries that have been increasing their output of goods and services at the rate of 10 percent per year, a 6 percent growth rate might be an unacceptable second- or third-best effort. Others, capable of growing at 6–8 percent per year, will prefer to risk the loss of a percentage point or two in the growth rate in order to achieve a more equitable income distribution, to build up backward regions, or to maintain a sizable defense establishment. Each nation will want and deserve considerable leeway in setting its own targets.

For the less developed world as a whole, political exigencies—among them, rising aspirations, a conviction that more can be done than has been done, and the demand for jobs by young people who will be coming onto the labor market in increasing numbers during the 1970s—will probably require higher targets than the 5 percent overall, 2.5 percent per capita rates that enjoyed a wide measure of acceptance during the 1960s. The less developed world as a whole will seek an inflow of resources sufficient to permit it to achieve an overall increase in GNP or GDP of not less than 6 percent per year, provided reasonably sensible domestic policies are followed.

There is no magic in any figure, though a 6–7 percent target would be high enough to be ambitious and not so high as to be implausible. As in the past, some nations will do better and some will do worse. In neither case are the political consequences in terms of stability, democracy, or a peaceful foreign policy axiomatic. (And this is one of the reasons that rich countries will resist commitments to particular rates of growth.) Yet increases of 6–7 percent per year, if shared with a modicum of social justice, could mean per capita increases of 4 percent per year—enough to provide a real sense of forward movement, a doubling of the standard of living in less than twenty years.

Though much depends on what is done in the field of trade policy

---

both domestic and foreign resources; structural and other changes necessary for longer-run economic, social, and political growth; and the effects of the foregoing on the level and distribution of income and welfare. They experiment with a few of the available economic indicators of good growth performance (more rapid export growth, smaller increases in cost of living, higher marginal savings, and so forth), indicators which they believe may be forerunners of a subsequent acceleration of GNP growth and which are in any event desirable features of the development process.

and in increasing the productivity of the capital and technical assistance that is made available, in my opinion it will be exceedingly difficult for the less developed countries to achieve the broadly shared 4 percent per person per year growth target that I favor for the 1970s without a substantial increase in current levels of foreign aid. By a fortunate coincidence, the targets can, I believe, be met with long-term capital inflows approximating 1 percent of the GNP of rich countries.

Although almost every study of aid requirements that has been made indicates that the less developed countries could put to productive use one and one-half to two times as much foreign aid as the current levels, it has become fashionable to dismiss these studies as pseudoscientific exercises. They suffer from two types of defects which are often confused. In the first place, the growth targets or other goals incorporate value judgments that are not universally accepted and are not provably ideal. The critic can rightfully ask, "Why a 6 or 7 percent per year rate of overall growth? Why not a 4, 5, or 8 percent gain?" Or, "Why not a rate of growth that will permit a 1 or 2 percent per year decline in the rate of unemployment until the level reaches 4 percent of the labor force?" In the second place, even if the goals are acceptable, the requirements estimates that follow from them may be unacceptable because of errors inherent in this kind of forecasting, particularly in the forecasting of export earnings.

Raymond F. Mikesell, for example, provides an excellent critique of the three basic approaches to the calculation of foreign aid requirements for less developed countries, namely, the savings-investment gap approach, the foreign-exchange-earnings–expenditure gap approach, and the capital-absorption approach. He rejects all three approaches and admits candidly that his own approach "does not provide the basis for a ready calculation of aid requirements."[12] I question whether we can talk seriously about a foreign aid program for the 1970s without such a basis.

---

12. Raymond F. Mikesell, *The Economics of Foreign Aid* (Chicago: Aldine Publishing Co., 1968), pp. 70–104, 281.

As John Pincus says,

The defects of all these methods are obvious to those who make projections and those who use them. . . . Despite the talent and ingenuity that have been devoted to these projection techniques, all we can say with confidence is that more aid is probably better for LDC growth than less aid, with any given set of political situations assumed constant. . . . The underlying issue is ethical, not technical. . . . There is always some total that is appropriate to a particular set of standards or targets. But it is important to remember that agreement on those standards is a pre-condition of agreement as to aid levels.[13]

Four frequently cited estimates of aid requirements are compared in the recently released report of the Perkins Committee. In these estimates, each of which takes the form of a range spanning several billion dollars, global needs "around 1973" run from a low of $13 billion to a high of $21 billion, whereas 1 percent of the GNP of members of the DAC is estimated to be $19.5 billion in that year.[14] My high growth target for the less developed countries, even coupled with high export earnings on their part, would doubtless result in an aid "requirement" closer to the $21 billion figure than to the $13 billion figure. The capital requirements of the less developed countries are currently being studied anew by a UN committee under the chairmanship of the Dutch economist, Jan Tinbergen.

I agree with John Pincus that, as an aid level, 1 percent of the GNP of the developed countries has acquired a certain appropriateness. This figure has been bandied about since the 1943 conference in Atlantic City that launched the United Nations Relief and Rehabilitation Administration (UNRRA), but frequently with little concern as to whether the target should be 1 percent of GNP or of national income. At the Atlantic City conference, it proved impossible to adopt a formula that would adequately reflect the capacity to pay of the various contributing countries. The rough-and-ready solution, introduced into the proceedings by Dean Acheson of the U.S. delegation, was to seek from countries whose territory had not been

13. *Trade, Aid and Development*, pp. 300–04.
14. *Report of the President's General Advisory Committee on Foreign Assistance Programs*, Oct. 25, 1968 (1969), pp. 35–36.

occupied by the enemy a commitment to contribute 1 percent of their national incomes.

Then in 1960, on the initiative of India, the UN General Assembly passed without dissent a resolution requesting the developed countries to transfer 1 percent of their national income to the underdeveloped countries for development. The UN Conference on Trade and Development (UNCTAD) held in Geneva in 1964 also couched its recommendation in terms of national income. Subsequently, a group of experts in a report to the UN Economic and Social Council on "The Measurement of the Flow of Resources from Developed Market Economies to the Developing Countries" recommended measuring aid against GNP at market prices, though they suggested that there probably ought also to be a series of measures of resource flows. The 1968 UNCTAD adopted a target figure of 1 percent of GNP but was unable to agree on a target date for reaching that figure.

National income differs from GNP mainly by excluding depreciation charges and other allowances for business and institutional consumption of durable goods, and indirect taxes. These exclusions in the OECD countries amount to nearly 20 percent of GNP—enough to have made a difference of well over $1 billion per year during the 1960s in the capital flow from the United States alone, under a 1 percent formula. The question of whether to use GNP or national income was therefore not just a technicians' quibble.[15]

With GNP in the OECD area growing at more than $100 billion per year, an implemented decision to step up the flow of long-term resources to less developed countries to 1 percent of GNP would mean a rise of more than $1 billion per year in the flow. Were the principle of progressivity introduced into the contribution scale, as it eventually will be, very rich countries such as the United States, Canada, and Sweden would be expected to contribute a larger fraction of their GNP than less affluent rich countries such as Japan, Austria, and Italy. Meanwhile, the flat 1 percent figure for all noncommunist industrialized countries is widely accepted.

15. See the discussion of the 1 percent target in Organisation for Economic Co-operation and Development, *Development Assistance Efforts and Policies: 1967 Review* (OECD, 1967), pp. 103–10.

The dawn of a new decade of development and the proposal for a World Development Charter, however, have sharply stimulated efforts to find more sophisticated indexes of requirements and ways of meeting them. The 1 percent target is too donor-centered, too aggregative, too fortuitously related to requirements, and too unrelated to the rationale for development assistance to last indefinitely.

By donor-centered, I mean such oddities as the resulting reduced aid flows during periods of recession in the donor countries, when requirements in less developed countries would in all probability increase because of reduced trade levels and other difficulties. The 1 percent figure is too aggregative in lumping together a lot of resource flows without distinction as to quality and effectiveness in stimulating development. While I believe it would permit requirements to be met, the target was not really derived from calculations of developmental requirements but inherited, *faute de mieux*, from an earlier relief program.

Though no one thinks of American foreign investment in Canada as foreign aid to Canada or Canadian investment in the United States as foreign aid from Canada, the inclusion of private investment flows to less developed countries in the 1 percent target carries an implication that the flows constitute aid when directed to low-income countries. A subsidiary target for what was referred to earlier in this chapter as "official development assistance" in relation to GNP would be more useful operationally.[16]

If the nascent sense of international community and conscience which makes it logically impossible to prosecute a war on poverty at home and abandon it at the water's edge is accepted as a basic rationale for development assistance, one could perhaps expect the magnitude of the effort on the foreign front to be linked in some direct way to the magnitude of the domestic effort. If the American people were asked to devote one dollar to the international war on

16. In this connection, the target recommended by the Pearson Commission is net disbursements of official development assistance sufficient to reach 0.7 percent of GNP by 1975 or shortly thereafter but in no case later than 1980. *Partners in Development*, Report of the Commission on International Development, Lester B. Pearson, chairman (Praeger, 1969), p. 148.

poverty for every four or five dollars devoted domestically to the same cause, the dichotomy between the two wars, the notion that one deserves an absolute priority over the other, might gradually be overcome.[17] At this moment, however, it is hard to see why any conceivable mathematical relationship between domestic and foreign expenditures for antipoverty programs by high-income countries should be more persuasive to parliaments in those countries than calculations of aid "requirements" in low-income countries.

Income Distribution within Less Developed Countries

Achievements such as a 6–7 percent per year overall increase in GNP or a 4 percent increase in the per capita growth rate of a less developed country tell us nothing about the internal distribution of the gains. The sharing problem is critically important. It is most unfortunate that data on income distribution within less developed countries are so meager and inadequate. The belief is widespread that development and development assistance to date have chiefly benefited small in-groups and barely touched the masses. If development efforts were more obviously devoted to improving the welfare of the lower and middle income groups in the population, not only the humanitarian argument for aid from rich to poor countries but other elements of the rationale as well would be greatly strengthened.

Is the feeling that the rich are becoming richer while the poor are being bypassed confirmed by evidence? Is this a price that has to be paid for growth? Would the more equitable distribution of income reduce rates of saving and add to aid requirements? Under what circumstances are expenditures for consumption in poor countries (for example, food to overcome hunger or malnutrition) a form of investment that is at least as likely to improve productivity as more conventional forms of investment?

Insofar as competent economists can judge, inequality in income distribution is greater in the less developed countries than it is today in the so-called developed countries, but probably no greater than

17. I am indebted to Patricia W. Blair for this idea.

it was in the latter before World War I. The explanation is that, in the earlier stages of development, those who have, or can lay their hands on, the resources to invest reap large profits that enable them to reinvest, and this increases inequality. The scarcity of talent adds to the special advantage of the few.[18] The inequality may be welcomed as proof that development is proceeding normally, and the conclusion may be drawn that introduction of more equity into the system too early in the game will affect adversely the long-term rate of growth. In due course, progressive taxation will take its bite and a better distribution of wealth will follow.

Gunnar Myrdal vigorously argues the opposite line: that a more equitable distribution of income at an early stage is not only favorable to development but almost a condition for it, at least in South Asia. The important question, he says,

is whether there is a conflict between economic equalization and economic progress, that is, whether a price must be paid for equalization in terms of retarded progress. Naturally, this issue cannot be settled by general and abstract argument. Even in the West today we lack detailed knowledge of how factors such as the savings ratio, labor input, and efficiency react to different systems of distribution; discussion of these matters is abstract and speculative. Knowledge of the relevant facts is even more meager in the South Asian countries. Nevertheless, it is possible to point to a number of conditions that suggest that there, much more than in the Western countries, an increase in equality would help rather than hinder development.[19]

The conditions to which he subsequently points are rather persuasive to me. But whatever judgment professional economists eventually reach, it seems almost certain that pressures for a more equitable distribution of the fruits of modernization in less developed countries will increase during the 1970s. Targets for per capita growth in the less developed world as a whole will be closer to 4 percent per year than 2.5 percent, and the increase will have to be

18. Maurice J. Williams and Richard J. Ward, "Aspects of the Income Inequality Problem in the Less Developed Countries" (Agency for International Development, Feb. 5, 1969; processed), p. 20.

19. *Asian Drama: An Inquiry Into the Poverty of Nations* (Twentieth Century Fund, 1968), pp. 646–47.

broadly shared among different regions, sectors of the economy, ethnic groups, and income classes within a country.

On the problem of how to restructure foreign assistance so that it will be least vulnerable to the charge of making the rich richer and will in fact help the middle- and lower-income groups at the earliest possible date, I would like to see a task force at work. To date, effective direct taxation of income in countries at an early stage of development has proved exceedingly difficult, but the difficulties may not be insuperable. Moreover, there may be indirect ways to tax income which aid programs could promote via technical assistance.

The network of economic controls maintained by many less developed countries—import controls, exchange controls, travel permits, work permits, licenses of all kinds—tends to benefit the haves rather than the have-nots, facilitates graft and corruption, and often hampers rather than expedites development. It can be pierced by foreign aid in the right amounts at the right times. (This was demonstrated a few years ago by U.S. aid to Pakistan in dismantling certain import controls.) In addition, more foreign aid can perhaps be channeled directly to the urban and rural poor, by providing small amounts of credit and technical assistance to organized community groups,[20] or by partial financing of major programs of public works. Any appearance of American support for a "trickle-down" theory of development, which provides benefits for the poor only after the rich have become conspicuously richer, must be avoided.

Corruption and maldistribution of income gains are not the same thing, but they often go hand in hand. Shocking examples of profiteering and conspicuous displays of wealth on the part of persons in high places—the accumulation of a $40 million fortune by Sarit Thanarit, former prime minister of Thailand, while in office; the meteoric rise of Ayub Khan's son, Gohar, from army captain in 1962 to big-time financier at the time of Ayub's downfall in 1969; the Manila entrepreneur who celebrated his wedding anniversary with a $500,000 party while the average Filipino ekes out a precarious

20. See, for example, William Sanders' discussion of the work of the Pan American Development Foundation in *International Development Review*, Vol. 11 (June 1969), pp. 2–4.

existence on $150 a year; and other less notorious cases—have done much to undermine confidence in the governments of less developed countries and to discredit foreign aid.[21]

Campaigns to reduce outright corruption in less developed countries will unquestionably have to receive increased attention during the 1970s. A prerequisite is to overcome what Myrdal refers to as the "taboo on research on corruption." Corruption, he suggests,

is rationalized, when challenged, by certain sweeping assertions: that there is corruption in all countries (this notion, eagerly advanced by students indigenous to the region, neglects the relative prevalence of corruption in South Asia and its specific effects in that social setting); that corruption is natural in South Asian countries because of deeply ingrained institutions and attitudes carried over from colonial and precolonial times (this primarily Western contention should, of course, provide an approach to research and a set of hypotheses, not an excuse for ignoring the problem); that corruption is needed to oil the intricate machinery of business and politics in South Asian countries and is, perhaps, not a liability given the conditions prevailing there (again, this mainly Western hypothesis about the functioning of the economic and social system should underline rather than obviate the need for research); that there is not as much corruption as is implied by the public outcry in the South Asian countries (this claim needs to be substantiated, and if it is true, the causes and effects of that outcry should be investigated).[22]

Even if corruption is rooted out completely, questions of equity versus growth will remain and keep the problem of income distribution high on the development agenda during the 1970s.

21. See Stanley Karnow, "Plight of the Poor Belies Philippines 'Growth'" and "Poverty, Violence, Corruption Infest Philippine Society," *Washington Post*, Dec. 25 and 26, 1968; Selig S. Harrison, "Social Inequalities Led to Ayub's Fall," *Washington Post*, Feb. 24, 1969; Bernard D. Nossiter, "Emphasis on West Pakistan a Factor in Ayub's Downfall," *Washington Post*, March 26, 1969; Joseph Lelyveld, "Pakistani Economic Panel Questions Own Plans," *New York Times*, Dec. 1, 1968; Myrdal, *Asian Drama*, Chap. 20: "Corruption—Its Causes and Effects," pp. 937–58.

22. *Asian Drama*, p. 939. Samuel P. Huntington is one of a growing handful of social scientists who are disregarding the taboo to which Myrdal refers. Huntington's book *Political Order in Changing Societies* (Yale University Press, 1968) includes (pp. 59–71) a stimulating and highly relevant discussion of "corruption and modernization," particularly with respect to the relationship between the prevalence of corruption and the absence of effective political parties. See also J. S. Nye, "Corruption and Political Development: A Cost-Benefit Analysis," *American Political Science Review*, Vol. 61 (June 1967), pp. 417–27.

Standard-Setting via a World Development Charter and Council

In order to help establish global standards for aid providers and aid receivers, the Netherlands delegation suggested to the General Assembly of the United Nations in 1966 that there should be a world charter for development. The assembly in due course adopted a lengthy two-part resolution: "Recognizing that the formulation of a consolidated statement of the rights and duties of peoples and nations might sustain and enhance international development efforts and co-operation and could help to enlist wider public support for the strengthening of development policies . . ." In the operative portion of Part A of the resolution, the secretary-general was requested "to prepare a concise and systematic survey of the various principles, directives and guidelines for action in the field of development." In Part B, he was requested to prepare also a "preliminary framework of international development strategy for the 1970s within which initial efforts could be concentrated."[23]

At the 1967 General Assembly session, the Netherlands delegation again put itself enthusiastically behind these efforts. It urged that the secretary-general prepare not only a survey of the various principles, directives, and guidelines in the field of development cooperation but also a preliminary outline of a charter of development. "Our expectation is that next year [1968] the General Assembly will appoint a governmental committee" which can take the secretary-general's preliminary outline as a starting point and draw up a draft charter.[24]

The U.S. delegation lukewarmly endorsed the Dutch proposal for a charter. According to its spokesman in the Second Committee: "The United States delegation supported that idea. Such a document might contain a larger number of targets than those set for the present

23. GA Res. 2218 (XXI), Dec. 19, 1966. United Nations, *Official Records* (GAOR), 21st sess., supp. 16 (A/6316) (1967), pp. 42–43.
24. Statement by B. J. Udink, minister in charge of development aid, in Committee II, UN General Assembly, Oct. 20, 1967. Udink returned to the fray in 1968 and in his speech of November 8 expressed the hope that his suggestion for an intergovernmental committee would "now be followed up."

decade. *But it was also necessary to avoid introducing precise commitments*, which might not be acceptable to many Governments."[25]

A successful charter-drafting exercise could supply a greatly needed fillip to the establishment of a rationale, framework, and level of international effort for development promotion in the 1970s. By spelling out succinctly the self-help obligations of the less developed countries, the level and character of the contributions to be made by the more developed countries, and the arrangements for monitoring the subsequent actions of both groups, it could provide a timely reason for the United States to abandon the short-term framework of the Foreign Assistance Acts of the 1960s in favor of broad implementing legislation.

However, given the enormous variations among countries in capacity and willingness to supply resources or use them efficiently, and given conflicting and constantly changing conceptions of national interest, the commitments in the charter are almost bound to be imprecise. As UN development specialists have noted:

It is probably desirable, and it may even be essential, to focus an international development strategy on quantitative global targets for desirable levels of development (in gross national product, education, health, employment and so forth) and on uniform measures (institutional reforms, economic planning, population policies and so forth) needed to overcome the obstacles to growth. To do so may be a necessary way of lending cohesiveness (and public understanding, which is vital) to the concerted attack on poverty, ignorance and disease and of establishing standards against which each developing country can determine and demonstrate the magnitude and plan the phasing of the efforts it must make.

There is, however, a danger—a risk of distortion, of inequality of commitment, of lack of credibility, and of eventual disillusionment—in any tendency to use such target averages and norms as, or to confuse them with, the goals to be sought at the country level. . . .

If the real purpose of defining quantitative global objectives is, as it should be, to establish some tangible and useful expression of the over-all purposes of the concerted efforts—a sort of universally acceptable international frame of reference—further work will need to be done to relate

25. UN General Assembly, 22d sess., Provisional Summary Record of 1,167th Mtg. (Dec. 8, 1967), Doc. A/C.2/SR. 1167, p. 4. (The italics are mine.)

the global targets as realistically as possible to the development potential of the individual countries.[26]

As reported earlier in this chapter in the discussion of growth rates, a 6–7 percent per year rise in overall growth may be a good target for the less developed world as a whole, but each country will want and deserve considerable leeway in setting its own growth targets. Similarly, donor countries as a group can afford to contribute ⅔ to ¾ of 1 percent of their gross national product in the form of official development assistance, but separately each can envisage circum- stances in which a legal commitment to do so year in and year out would be embarrassing.

Though governments will refuse to commit themselves in ironclad fashion to a set of numerical targets, they may be willing to announce such targets, pledge their best efforts to achieve them, and establish a mechanism for appraising national efforts and publicizing the ap- praisal. The World Development Charter, in other words, could provide for a World Development Council or some other prestigious group to monitor fulfillment of obligations undertaken, progress made, requirements that are emerging, and problems that need atten- tion. If created, the council should consist of outstandingly qualified independent experts, appointed by the secretary-general of the United Nations (provided he can appoint them without having to rely too heavily on "consultations with member governments") or by the president of the World Bank. Experts serving in their individ- ual capacities can produce franker, livelier, more trenchant reports than a group of government representatives burdened with bulky briefs from their home offices or a council of international agency directors understandably interested in puffing up the achievements of their agencies, staking out claims for additional responsibilities, and glossing over shortcomings that should be exposed.

The appointment of the Pearson Commission by Robert S. Mc- Namara, president of the World Bank, is evidence of the latter's ability to appoint men of distinction. Headed by Lester B. Pearson,

26. Comments of UN Development Programme on International Development Strategy for the 1970s, Doc. E/AC.56/L.1/Add. 3, E/AC.54/L.32/Add. 3, Feb. 4, 1969, pp. 25–26.

former prime minister of Canada, the commission was named in late 1968, pursuant to proposals for a one-shot "grand assize" made a year earlier in Stockholm by McNamara's predecessor, George D. Woods. A World Development Council, whether set up by means of a World Development Charter or independently, should be a continuing body. It should have a small professional staff and a panel of experts that it can call on for individual country reviews. It need not have development funds at its disposal, but its overall report (like that of our own Council of Economic Advisers) and its country reviews should be authoritative enough to influence the agencies that do have funds. After publication, the overall report could perhaps be placed on the agenda of the UN Economic and Social Council for discussion.

With the exception of the unpublicized but useful country reviews conducted within the framework of the Development Assistance Committee of the OECD, the performance of aid-providing nations tends to be far less closely scrutinized than that of aid-receiving nations. Some years ago, the distinguished Indian economist, I. G. Patel, called it "a curious commentary on our international institutional framework that while the IMF 'consults' its poorer members every year with all the thoroughness of a judicial inquiry and with specific recommendations in regard to removal of exchange restrictions, no such machinery with the same authority exists for bringing about the necessary reform in the commercial policy of the advanced nations."[27]

The International Monetary Fund (IMF) and the General Agreement on Tariffs and Trade (GATT) are technically equipped to deal with monetary and commercial policy issues; the World Development Council should not do their work for them nor duplicate the work of functioning consortia and consultative groups. It should concentrate on overall development performance, with particular reference to the fulfillment of obligations implicit in the World Development Charter or other formal undertakings.

At the same time, the council should be capable of expressing its findings in easily understood terms worthy of the attention of intelli-

27. "Exports by Countries in Process of Industrialization," in *New Directions for World Trade: A Chatham House Report* (Oxford University Press, 1964), p. 104.

gent laymen throughout the world. Part of its role, in other words, should be to keep the public well enough informed to put pressure on national political leadership to live up to its development obligations. This applies to rich countries and poor countries alike.

If church groups, chambers of commerce, labor unions, farm organizations, and others had authoritative reviews of national efforts by the council, they could do much to educate the public. Without backing of this sort, an American President may hesitate to invest the time and political capital required to keep development assistance programs alive and effective. With it, he can in effect say to the Congress, "Consistent with the recommendations of the World Development Council and the expressed desires of various well-known groups, I ask this year for a program of the following magnitude and scope."

A conviction that development of the low-income world is important, is in the long-term interests of the United States, and can be helped by financial and technical assistance from abroad would be a prerequisite for rather than a consequence of active American participation in a charter-drafting exercise. The consequence, if the exercise were reasonably successful, would be a firm indication to the Congress and the American people that other high-income countries were prepared to "share the burden" with the United States, that poor countries recognized their obligation to use resources efficiently, and that requirements and performance were authoritatively reviewed on a regular basis.

One of the difficulties of the World Charter-World Council idea is that it could so easily become neither a spur nor a guideline but an exercise in futility, irrelevant to the real world of policy making. Considerable time and money could be spent, with the end result a charter filled with pious platitudes committing nobody to anything and a council that became one more otiose bit of international machinery. The reverberations of even the most ringing declarations soon grow dim. Prestigious council members have a tendency to lose their halos on entering the marketplace and ultimately to be succeeded by less prestigious appointees.

An alternative approach, lower key but more likely to evoke support in the foreign ministries of the larger donor countries, is to work upward from the operational level rather than downward from the inspirational; in other words, to concentrate on improving the machinery already in existence. The United Nations has put a number of commissions, committees, and ad hoc groups to work on preparations for the second decade of development (DD II) and out of these may come useful proposals for invigorating the international development effort. Independently of these activities, the consortia and consultative groups already in existence for key developing countries can be built up into authoritative sources of information on the performance and requirements of aid-receiving countries and the specific roles that different donors and multilateral agencies should play in meeting requirements. Eventually, the World Bank or some other appropriate agency could consolidate the country reports into an influential overall report.

Overcoming America's Aid Weariness

The novelty and glamour of aiding exotic lands have worn off. The larger, longer-lasting outflow of development assistance from the United States that most experts consider essential faces almost insuperable domestic political hurdles. The reasons are familiar and many of them have little to do with imperfections in the aid program; the program is more victim than cause of disenchantment and frustration.

The Congress has no desire to authorize back-door financing and has become increasingly hostile to front-door financing. The American public appears massively indifferent, perhaps because its humanitarianism and fundamental decency have not been properly appealed to. According to public opinion polls, a majority of the American people has consistently backed foreign aid in principle. Yet the nation's sense of outrage over the beating that the program has taken in the Congress during the last few years has to date been fairly well confined to the editorial pages of the *New York Times* and the *Washington Post*.

Groping for clues to substantive or administrative improvements in the U.S. effort, a distinguished AID administrator confessed frankly before leaving office:

The loudest signal that I get from Capitol Hill is not that the program is insufficiently concentrated; not that it is insufficiently multilateral; not that it isn't working and not that aid is ineffective. The main signal from the Hill, it seems to me, is one of indifference.

Attribute this indifference to anything you like: Vietnam, the problems of our cities, higher taxes, lack of understanding of what development means, dissatisfaction with the state of the world, general frustration, neo-isolationism. You name it. The result is the same: our foreign assistance efforts are lagging badly and nobody seems to care.[28]

How can people who should care learn to care? When raucous demonstrations, physical occupation of public buildings by demonstrators, and the hurling of rocks, stinkbombs, and obscenities have become the most fashionable ways to shock the establishment and register discontent, less dramatic prescriptions seem painfully bland. But a call to the barricades would be premature. The more conventional remedies have not been exhausted. Education to overcome American apathy about development assistance remains a better, more democratic answer.

Initially, the educational effort should be directed toward opinion leaders and key congressmen—the mass market for detailed information on foreign policy issues is practically nonexistent. Because the public at large is indifferent, the individual legislator has great latitude on foreign aid. If he is educable at all, he can be influenced by the views of a few people whom he genuinely respects.

In the long run, the mass market cannot be ignored. Nothing is more dangerous to democracy than the tendency of opinion leaders to talk to each other and leave to someone else the job of talking to the people. Pressure from below is needed to guide and ratify the broad thrust of public policies.

Unfortunately, during most of the 1960s, there was no national, nongovernmental citizens' organization engaged on a full-time basis

28. William S. Gaud, address to the American Assembly on World Hunger, Nov. 2, 1968.

in research and education on the problems and needs of the less developed countries and the U.S. response thereto. No public support group was dedicated to evaluating development assistance programs and making policy recommendations, preparing educational materials on these matters and disseminating them, or maintaining liaison with leaders in the executive and legislative branches of the U.S. government, in mass membership agencies such as labor unions, in farm and business groups, and in universities and private organizations at home and abroad. Early in 1969 such an organization was launched under the name Overseas Development Council. It has impressive business and foundation support and may be expected gradually to exercise considerable educational influence.

Presidential leadership in building political support for a more liberal, more sustained, and more sustainable development assistance program is, of course, essential. The present arrangements—lack of readable, objective appraisals to which the President can refer in justifying the size and scope of his request, absence of basic authorizing legislation for aid, strained relations between executive and legislative branches of the U.S. government, cumbersome congressional procedures—maximize the amount of time and effort the President must devote to his foreign aid program and make it hard for the country to assume a stance appropriate for the 1970s. The debates on the authorization and appropriation measures have regularly given the Congress its greatest opportunity to vent its frustration and irritation over the President's conduct of domestic and foreign affairs and the unmanageable onward rush of events in a troubled world. In the never-ending struggle for power between the legislative and executive branches, they offer the former scope and rope for hobbling the latter.

The Congress, in addition to providing the public funds that are needed, should provide some broad guidelines for their use. The national interest will be best served, however, if the legislative branch gives to the larger, better-staffed executive branch considerable discretion with respect to how much, to whom, and for how many years—and if both branches keep at least one eye fixed on the long-term outlook, regardless of the irritations of the moment. The reason for a broad grant of discretionary authority is not that the executive branch is wiser but that legislation is a much more explosive, unilateral, and inflexible device than negotiation for securing, for instance, a more peaceful Egyptian foreign policy, compensation for nationalization of American property, or preference for the small business enterprise.

The check list of statutory criteria that must be satisfied before loans from aid appropriations can be approved includes 63 items, many of which, viewed separately, may appear defensible. Together they constitute a straitjacket. When foreign aid legislation is expanded by the Congress from the establishment of general guidelines into the preparation of a manual of detailed instructions to the aid administrator, the results are more likely to serve local than national interests. The national interest will also suffer if aid legislation is allowed to become a vehicle for the ventilation of congressional irritation with the conduct of other aspects of foreign or domestic policy.

None of this is intended to imply that the executive branch never needs a kick in the pants, that shock treatment for a designated foreign government will not sometimes prove helpful, or that the withholding of aid is always an antisocial act. It *is* intended to imply that the much-amended, highly restrictive Foreign Assistance Act of 1961 is inadequate as a framework for development assistance in the 1970s.

CHAPTER FIVE

Four Special Problems

THE PRINCIPAL PREREQUISITES for a more durable, mutually satisfactory relationship during the 1970s between the richest of the rich countries and almost ninety poor countries have already been mentioned. On the American side, they include acceptance of a rationale for development assistance that, inter alia, recognizes the drive to conquer poverty abroad as a logical extension of the same pressures and considerations, moral and material, that make urgent the conquest of poverty here at home; reversal of the cynicism and boredom that have somehow shrouded the amazing headway made since the end of World War II; provision of external resources on a scale sufficient, when combined with mobilizable domestic resources, to raise still further the pace and quality of development in the low-income countries; and institutionalization of relationships in ways that minimize the strains inherent in confrontations of rich donor and poor recipient and maximize the self-respect of both parties.

Related in various ways to the above are four special, somewhat disparate problems that merit mention at this point: the country-programming process that has been evolved by the United States government to facilitate the allocation of aid; the debt burden of the less developed countries and the financial terms on which future assistance is provided; the population problem and the need for a breakthrough in the 1970s comparable to what appears to have been achieved in agriculture in the 1960s; and that hardy perennial, the multilateral-bilateral mix. Other problems could be mentioned—how to assist less developed countries in building effective educational systems is almost as important as controlling the population explosion—but this book was never intended to be a comprehensive treatise on all aspects of development.

The Country-Programming Process

In practice, the magnitude and composition of the American aid program in an aid-receiving country in any given year are determined primarily by the size and scope of the program in the preceding year.[1] In theory, they are determined by an elaborate program planning process, which began as an effort to get away from the piecemeal approach of the 1950s and to substitute for it a more comprehensive analysis of needs and priorities. The process for a given year normally takes fifteen to eighteen months,

spanning field mission analysis and discussions with host government, Washington review, Congressional action on the appropriations request, final allocation of funds to regions and countries, and commitment of funds for specific projects or programs. Radical changes in a country's economic or political situation may make necessary a readjustment of country program proposals at any time during this process.[2]

The exercise is supposed to help allocate U.S. resources in the light of relevant information about what the receiving country has done

1. "At any one time, the bulk of most country assistance programs consists of projects started several years earlier and not yet completed. The country situation, or U.S. judgment of priorities, or the nature of the U.S. interest in the country may have changed in the interim. But the projects cannot be abruptly broken off or modified without badly damaging mission morale, violating contractual obligations, and, in all likelihood, straining relations with the aided country." Joan M. Nelson, *Aid, Influence, and Foreign Policy* (Macmillan, 1968), p. 48.

2. Agency for International Development, *Principles of Foreign Economic Assistance* (September 1965), p. 9.

and will do with its own resources; it is not supposed to be a substitute for development planning on the part of the country itself. The process need not be spelled out here, since it has already been described with great perspicacity by a former member of the Program Coordination Staff of the Agency for International Development (AID).[3] It is indeed "the major conceptual means of providing substantive content to the American desire to influence the development policies and plans of the recipient countries."[4]

Some of the principal advances of the 1960s in techniques for the use of outside assistance to expedite development can be attributed to the deep U.S. involvement in the programming process. Nevertheless, the point of diminishing returns has, I suspect, been reached, and a more indirect U.S. involvement during the 1970s would be preferable. This view is violently disputed by some of the ablest professionals in the AID.

The programming process begins with a statement of U.S. objectives in the low-income country. That statement "is almost always a pro forma quotation from earlier submissions or from State Department documents on U.S. policy toward a country. . . . It is seldom an independent statement of policy. This is as one would expect. The A.I.D. programming process is not the appropriate channel through which to determine basic U.S. policy toward a country."[5]

Yet the starting point makes it almost inevitable that the end result will be a program more attuned to U.S. interests in the area than to the objectives and interests of the country itself. Is this a good thing, a bad thing, or, as is usual in such situations, sometimes good and sometimes bad? Is the process essential to give the United States the leverage which the exercise is alleged to confer (by revealing required changes on the part of the receiving country in monetary, fiscal, foreign exchange, and other development policies and permitting aid to be related to policy changes)? If the United States

3. Nelson, *Aid, Influence, and Foreign Policy*, pp. 48–67. Official sources include pp. 8–13 of *Principles of Foreign Economic Assistance* and portions of Agency for International Development, *AID Manual*, Chap. 1000.

4. National Planning Association, *A New Conception of U.S. Foreign Aid*, Special Report 64 (Washington: March 1969), p. 21.

5. Nelson, *Aid, Influence, and Foreign Policy*, p. 60.

lacked its present imposing country-programming apparatus, replete with resident field missions to cushion relations between Washington and the capitals of key less developed countries, would the Congress try to maximize U.S. leverage through the even clumsier device of legislating the size and scope of the U.S. effort, country by country?

In trying to clarify problems connected with country programming, it will be helpful to consider three issues separately: (1) whether the basic principles implicit in country programming are still valid; (2) if so, whether the locus of country programming should be changed; and (3) the relationship of country programming to leverage on the low-income country.

Development assistance could be allocated with little ado by adopting a formula for distribution based on population, or population and per capita income, or population, per capita income, and foreign trade as a fraction of gross national product (GNP). Though there is much to be said in favor of entitlement by formula, at present most donor governments will recoil in horror at anything so simple and straightforward. In its pristine form, the project approach was also a substitute for country programming; donors needed only to approve and finance "good" projects and reject "bad" ones.

If, however, overall resource use by the less developed country is to rank as a major consideration, some system for reviewing past, present, and proposed uses of its resources is necessary. The idea of regularly looking ahead for several years at a time, of trying to ascertain whether the country's policies are sufficiently conducive to development and how the host country's resources can best be combined with external resources in order to achieve priority goals, can only be lauded. Country-programming arrangements are deficient, not because the basic objective is obsolete, but because current procedures are so ponderous, make so many superfluous demands on scarce and overworked decision makers, and are not designed to satisfy simultaneously a larger number of interested parties. The substantial investment of U.S. time and energy in independently amassing detailed information tends to downgrade the developing country's assessment of its own needs and priorities, encourage a Papa-knows-best attitude on the part of the United States, and involve the United States too intimately in the internal affairs of other countries.

In renewing aid to Indonesia after the fall of Sukarno, the United States has skillfully avoided some of the pitfalls of its earlier relations with that large, strategically situated nation. The United States is now a member of a group of donor nations known as the Inter-Governmental Group for Indonesia. The IGG, in cooperation with the government of Indonesia, asked the International Monetary Fund and the World Bank to take the lead in coordinating aid to Indonesia, determining requirements for stabilization and project assistance, and reporting on performance. The leadership of the Fund and Bank, and of the Dutch chairman of the IGG, "has been outstanding."[6]

The better a country's own development program is, the easier it should be to reach a decision concerning the U.S. role, if any, and that of other external sources of assistance in fulfilling the program. As multilateral assistance programs and other bilateral programs expand in relation to the U.S. program, a collective review of the plans and priorities of each developing country and of who should do what toward meeting them is increasingly necessary. In the case of consortia and consultative groups serviced by the World Bank, it would seem to me preferable to have the World Bank staff take over the essential features of the country-programming exercise, with the decisions about who does what worked out in meetings of the consortia. In the case of the Latin American countries, the review of country progress and programs by the Inter-American Committee on the Alliance for Progress (CIAP) might serve a similar role, though decision makers in donor countries will probably have more confidence in the staff work of the World Bank. If the United States believes that a country is neglecting its agriculture, controlling imports in counterproductive fashion, or failing to push marketable exports, it can say so during the course of the performance review.

Leverage and country programming have been closely connected

6. Statement of June 17, 1969, by Marshall Green, assistant secretary of state for East Asian and Pacific affairs, before the House Foreign Affairs Committee (processed), p. 12.

in the minds of U.S. aid officials, but there is an obvious difference between the use of aid to induce sensible development policies in the less developed countries and the use of aid to promote other U.S. interests.

Given the growing resistance of developing countries to the attempts of donor governments to influence their policies, I would hope that the United States will be able to rely more heavily on multilateral agencies, and on mechanisms sponsored by those agencies, for exercising such outside influence on the development policies of individual low-income countries as is feasible. Endowing the multilateral agencies with greater resources ought to be an integral part of the arrangement. Given man's limited understanding of the development process, humility is strongly commended to all agencies and groups having prescriptions for expediting development.

The Debt Burden and the Terms of Aid

Although decisions concerning the capacity of any given country to service additional foreign debt depend on careful analysis of the local situation and prospects, it was evident before country programming became a central feature of the U.S. aid effort that the financial terms on which aid was being made available to the less developed world as a whole spelled trouble ahead. The published work of Dragoslav Avramovic and Ravi Gulhati made it clear a decade ago that the foreign debt of the low-income countries was climbing at an alarming rate.[7] A principal message of my 1961 book on grants, loans, and local currencies was that the terms of aid should become softer, not harder, that much of the antigrant sentiment was irrational, and that the character-building virtues alleged to be inherent in development via the loan route were not a function of the rate of interest;

7. Dragoslav Avramovic, assisted by Ravi Gulhati, *Debt Servicing Capacity and Postwar Growth in International Indebtedness* (Johns Hopkins Press, 1958); Dragoslav Avramovic and Ravi Gulhati, *Debt Servicing Problems of Low-Income Countries, 1956–1958* (Johns Hopkins Press, 1960).

self-help requirements and mobilization of local resources could be incorporated into a 100 percent grant program.[8]

There is no necessary connection between the financial terms on which the United States makes aid available to a foreign country and the financial terms on which such aid subsequently becomes available to business enterprises and private citizens in the country aided. The government receiving aid can sell at prevailing prices the commodities it has received on a grant basis. It can give away commodities for which it has had to pay. It can use either grant or loan aid, or both, to establish a lending institution within its boundaries which makes loans at rates of interest higher or lower than the cost of the capital obtained from abroad.

The so-called two-step loan can be an integral part of the intergovernmental loan agreement. The terms appropriate for AID assistance to the government of India, for instance, were not considered appropriate for Hindustan Motors, Ltd., a profit-making enterprise within India. In this case, the loan agreement itself provided concessional terms to the government of India (related to its ability to repay in foreign exchange) but different and harder terms to Hindustan Motors (related to its ability to make repayment in rupees out of its future earnings).

If imports are financed by grant aid but sold within the country, the foreign government will have been required by the United States to establish a counterpart fund into which it deposits the local currency proceeds derived from sales of imported commodities. The possibility of drawing on an account that does not have to be raised by taxation or by borrowing from its own citizenry can be demoralizing to a government in the sense of relaxing pressures for frugality and careful husbanding of resources. The built-in protection against inefficient use of these resources is the requirement for U.S. consent to expenditures from counterpart and local currency accounts.

All in all, the distinctions among grants, hard loans, and soft loans are very important in evaluating realistically the contributions being

8. Robert E. Asher, *Grants, Loans, and Local Currencies: Their Role in Foreign Aid* (Brookings Institution, 1961).

made by different aid donors, or by the same donor at different time periods, in determining the burden of debt service placed on aid receivers, and in certain other respects. They are quite unimportant in determining how the producer in the aid-supplying nation gets paid for the goods he ships or how the end user in the receiving country makes payment for the goods he receives. The end user normally pays commercial prices in local currency for what he gets. Neither his morality nor the efficiency of his enterprise is directly affected by the form of aid his government has negotiated.

Foreign importer and American exporter can usually deal directly with each other. The purchaser has all the customary incentives to buy only what he needs and in the process to expend the minimum amount of local currency. The seller has all the customary incentives to charge reasonable prices, to dispose expeditiously of his wares, and to obtain from sales the dollars he needs to remain in business.

Despite the irrelevance of the loan versus grant issue insofar as buyer and seller of aid-financed goods are concerned, it has been almost an article of faith in the legislative branch of the United States government that government-supplied capital for foreign economic development should take the form of loans. More than 90 percent of the aid provided under the Marshall Plan was in the form of grants, but grant aid, it was increasingly felt by the administration and the Congress, should not become a permanent feature of international economic assistance.

Since the end of the Marshall Plan, the history of American foreign aid has been a shift in emphasis from grants to loans, a shift from loans repayable in local currency to loans repayable in dollars, and a very substantial increase in the minimum interest rates on loans repayable in dollars. Today, approximately 60 percent of AID assistance to countries other than Vietnam is furnished on a loan basis.[9] Although the forty-year maximum on length of AID loans and the ten-year maximum grace period before repayments of principal must

9. The percentage of country and regional programs financed by loans was 6 percent in 1953–55 and 36 percent in 1959–61, according to Agency for International Development, *Summary Report on Loan Terms, Debt Burden and Development* (April 1965), p. 2.

begin have survived intact, the following changes in interest rates have been made by the Congress during the 1960s without vigorous opposition from the executive branch or the public:

Year	Minimum interest rate during grace period (in percent)	Minimum interest rate after grace period (in percent)
1961	0.75	0.75
1963	0.75	2.0
1964	1.0	2.5
1967	2.0	2.5
1968	2.0	3.0

The reasons behind the congressional actions include one incontrovertible fact—that capital everywhere costs more to raise than it did ten years ago—and a variety of beliefs. Among the latter are a belief that the United States was unnecessarily generous during the Marshall Plan period, that lending is more "businesslike" than granting, that loans are more likely to evoke "sound" economic and financial policies in the borrowing country than other forms of aid, and that the discovery of oil or an economic miracle comparable to the postwar recoveries of Germany and Japan will make repayment relatively painless. Finally, there is the belief that, just as an individual should limit his acquisitions to items he can pay for outright or buy on credit, so each nation should tailor its ambitions to its resources and earning capacity. If credit is obtained and put to productive use, output will rise and incomes will increase. If the loan was worth making or taking, the increase should be more than sufficient to provide for amortization of principal and payment of a reasonable rate of interest.

The rise in domestic output, however, may not generate the necessary amount of foreign exchange. Furthermore, resources that have to be devoted to external payments will not be available for consumption or investment at home. The transfer will slow down the potential rate of growth below what it would be if the aid were as efficiently used with no obligation concerning repayment.

As loan terms harden, debt service charges mount, and more aid must be provided each year to maintain the same net flow of resources to a less developed country (that is, to leave the same amount in its possession for development). The growing debt burden of the less developed countries is now recognized as one of the inescapable problems of the 1970s. The Organisation for Economic Co-operation and Development (OECD), the World Bank, the United Nations Conference on Trade and Development (UNCTAD), and the AID regularly release statistical compilations and analyses; no private report (such as this one) is allowed to appear without a summary of the situation and suggestions for a course of action.

For 91 developing countries, public and publicly-guaranteed debt outstanding at mid-1967 amounted to $43.6 billion. . . . Service payments on the public and publicly-guaranteed external debt of these countries are estimated by IBRD [International Bank for Reconstruction and Development] at $4 billion, of which roughly $2.8 billion are amortization payments and $1.2 billion interest payments. Between 1962 and 1967, debt outstanding grew at an average rate of 10 percent a year, and service payments by 12 percent a year, or significantly faster than the export earnings of the less-developed countries as a group. The most significant trend in the past five years has been the sharp increase in debt service payments of developing countries in Asia and Africa; their debt obligations have more than doubled. There was an increase of about 50 percent for Latin America . . . but no increase for countries in the Middle East.[10]

As in every other aspect of development, the problem varies in intensity not only from region to region but, more importantly, from country to country and includes sharp intercountry variations within each region. Some less developed countries have fairly rosy export prospects and should not get into early difficulty. Others are in trouble primarily because of the sluggish performance of their exports.[11] Some, like Argentina, have had excessive recourse to short-term debt. Some—Indonesia under Sukarno and Ghana under Nkrumah are the

10. Organisation for Economic Co-operation and Development, *Development Assistance: 1968 Review* (OECD, 1968), p. 134. The table on p. 136 indicates that the bulk of debt-service payments in 1967 were on publicly guaranteed private debt, particularly private export credits, rather than on official debt. During the 1970s, however, service payments on official bilateral and multilateral loans will rise, as grace periods on outstanding loans come to an end.

11. For more on the importance of export earnings, see Chapter 7 below.

classic cases—have encountered debt-servicing difficulties because of wholesale mismanagement of their economies. Nevertheless, even with good export growth, avoidance of additional short-term suppliers' credits, and Sunday school behavior in management of their domestic economies, the debt-servicing outlook for ten or twenty less developed countries, including India, Pakistan, and some large Latin American nations, is bleak.

What should be done? The answers are easier to tick off than to put into effect: provide more aid in the future on terms that minimize the burden on the foreign exchange earnings of less developed countries; reschedule outstanding debt in special cases and be prepared in very special cases to write some of it off completely; institutionalize the procedures for convening and managing negotiations aimed at the rescheduling, rolling over, or write-off of outstanding debt.

While the United States must, of course, try to provide enough assistance to meet the international targets being set for the 1970s, it should recognize more clearly the contribution to this objective that can be made by reversing the trend toward harder terms in its bilateral aid. On the theory that the climate for major policy changes is at present unpropitious, the specific proposals for liberalization made to date have been modest: authorize lower rates of interest during the grace period, substitute an average-terms criterion for the present minimum-interest requirements, make Public Law 480 credit terms as generous as those permitted under the Foreign Assistance Act, and keep the grant channel open. The average-terms criterion would permit the United States to offer softer than average terms to a nation such as India but harder than average terms to, say, Peru or Jamaica. None of these proposals seems to me sufficiently far-reaching.

Given the "requirements" of India, Pakistan, Indonesia, and certain other major candidates for assistance in the 1970s, much more of the world's aid is going to have to be made available on terms no harder than those of the International Development Association. It will be recalled that IDA terms are fifty-year credits with a service charge of $\frac{3}{4}$ of 1 percent on the principal amount that is withdrawn and outstanding. The credits have carried grace periods of ten years before repayments begin. Thereafter, 1 percent of the credit is repayable annually for ten years and 3 percent annually for the final thirty years. In such credits, the concessionary element, at a 10 percent discount rate, is equal to 83.64 percent of the credit; that is, a $1 million credit is equivalent to a grant of $836,400.

How will a Congress that is reluctant to authorize bilateral lending at 3 percent rates be persuaded to authorize loans at ¾ of 1 percent? I do not pretend to know. It is the same Congress, however, that authorizes IDA replenishments, that has always provided technical assistance on a grant basis, that provided military assistance on an overwhelmingly grant basis, and that has rarely remained totally deaf to rational argument.

Public preoccupation during the 1960s with gross levels of assistance may have resulted in insufficient attention to net levels and, more specifically, to the grant-equivalent of different aid levels. A succession of seemingly small increases in interest rates can reduce substantially the grant-equivalent of a given nominal level of assistance. If the executive branch began presenting its appropriation requests in terms of the grant-equivalent total it was seeking, together with actual grant-equivalents for preceding periods, attention would be focused on a more realistic measure of effort. A rise in interest charges to less developed countries would then require a higher overall appropriation to provide the same grant-equivalent level of assistance.[12] If the term "grant-equivalent" is regarded as a political liability, the calculations could be made in terms of "IDA-equivalents," thus making IDA credits a kind of international norm.

Discussion may uncover more efficient ways of meeting the debt-service problem than a sharp increase in the amount and proportion of aid on IDA terms. Raymond F. Mikesell, for example, suggests that fifty-year loans at little or no interest are inconsistent with a major function of concessionary aid, namely, constraining a country to make essential structural adjustments in its economy, including a

12. See Charles R. Frank, Jr., and William R. Cline, "Debt Servicing and Foreign Assistance: An Analysis of Problems and Prospects in Less Developed Countries," Agency for International Development, Discussion Paper 19 (June 1969; processed).

rise in the savings rate and an expansion of export earnings, "so that within a reasonable time it may obtain its external capital requirements in the international capital markets, either directly or through a public international intermediary." More appropriate, he argues, would be an interest subsidy for a much more limited period. He also makes a strong case for longer grace periods for amortization payments as the most feasible means of temporarily limiting a rise in debt–service ratios.[13]

Even if the terms for new assistance are significantly liberalized during the 1970s, debt rescheduling will have to be undertaken in a number of cases. With service charges on outstanding loans to less developed countries running at $4 billion per year and still increasing, a reduction of 10 percent in this reverse flow is equivalent to $400 million or more in additional aid. It is aid, moreover, that does not have to run the full legislative gauntlet.

The technical problems of working out sensible rescheduling arrangements are formidable, however. In economic terms, there may be little difference between (1) giving fresh aid to countries like India or Indonesia that have serious balance-of-payments problems caused in part by heavy service charges on outstanding foreign debt and (2) reducing the service charges by rescheduling the debt. The rescheduling negotiations nevertheless seem to highlight the question of the extent to which a creditor like the United States, instead of helping the needy in India or Indonesia, may merely be making it easier for those countries to repay short-term commercial credits that never should have been extended or medium-term loans from the Soviet Union and Western Europe that were made on stiffer terms than those of the United States.

In spite of all the technical difficulties, the India Consortium, under the leadership of the World Bank (as chairman of the consortium), managed to reach agreement "in principle to provide relief of about $100 million (or roughly 25 percent) of debt service payments due to consortium members for each of the three Indian fiscal years be-

13. "External Debt and Borrowing Service," a paper prepared in the summer of 1969 for the Organization of American States. For more on interest subsidies, see also Chapter 6 below.

ginning April 1, 1968, and to take action on debt relief in the first of the three years."[14] Other rescheduling operations have also been successful.

Consortia or consultative groups for a dozen other countries have been established under World Bank leadership, and the Bank is a participant in the five coordinating groups organized under OECD or other non-Bank auspices. The Bank is also, by general agreement, the principal source of information on external debt. It is therefore the logical candidate for convening and managing rescheduling exercises in the 1970s, even though in some cases this may involve postponing payments due the Bank itself as well as payments due other creditors. Rescheduling sessions should be as infrequent as possible but should not be delayed until the situation reaches crisis proportions.

Management responsibilities should include the development of indexes that will help predict the need for rescheduling, the development of criteria for reasonable equity among creditors in sharing the burden when and if rescheduling becomes necessary, and measures to help debtors that are bailed out from again getting into trouble by overborrowing. It is only realistic to note in closing this section that rescheduling will not always suffice and complete write-off of some portion of the debt may ultimately become necessary—and no more costly or painful than providing new grants to pay off old loans.

The Population Problem

During the early postwar years, the population problem could be more or less ignored. The spectacular decline in mortality rates resulting from public health campaigns—one of the forgotten triumphs of foreign aid—had not fully manifested itself. Economic development was considered easier to achieve than turned out to be the case, and since a decline in the birthrate was considered a corollary of development, rapid population growth would at worst be a tempo-

14. *World Bank, International Development Association, Annual Report 1968* (WBIDA, 1968), p. 36.

rary phenomenon. In any event, family planning was too delicate a subject to incorporate into development strategy.

A major rupture in the official silence about the problem of population growth came in 1959 with the publication of the report of the Draper Committee. Its third interim report dealt with economic assistance programs and included a brief chapter on the population question, which ended with a forthright recommendation for action "to meet the serious challenge posed by rapidly expanding populations."[15] Action did not follow with lightning speed and it was largely the specter of mass famine in the 1970s and 1980s that heightened official interest in family planning programs during the 1960s.

The rate of population growth in the less developed world in the 1950s was about double that of the developed noncommunist world and in the 1960s it has been almost treble. During the decade 1955-65, 21 developing countries, including Colombia, Costa Rica, the Dominican Republic, Jordan, Libya, Mexico, the Philippines, Taiwan, and Venezuela, had annual rates of population growth of 3 percent or more.[16] While some of the countries with very high rates of population growth have also had superb overall growth records, the handicaps of a high rate of population increase are becoming more apparent each day. It reduces the per capita rate of improvement to a much more modest total. It saddles each wage earner with a far heavier load of dependents than he would have in a developed country: in the Philippines the average number of children per family is 6.8 as compared with 2.5 in the United States. It reduces the resources available for investment in industry and agriculture, contributes to the fragmentation of land holdings, and increases mightily the annual claim on the education, housing, and welfare budgets. It steps up the number of jobs that will have to be created each year well beyond the number foreseeable on the basis of present trends.

In early 1967, nearly eight years after the release of the Draper Report, a Population Service was established within the Office of

15. *Economic Assistance Programs and Administration*, Third Interim Report Submitted to the President of the United States by the President's Committee to Study the United States Military Assistance Program (July 13, 1959), p. 45.

16. United Nations, *World Economic Survey, 1967, Part One* (UN, 1968), pp. 33-34.

the War on Hunger in AID headquarters. More than twenty less developed countries had requested and were receiving U.S. assistance in population problems; advocacy of dramatic increases in the resources devoted to family planning had become de rigueur. The AID was supplying training for foreign demographers, statisticians, and technicians, and advice to less developed countries in establishing educational programs; and it was furnishing educational materials, medical instruments, and equipment and supplies for use in health clinics and family planning centers. Contraceptives and the materials to manufacture contraceptives, which had been on the ineligible commodity list of the AID and its predecessors since 1948, were removed from the list in May 1967. Finally, in November 1967, the administrator issued a formal Policy Determination to all AID offices, directing them to give the highest priority—along with food production—to encouraging, supporting, and strengthening family planning programs in the developing countries.[17]

This implied substantially stepping up AID obligations for family planning from the $4.25 million level of the preceding fiscal year. The Congress was more than willing; it was actually prodding the AID. As usual, however, legislative delays jeopardized the expansion. The authorization act for the fiscal year that began on July 1, 1967, did not become effective until November 14 and the appropriation act, which earmarked $35 million of economic aid funds solely for programs relating to population growth, became effective only on January 2, 1968. Nevertheless, the AID managed to commit about that amount and to raise the level of obligations for population and family planning programs above $45 million in fiscal year 1969.

The situation in family planning at the threshold of the 1970s is vaguely analogous to the situation in agriculture a decade earlier. The shift in congressional and AID priorities has given impetus to parallel shifts elsewhere—in the United Nations, at the World Bank, and above all in the less developed countries themselves. Massive research and an even more massive effort to disseminate the technology that is already available are still required. What breakthroughs will be

17. P.D. 39, Nov. 3, 1967.

made cannot yet be foretold.[18] The most valuable would probably be the development of an effective, once-a-month oral contraceptive. To expedite research relating to this development, the AID recently announced a grant of $4.5 million.

Since mere knowledge of the availability of low-cost, foolproof contraceptives may not suffice, further experiments with positive financial incentives and rewards for keeping down the number of children per family are also needed. The problem is to keep the subject of family planning close to the top of both the research and the action agenda during the coming decade.

Only in a handful of less developed countries—most notably Taiwan, Hong Kong, Korea, and Singapore—have birthrates actually begun to fall markedly. The average for the less developed world as a whole still exceeds 40 births per thousand as compared with rates of 14–20 per thousand in Western Europe and the United States.

Under the most favorable assumptions, the rate of population increase (birthrates minus death rates) is likely to be somewhat higher for the less developed world as a whole during the first half of the 1970s than during the 1960s. The last half, 1975–80, should tell a different story. Since so much of the population of the less developed world lives in South Asia, the keys to success are India and Pakistan. Both countries are now alert to the problem and committed in their own self-interest to programs of action. Trends in Communist China may be equally important, but influencing them remains beyond the capacity of the outside world.

The Multilateral-Bilateral Mix

For many years now, knowledgeable people have been advocating greater reliance on multilateral channels of development assistance—on the World Bank Group, the Inter-American Development Bank,

18. See Richard N. Gardner, "Toward a World Population Program," in Gardner and Max F. Millikan (eds.), *The Global Partnership: International Agencies and Economic Development* (Praeger, 1968), pp. 332–61.

the UN Development Program, and other intergovernmental agencies. Nevertheless, the U.S. foreign aid program, like that of other donors, remains overwhelmingly bilateral. Rhetoric escalates, more international machinery gets created, some valuable halfway houses to multilateralism such as consortia and consultative groups come into being, but the basic division of labor changes at a rate that is barely perceptible. Concrete proposals for attaining a radically different division of labor are seldom made.

There are, of course, valid reasons for retaining a bilateral development assistance program. Those valid reasons obviously have a good deal to do with why the United States still has one. In my view, the United States should continue to operate a bilateral aid program during the 1970s. Instead of the present 85 percent bilateral to 15 percent multilateral ratio, however, I recommend transition by 1975 to a mix that is 40 percent bilateral and 60 percent multilateral. The situation should then be reappraised with a view to determining whether to hold at 60 percent, to set a new target of, say, 75 percent, or to reverse the trend by allocating further increases primarily to the bilateral program. Since there are now regional as well as global multilateral institutions, the United States can choose a predominantly multilateral approach without either putting too many of its eggs in one basket or depriving itself of an effective voice in the regional distribution of its assistance.

As I have said about every other target discussed in this book, there is no compelling logic that leads inexorably to the specific figures mentioned—in this case, a 40–60 ratio within five years. The important thing, in my view, is to publicize a goal that facilitates purposeful movement toward a "lower political profile" for the United States and a simultaneous beefing up of suitable international agencies for promoting development.

For a short, big-push, regionally focused effort like the Marshall Plan, the bilateral approach has much to commend it. It is considerably less appropriate for the long haul, during which all the strains inherent in the relationship between rich donor and poor recipient, each pursuing a variety of objectives, can come to the surface.

Multilateralization, to use an awkward word, would be consistent with what Senator Fulbright and some of the most articulate members of the Congress have advocated. Impressed by the need for a change in the political context of the relationship between aid-giving and aid-receiving nations, the chairman of the Senate Foreign Relations Committee said in 1966, "The way to bring about this change is to multilateralize—and thereby to institutionalize and depersonalize—the aid relationship. For several years, I have advocated that greater use be made of the World Bank and its affiliated institutions. . . . The Senate has approved this view at least twice, only to see it frustrated by the Appropriations Committee of the other body."[19]

Most, but not all, of the less developed countries favor the multilateral approach. They do so not because they want to take politics out of the aid relationship, but because they want to place the aid relationship in a new and different political context. They want to publicize their problems, air their grievances, share the driver's seat with the donors, and alter the balance in what Barbara Ward has referred to as a "lop-sided world." The drive toward greater participation in the political process is destined to gain momentum, domestically and internationally, and I see no good reason to fear it. Its rationale is "the not unreasonable assumption that the poor have a right to participate in policymaking which affects their own future and an obligation to take some responsibility for the result. (Institutionalizing the participation of the poor in policymaking is not the same thing as is currently meant by 'self-help' in aid jargon; the latter usually signifies changes in recipient-government policy recommended—nay, insisted on—by donors.)"[20]

The views of the United States will not be given short shrift in international forums. Some opposition may arise simply because of the source, but offsetting this will be sober second thoughts based on the economic and political power of the United States, the justice or merit of the views it espouses, and the skill with which it espouses them. Nevertheless, Senator Fulbright's pro-multilateral views have

19. Senator J. W. Fulbright, on "Suggested Basic Changes in Foreign Aid Programs," *Congressional Record*, Vol. 112, Pt. 6, 89 Cong. 2 sess. (1966), p. 7464.

20. Patricia W. Blair, "The Dimension of Poverty," in *International Organization*, Vol. 23 (Summer 1969), p. 694.

not been vigorously echoed in the House of Representatives. Despite the absence of enthusiasm among House leaders, the multilateral programs have fared reasonably well in the Congress by comparison with the larger bilateral aid requests.

During the 1940s and 1950s, when appropriations for foreign aid were far more generous in relation to U.S. gross national product than at present, one of the most effective arguments against the multilateral approach was that the shift would entail a substantial decrease in the amount of aid made available, with resultant severe setbacks to progress in the areas being aided. With appropriations down to their present levels, that argument loses a good deal of its force. Insofar as its own bilateral assistance program is concerned, the United States is already caught in a trap of its own making; it has stretched the list of irritating regulations to be complied with and shrunk the amount of help that can be obtained by complying.

Preventing further reductions in the flow of U.S. aid will be an insignificant achievement compared to expanding the flow to a level at which it can again make an appreciable impact on the pace and course of development. Persuading the Congress to increase the flow substantially will be difficult enough; asking it simultaneously to channel a much larger share of it through international agencies, thereby sacrificing some measure of control over the allocation and use of funds originating in the United States, may be asking too much. As a student of development and international relations, however, I consider the request worth making.

Greater reliance on multilateral machinery should be viewed primarily as a response to encouraging rather than discouraging changes in the aid environment. The United States pioneered in developing the technical assistance concept, in introducing soft lending, in utilizing surplus agricultural commodities to promote development abroad, in providing nonproject, or program, assistance, and in demonstrating the potentialities of aid on a generous scale. It led the way in stationing well-manned—some would say overmanned—resident missions in key countries. It established the Peace Corps. It proved the feasibility of contracting with universities, nonprofit private organizations, and engineering firms for the performance of certain functions. It consistently emphasized agriculture, education, and health programs. Others have gradually followed the American lead and, in some respects, surpassed the leader. The lonely trailblazing course trodden by the United States has become a highway on which multilateral vehicles are more numerous, better designed, and more thoroughly road tested than once they were. Traveling in multilateral vehicles may involve some sacrifice in the "influence potential" of U.S. aid but will also reduce the "boomerang potential."

By utilizing international machinery, the United States can to some extent avoid the strains inherent in direct donor–recipient relations, the injection of irrelevant side issues into the mainstream of negotiations, and the competitive follies implicit in numerous overlapping, uncoordinated, bilateral efforts.[21] For these advantages, there are of course offsetting costs. International agencies can wade into waters too deep for wading and side issues can poison multilateral as well as bilateral discussions. Nevertheless, multilateralism is widely believed to be the pathway of the future. It assumes a growing consensus, not only about development as a goal, but also about the nature of the development process and the desirability of promoting growth in nondiscriminatory fashion.

Recognizing that too much of the debate has been conducted in terms of generalities, I have tried elsewhere to review in detail the arguments for and against greater reliance on multilateral channels. Permit me here (and in the next chapter) only to remind the reader of a few points.[22] The first, of course, is the absence of homogeneity in the picture. The international agencies vary significantly in voting arrangements, command over resources, professional competence, and flexibility. Less developed countries are no more eager to become

21. What I call irrelevant side issues—how an aided country votes in the United Nations, with whom it chooses to trade, what posture it assumes toward particular foreign investors, whether it will allow any of its territory to be used as a U.S. military base—are usually considered relevant by those who raise them.

22. See Robert E. Asher, "Multilateral Versus Bilateral Aid: An Old Controversy Revisited," *International Organization*, Vol. 16, no. 4 (1962), pp. 697–719 (Brookings Institution Reprint 66). See also Frank M. Coffin, "Multilateral Assistance: Possibilities and Prospects," *International Organization*, Vol. 22, no. 1 (1968), especially the suggestion on page 284 for a forum for parliamentarians in which questions of trade, aid, and monetary policy can be systematically discussed.

wards of the World Bank or the United Nations than of the United States or the USSR. Donors are as pathologically insistent as receivers on that will-o'-the-wisp, maximum freedom of action. They, too, vary in the strength of their attachment to the bilateral channel, in their enthusiasm for particular multilateral agencies, and in their commitment to development as an objective of policy. The willingness of Germany, France, the United Kingdom, Japan, and the other leading aid-providers to collaborate in multilateral arrangements determines the degree to which the United States can channel more of its aid multilaterally without depriving the multilateral agencies of their international character. United States leadership and policy in turn will influence the views of the principal donor nations.

At the moment, the dynamism of the principal multilateral source of development assistance, the World Bank Group, stands in strong contrast to the weariness that has overtaken the major bilateral programs. How to retain and capitalize on that dynamism is a principal challenge of the 1970s.

CHAPTER SIX

Toward a Predominantly
Multilateral Program

In preparing for the predominantly multilateral aid program recommended in the preceding chapter, a distinction should, in my view, be made between capital assistance and technical assistance and, within the capital assistance category, between normal, or basic, development assistance and special, or supplementary, assistance. The bulk of U.S. capital assistance other than purely private investment should be thought of as basic development assistance and transferred to multilateral auspices in accordance with an announced timetable.

The Proposal in Brief

The proposed transition is best summarized in Table 4. In brief, the new approach would include the following:

1. The United States would indicate its intention to raise its net outflow of long-term resources to less developed countries to the familiar 1 percent of U.S. gross national product (GNP) by 1975. Given the other claims on U.S. resources and the absence as yet of a

credible U.S. commitment to development of the low-income world as a policy objective worthy of high priority, fulfillment of this pledge will not be easy, despite the fact that GNP in current dollars should approximate $1.42 trillion by 1975.

2. One percent of $1.42 trillion is $14.2 billion. This sum should be the target figure for the net outflow of long-term resources, public plus private, in 1975. It would require a 2½-fold increase in the 1968 outflow.

3. The difference between the 1 percent ($14.2 billion) and the estimated private flow will be the public or official flow; in other words, what is popularly called foreign aid. Taking into consideration such new incentives to private foreign investment as may come into being by 1975, an optimist might project a 15 percent per year increase in private foreign investment, inclusive of private purchases of the securities of multilateral institutions such as the World Bank and the regional development banks. The projected fourfold increase over the 1968 total in private U.S. purchases of the securities of multilateral development financing institutions would be dramatic but surely not beyond the realm of possibility. The total private flow would thus rise from slightly above $2 billion in 1968 to $4.5 billion in 1975.

4. In that event, the official flow in 1975 ought to be $9.7 billion, as compared with $3.6 billion in 1968 (and $3.7 billion in 1963). Since the official flow now includes Food-for-Freedom, supporting assistance, and other items unlikely to increase significantly during the 1970s, the increase will have to be concentrated primarily in the categories currently known as development loans and development grants.

5. If the program is to become predominantly multilateral by 1975, the multilateral component of the official flow will have to rise to more than 50 percent. The multilateral institutions, with $5 billion in official resources from the United States and $1 billion from bond sales to private U.S. investors, could then collectively be larger than the 1975 U.S. bilateral program of $4.7 billion in official resources plus such sums as might, with new legislation, be raised for U.S. development financing agencies by bond sales to private investors.

TABLE 4. *An Illustrative U.S. Development Assistance Program for 1971–75*[a]

(In billions of dollars)

	Calendar year					
Item	*1968*	*1971*	*1972*	*1973*	*1974*	*1975*
1. U.S. gross national product	861[b]	1,070	1,160	1,240	1,330	1,420
2. One percent of gross national product	8.6	10.7	11.6	12.4	13.3	14.2
3. Total net flow of financial resources to less developed countries, official plus private[c]	5.7[d]	6.8	8.0	9.4	11.6	14.2
4. Official flow[e]	3.6[d]	4.2	5.1	6.1	7.8	9.7
5. Bilateral component	3.3[d]	3.4	3.5	3.6	4.1	4.7
6. Multilateral component	0.3[d]	1.8	1.6	2.5	3.7	5.0
7. Private purchases of multilateral securities	0.3[d]	.4	.5	.6	.8	1.0
8. Other private investment	1.8[d]	2.2	2.4	2.7	3.0	3.5

a. For the period 1971–75, the figures are crude estimates based on the assumptions that (1) GNP in the United States, in real terms, will increase by about 4.4 percent per year and price increases will taper off to 2.5 percent per year by 1973; moreover, there will be some slack in the economy in 1970 and early 1971; (2) it is desirable to raise the total net flow of U.S. resources to less developed countries to 1 percent of GNP by 1975; (3) private investment (inclusive of private purchases of the securities of multilateral institutions) should rise during the 1970s but can hardly be expected to rise by more than 15 percent per year during 1971–75; (4) the official flow of financial resources should be sharply increased, with the bulk of the increase going to multilateral institutions; (5) the multilateral component of official assistance plus private purchases of multilateral securities will permit the U.S. program, if other donors also step up sharply their contributions to multilateral agencies and their purchases of multilateral securities, to be considerably smaller than the multilateral effort by 1975.

b. From the *Economic Report of the President, January 1969*, p. 227.

c. Line 3 = 4 + 7 + 8.

d. Lines 3–8 of the 1968 data are from the Organisation for Economic Co-operation and Development, Press release of July 11, 1969. The official flow in 1968, it may be noted, is substantially below the figure in Table 1 for economic aid to less developed countries in that year. The reason is not only because the figures in Table 1 are fiscal year totals whereas the above are calendar year totals, but more importantly because the OECD figures represent net disbursements (not commitments or authorizations) and have been adjusted to take into account loan repayments, reverse grants, and so forth.

e. Line 4 = 5 + 6.

6. Of the funds provided for multilateral institutions, as least half should go to the World Bank family, most specifically, to the International Development Association (IDA). It is important on the one

hand to concentrate resources at a point at which some leadership and leverage can be exercised and on the other hand not to give any agency a monopoly position or delusions of grandeur. As the most experienced and respected international body in the development business, the World Bank Group would seem to be a logical candidate for half of the total to be transferred to multilateral auspices by the United States. The other half should be shared by the Inter-American Bank, the UN Development Program (UNDP), the Central American Bank for Economic Integration, the Asian and African development banks, and any competently managed new international institutions designed for the promotion of development.

7. While there are strong reasons for putting the bulk of capital assistance under multilateral auspices, the case for doing the same with technical assistance does not appear to be equally persuasive. Technical assistance is not an explosive issue. Rarely does it give rise to the political headaches that accompany capital assistance. Nevertheless, the multilateralization of capital assistance proposed above will almost automatically raise substantially the volume of technical assistance that is provided multilaterally. Unnoticed by most observers, the World Bank Group, the Inter-American Development Bank, and the International Monetary Fund have gradually increased the amount of technical assistance they furnish. Much of it is related to specific loan projects, thereby providing the integration of technical and capital assistance to which lip service is universally paid. The rest is in the field of economic planning, national accounts, fiscal and monetary policy, feasibility studies, development institutes, and other areas logically within the competence of the international financial agencies.

It would be desirable also to see the UNDP expanded as a source of technical assistance and preinvestment help. More important than a phased transition to a predominantly multilateral technical assistance program, however, is making the consumers of technical assistance more "product conscious," more determined to get the kinds of help they need most at the times and places they most need them. Technical assistance is still accepted all too casually by less developed countries.

The reason is not primarily because technical assistance is normally provided on a grant basis, but because discovery of the magic of capital–output ratios by the less developed countries made technical assistance seem almost undesirable, hardly worth bothering about, in comparison with capital assistance. If every $2, $3, or $4 invested in a developing country could be relied on to add $1 or so per year to its gross national product, beginning almost immediately, while the payoff on technical assistance would be more distant and uncertain, then the job of the developing country should be to maximize the inflow of capital assistance rather than technical assistance. Moreover, it was easier to think of capital assistance in terms of hundreds of millions of dollars than to think of technical assistance running into comparable sums per country. Therefore, a moderately productive capital assistance program seemed to promise more development than a more productive though much smaller technical cooperation program.

Fortunately, technical assistance continued to be a component of aid programs and the value of high-quality technical assistance has been demonstrated again and again. Since it is such a small fraction of the total cost of a development program, it would seem to me that requiring more of it to be paid for outright or obtained on a loan basis would help put it in proper perspective. If loans and credits in the $1 million to $10 million range were made available to poor countries on easy terms, the borrowers would do much more about hiring their own experts, integrating them into their own institutional structures, and developing a greater stake in the success of technical assistance projects.

The recommendation to put more technical assistance on a soft loan basis admittedly runs counter to my overall desire to hold down the debt-servicing burden of the less developed countries. If loan terms were sufficiently soft, however, the additional burden would be bearable and technical assistance would, I surmise, be better organized. Some technical assistance programs, including the UN program, expect recipient governments to make a counterpart contribution and thus impose a cost, though not a foreign exchange burden, on those governments. The counterpart may cover office

space, secretarial service, domestic transportation, and other ameni-
ties, but normally it does not enable the receiving government to hire
and pay the expert, as would be possible with the proceeds of a loan
in convertible currency.

8. To recapitulate, the foregoing proposals envisage stepping up
to 1 percent of GNP the overall flow of public and private U.S.
resources to low-income countries, multilateralizing the bulk of the
development assistance coming from the United States by 1975, retaining a significant supplemental bilateral capacity, and putting
more technical assistance on a loan basis. Stated in such summary
fashion, the recommendations have innumerable loose ends. In discussing a proposed course of action, however, there is merit in em-
phasizing its main thrust without obscuring the view by including all
the qualifying details. The main thrust is toward a program large
enough to matter and multilateral enough to give less developed
countries a voice in determining the ground rules under which most
of the assistance will be made available. The United States may then
be spared some of the obloquy that is a corollary of a large, predominantly bilateral effort. For reasons given in Chapter 2, it is unrealistic
to think the obloquy can be avoided by curtailing the aid program
and concentrating on domestic problems.

Obstacles and Problems

Robert Browning wrote the lines

> And yonder soft phial—the exquisite blue,
> Sure to taste sweetly, is that poison, too?

in 1845, long before the sky-blue flag of the United Nations came
into existence. Yet the question asked by the jealous, rejected woman
in his poem "The Laboratory" may properly be asked of those who
today recommend placing the bulk of development assistance under
UN or other multilateral control.

Will the multilateral alternative be disillusioning, too? Are multilateral institutions adequately equipped to promote development?

Though some of them provide a better political context for the aid relationship than the large bilateral programs, others do not, and the multilateral approach also poses formidable problems.

Early in the first decade of development, Hans Morgenthau suggested that "the problem of foreign aid is insoluble if it is considered as a self-sufficient technical enterprise of a primarily economic nature."[1] Yet this is precisely the framework within which it has most frequently been considered internationally. International agencies can decide not to provide aid for certain purposes or unless certain eligibility requirements are met—and those decisions may be the product of bitter political infighting. Once they decide the terms on which aid should be available for the build-up of industry or agriculture or the public service, however, international agencies cannot afford to discriminate among members on political, ideological, or military grounds.

Nevertheless, international agencies can become instruments for the greater glory of their secretaries-general, or agents of particular political constellations. The Development Assistance Committee of the Organisation for Economic Co-operation and Development (OECD) has been referred to as a donors' club, the United Nations Conference on Trade and Development (UNCTAD) as a forum in which aid receivers try to impose conditions on aid donors, the World Bank as an Anglo-American institution. For the most part, however, actions taken by international agencies reflect a broader consensus and are more acceptable than those of a single foreign office; in the global agencies, receivers as well as donors of aid have had a say in shaping the policies of the agency and an opportunity to place in the secretariat fellow-nationals in whom they have confidence.

If multilateral machinery is to remain multilateral—that is, not to become overwhelmingly dependent on the United States for its resources—other developed countries too will have to be willing to step up very substantially their subscriptions and contributions to, and their purchases of the securities of, multilateral agencies. In one sense

1. "A Political Theory of Foreign Aid," *American Political Science Review*, Vol. 56 (June 1962), p. 309.

they have less incentive to do so than the United States: their bilateral programs are in less trouble at home and abroad than the U.S. program and their influence in the international machinery is likely to be less than that of the major contributor. In another sense, they have a greater incentive: individually they cannot hope to play very significant roles in the transformation of the less developed world, but collectively they can. As the Netherlands minister of foreign affairs said a few years ago:

Being a small country, the Netherlands has not sufficient financial means at its disposal to give extensive bilateral assistance to underdeveloped countries. So only a very limited number of such countries could be considered for assistance, and that might affect our relations with other countries adversely.... There is therefore a danger that if the Netherlands should arbitrarily decide to give bilateral assistance to a few countries, we should be subjected to political and economic pressure to induce us to give assistance beyond our financial capacity.[2]

The problems of France, Britain, Germany, and Japan are in a somewhat different category than those of the Netherlands, the Scandinavian countries, Australia, and Canada. The recommendation in this study, however, is not that donors give up their bilateral programs but that as they move toward the 1 percent target they channel most of the increase into multilateral agencies. If they are unwilling to move as rapidly as proposed herein, the timetable can probably be stretched; my hope is that it will not have to be abandoned because of resurgent nationalism, frustration with international machinery and cooperation, or other divisive forces.

Although orderly development requires simultaneous headway on many fronts, governments cannot give equal priority to all claims for attention. One of the lessons of the past decade, mentioned in Chapter

2. "Netherlands Policy for Aid to Developing Countries," memorandum sent by the minister of foreign affairs to the chairman of the Second Chamber, Aug. 18, 1962, p. 4 (of English copy at the Netherlands embassy, Washington, D.C.). A similar statement has been made by a noted Canadian economist. "When viewed in this perspective as well as in the perspective of the needs of the LDC's, it is apparent that Canadian foreign assistance by itself can be expected to make only a minor dent on world poverty, and by itself Canadian assistance is unlikely to make a significant difference to long-run political and economic developments in the world," wrote Grant L. Reuber in "Canada's Economic Policies Toward the Less Developed Countries," *Canadian Journal of Economics*, Vol. 1 (November 1968), p. 671.

3, has been the need for each less developed country to concentrate on a limited number of goals achievable within a specified time—self-sufficiency in rice in five years, a tripling of earnings from tourism in four years, the development of some suitable processing industries within three years. The multilateral machinery, with its many autonomous parts and its somewhat technocratic approach, is at present more ill equipped than is the U.S. government to reach agreement with the political leaders of developing countries on such targets and to concentrate its efforts on the agreed goals. Neither the UNDP resident representative in a less developed country nor any other international official serves in a true sense as captain of a team.

The international financial agencies, it has been alleged with considerable justification, are too financially oriented and insufficiently development oriented. (Institutions called banks will try to behave like banks; it is perhaps unfortunate that the World Bank antedates the IDA, thereby making the latter a part of the World Bank Group instead of the Bank a member of the IDA family.) Given its articles of agreement, the World Bank Group has to date found it extremely difficult to make nonproject, or program, loans, although the lubricating and broadly stimulating effects of program aid to countries no longer at the very earliest stage of development are widely recognized. Even in project assistance, the World Bank and IDA are still more encumbered than the AID with arcane doctrine to the effect that the financing of consumable goods cannot be developmental. This means that loans for importing turbines and generators are development loans, but loans for importing fertilizer are not.

Some of the advantages of program loans could be achieved by greater liberality in meeting the local currency costs of project loans, but this the Bank and IDA have also been reluctant to do. Their preferred compromise between program and project lending is the sector loan—for imports and undertakings that will help modernize agriculture, education, or transportation in the low-income country. The sector loan is a promising device, deserving wider usage in the 1970s. Sector lending can readily include the convening of groups such as consortia to consider large sector programs suitable for financial inputs from various external sources.

The defects in multilateral machinery are, I believe, remediable. Although the articles of agreement of the World Bank should not be changed annually, the fact is that they have not been changed in a quarter of a century except to authorize the Bank to make, participate in, or guarantee loans to its first affiliate, the Internationl Finance Corporation. Moreover, the very soft terms for credits from the Bank's second affiliate, the IDA, mean a lighter debt-servicing burden on less developed countries than they acquire under most bilateral programs. It may be easier to convince Germany, Japan, and some of the harder lenders to increase their IDA replenishments than to relax their own terms. Further, the competitive bidding procedures of the international agencies procure more aid per dollar than the bilateral procedures tying aid funds to purchases from the nation supplying the funds.[3] Tied aid is poor-quality aid, not only because it decreases the real value of aid to the receivers and sets a bad example for donors not already wedded to the practice, but also because it is inconsistent with the import-liberalization and other economic policies the United States recommends to less developed countries. If prospective improvements in the international monetary system do not alleviate the persistent balance-of-payments problems of industrialized countries, some safeguards can be negotiated for their protection without requiring the international agencies to abandon the practice of buying from the lowest-cost producers.

Whereas the Agency for International Development (AID) is wholly dependent on congressional appropriations, the World Bank and the regional development banks can obtain loanable funds by selling bond issues in private capital markets. The World Bank can subsequently authorize the transfer of funds from its net income to the IDA—as it has already done for a total of $285 million—thereby also reducing the dependence of that agency on direct governmental appropriations. Were it to authorize future transfers as interest subsidization funds for IDA bonds, IDA's dependence on parliamentary appropriations could be still further reduced.

Looking further into the future, there are at least two other independent sources of revenue that could become available to interna-

3. See also Chapter 9.

tional development agencies during the 1970s but are unlikely to be awarded to national agencies. I refer to the registration or licensing of rights to exploit for oil and other valuable resources the oceans and ocean beds beyond present national jurisdiction, and the forging of a stronger link between the creation of monetary reserves and the extension of development assistance.[4]

Irrespective of the channels through which aid is permitted to flow, which less developed countries should receive assistance and in what volume? For practical purposes, the decision as to whether eligibility standards are being met by Egypt or Burma or Haiti or Paraguay, or how much of the available aid should be allocated to Brazil or India, or whether aid to Pakistan or Korea should be terminated in x or in y years, must be made by those administering the various programs, preferably on the basis of international reviews of some kind. The international climate to be sought through such reviews should be one in which less developed countries are eager to cease being net recipients of assistance and proud to become net providers.

In that climate it seems to me reasonable to look forward to the gradual evolution of rough and ready norms for import and export policies, investments in growth, expenditures for defense, treatment of minorities, dispensation of justice, concern for the genuinely needy groups in the population, and other criteria that will help to show which countries are seriously interested in development and what the laggards might do to prove their seriousness. To be eligible for assistance, a country should be development-minded, be capable of benefiting from external assistance, and behave decently, domestically as well as internationally. I see no early acceptance of formulas to answer the question: How much to each eligible?

However, judgments concerning qualifications, needs, and performance may be multilateralized by using consortia, panels of "wise men," a World Development Council, the Alliance for Progress machinery, the World Bank Group, regional banks, or other international mechanisms. Multilateral machinery cannot be expected to shore up shaky governments because the United States wants them

4. See Chapter 9.

shored up, to promote the sale of noncompetitive U.S. exports, to adopt the political or economic philosophy of the United States, or to oppose political doctrines simply because the United States is opposed to them. Multilateral agencies, on the other hand, may be better equipped than the United States to operate in certain sensitive areas of economic and social policy (for example, exchange rate policy, import and export controls), though this is not true of all sensitive areas.

With respect to policy guidance, Andrzej Krassowski has stressed the need for outside donors to find a middle ground somewhere between giving advice and exerting pressure. He calls it "the role of devil's advocate or loyal opposition."

This sort of donor role falls somewhere between giving advice and exerting pressure. Advice is normally offered with the expectation of action being taken in accordance with the advice given. The devil's advocate role is to advise, but without expecting or necessarily wanting, acceptance. Pressure is normally backed by some form of sanction to ensure that certain actions follow. Again the devil's advocate role is a form of pressure for action, but there is no threat of sanctions if no action follows. . . .

Since in the majority of developing countries there is no genuine debate on policy or the debate is confined to a very small, and unrepresentative, inbred circle, the lack of serious and broadly-based discussion leads to a lack of critical appraisal, a dogmatic following of certain concepts, and a lack of innovation and of challenge to familiar and traditional methods. The donor government's aid and development personnel can, in many cases, perform the role that one would expect a loyal opposition to perform—the role of a partner for a necessary exchange of views, and one whose outlook is likely to be sharply different and, therefore, inherently critical.[5]

If multilateral machinery replaces the U.S. government as the principal source of external assistance, its capacity to play this role should be improved. An authoritative task force, building on the foundations laid by the Pearson Commission, ought to review the situation and come forward with additional recommendations designed to equip the multilateral machinery to function in optimum

5. Andrzej Krassowski, *The Aid Relationship* (London: Overseas Development Institute, 1968), p. 13.

fashion (1) as a fount of policy proposals and guidance; (2) as a partner in the selection of a few high priority targets on which to concentrate the development drive in each country; and (3) as a source of external resources to help realize those targets.[6] Since bilateral assistance will not disappear, the task force should also consider who is best equipped to do what.

Would American goodwill toward the multilateral agencies fade if those agencies were in business in a much bigger way, if they failed to favor the countries we liked, rewarded some that we do not like, and generally moved out of the shadow of the larger U.S. program into the limelight? Would the goodwill of less developed countries toward the multilateral agencies fade if those agencies became the major arbitrators of "who gets what, when, and how"? What serious losses in flexibility and concentration of effort would the United States suffer by relying predominantly on multilateral aid? What losses in flexibility would the multilateral machinery suffer? How significant, for example, is the 1967 effort in Congress to involve the General Accounting Office in the auditing of the expenditures of the Inter-American Development Bank? Is the resultant Selden Amendment a warning that executive branch efforts to multilateralize aid will be accompanied by congressional efforts to treat the multilateral programs as if they were bilateral?[7]

6. See *Partners in Development*, Report of the Commission on International Development, Lester B. Pearson, chairman (Praeger, 1969), especially Chaps. 6 and 11.

7. The 1966 decision of the National Advisory Council on International Monetary and Financial Policies—an executive branch rather than a congressional body—reaffirming the United States policy of opposing assistance by any international financial institution to any country ineligible for U.S. bilateral assistance because of its expropriation of American-owned private property is, to me, disquieting. Since an affirmative U.S. vote is required for dollar financing provided by the Fund for Special Operations of the Inter-American Development Bank, U.S. opposition in such cases is tantamount to a veto. See National Advisory Council on International Monetary and Financial Policies, "Special Report to the President and to the Congress on the Proposed Expansion of the Fund for Special Operations and on the Proposed Modification of Provisions for the Election of Executive Directors of the Inter-American Development Bank" (April 1967; mimeographed), pp. 17–18. Note also the congressional attitude toward multilateral programs expressed in Sec. 301(b) of the Foreign Assistance Act of 1967: "The President shall seek to assure that no contribution to the United Nations Development Program authorized by the Act shall be used for projects for economic or technical assistance to Cuba, so long as Cuba is governed by the Castro regime."

In the United States, the acceptability of the multilateral alternative is based largely on the vision of a handsome pyramid with the World Bank, headed by a dynamic American president and governed by weighted voting, at the apex. The rest of the development machinery is assumed to fall neatly into place somewhere below. At present, most of the rest of the low-income world would also accept (and regard as a significant step forward) multilateralization of the administration of capital assistance along the lines proposed herein—that is, with a leading role for the World Bank Group.

To Americans, however, it is only fair to point out in closing this discussion that the emerging world economic order is not destined to be headed permanently by an American bank president or by an international technocracy safely insulated from the political winds sweeping across Asia, Africa, and Latin America. The one-nation, one-vote arrangements of the UN General Assembly give 300,000 people in Malta the same vote as 200 million people in the United States. The weighted voting in the World Bank gives 200 million Americans nearly thirty times as strong a voice as 115 million Pakistani. The problems of preserving the professional integrity of international agencies while simultaneously making them appropriately responsive to the will of the people of the world are unlikely to have been solved before the 1970s draw to a close.

Despite the many foreseeable problems, greater U.S. reliance on multilateral arrangements for the promotion of development seems to me, on balance, a clearly desirable course of action. As an integral part of the multilateral thrust herein recommended, an effort should be made to have the multilateral agencies take on some of the ablest and most experienced American personnel, engage in country programming to the extent necessary, coordinate capital with technical assistance more effectively, provide more program and sector aid, and enhance their impact by an integrated approach to some judiciously selected targets. They should also make greater use of such successful American practices as contracts with universities, nonprofit private organizations, and engineering firms. I would still expect the multilateral approach to be less missionary than that of the United States, less concerned with maximizing its influence potential in any given country, more service oriented. I would welcome the change, not only because of my conviction that hopes of exercising substantial amounts of leverage on nominally sovereign governments are for the most part doomed to disappointment, but also because less developed countries are gradually becoming better judges of their specific needs.

The Accompanying Bilateral Program

To accompany a phased transition to a predominantly multilateral capital assistance program, there is need for a phased transformation of the remaining bilateral effort, which will have to be larger than the current program if target figures for official flows of development assistance are to be approached by 1975. The purpose of the transformation should be to make the bilateral program more flexible; better able to serve those American foreign policy interests that may not be adequately served by the orientation, present or future, of international machinery; less dependent on the annual authorization and appropriation cycle; and able to rely on institutions more specialized and permanent than the AID.

As a major world power, the United States is inevitably interested, not solely in rapid economic progress on the part of less developed countries or even in balanced economic, social, and civic development, but also in a host of short-term and long-term objectives, the attainment of which might be eased by the ability to put in additional aid, to withdraw it, or to direct it to particular projects or activities in a less developed country. If basic development assistance in amounts sufficient to affect the rate of progress were available from international institutions, the United States would no longer be a hulking giant among Lilliputians and its image could be improved by consciously concentrating its bilateral assistance on activities that seem useful to it and the recipient country but that the international agencies are unready or unwilling to provide.

There is nothing reprehensible about maintaining freedom to be more generous to a decent, friendly government than to an indecent, unfriendly one. If the United States can become identified with support for progressive forces abroad and establishment of the better world order it purports to seek, its prestige should rise. If it allows itself to become identified with support for reactionary regimes, for blatant anticommunism, or for the status quo, it will suffer.

Thus, a principal purpose of the bilateral program retained by the United States would be the opportunity for the United States to give a special push to help make Latin America self-sustaining, or to involve itself more directly in Tunisia than in Algeria, in Chile than in Cuba, in India than in Laos—if and when it thought its interests would be better served thereby. Because of the political and security interests, regional loyalties, and cultural ties previously alluded to (as well as whim, accident, and economic concern), the United States will in all probability wish to continue doing more than promote democracy and help fulfill agreed development programs. It has in the past provided famine relief, budget and balance-of-payments support, strategically timed announcements of project approval, and other tangible evidences of goodwill. Demands for special consideration will not disappear. Other rich countries will promote their interests by every device at their disposal and the pragmatic United States will not wish to withdraw from the competition.

Ideally, no U.S. bilateral aid should go to repressive, undemocratic regimes, but we do not live in an ideal world. When allegedly overriding political, economic, or security considerations require the release of resources to undeserving regimes, let it be done "with a handshake rather than an embrace."

In view of the multipurpose character of bilateral aid, should direct American assistance be considered development assistance or some more general form of contingency aid? I would urge that the resources be treated as supplementary assistance for development, while recognizing that some nondevelopmental activities would also be supported. The dilemma is that, if nonmilitary bilateral efforts are treated as supplementary assistance for development, the Congress and the public have a right to expect economic, social, and political growth as a result of those efforts and to react negatively if growth does not occur. If even the pretense that they represent development assistance is abandoned, the shenanigans in terms of nondevelopmental uses are almost certain to be overdone and, before long, to cause the downfall of the whole program.

Innovation and specialization should also figure in the rationale for bilateral programs. Attention has already been directed in this study to the fact that much of the trailblazing in the field of development assistance has been done bilaterally, most notably by the United States. It will surely continue to be easier to line up one donor and one receiver behind a new idea than to persuade large numbers of each that the idea has merit. The U.S. bilateral program might therefore seek to concentrate more on innovations and on projects that the United States is peculiarly well equipped to help execute. After the feasibility of such projects has been satisfactorily demonstrated, an effort should be made to shift responsibility for further work in those fields to an appropriate multilateral agency.

I noted some years ago that Sweden was splendidly equipped to pioneer in the field of family planning, that Denmark was a leader in modern dairying and Norway in fishery, that American public administrators tended to be rather narrowly specialized whereas the British excelled in producing generalists—responsible, honest, competent executives who could fill a variety of posts. "Is it not time," I asked, "for the United States to think through carefully wherein its genius lies?" And I suggested a few fields in which the United States might enjoy some comparative advantage.[8] Experts could easily expand the list.

Consortia and consultative groups have already been mentioned as halfway points between multilateral and bilateral assistance that in some respects provide the best of both worlds. Eighteen such groups had been formed by mid-1969 and the United States will doubtless wish to retain freedom to participate in these efforts. Typically, the World Bank or the OECD will convene government representatives

8. Robert E. Asher, "Multilateral Versus Bilateral Aid: An Old Controversy Revisited," *International Organization*, Vol. 16, no. 4 (1962), p. 716 (Brookings Institution Reprint 66).

from selected countries to review the development prospects and aid requirements of particular low-income countries and to see what can be done about meeting agreed needs. A portion of the necessary financing will be provided multilaterally by the World Bank Group and a portion by participating governments in accordance with arrangements worked out bilaterally between borrower and lender. The coordination of technical assistance, unfortunately, is rarely discussed in these groups, and as of mid-1969 half a dozen of them had not met for two years or more, thereby raising a real question as to whether they were in fact performing the service for which they were created.

The purpose of the consortium or consultative group is to enable donors to become informed collectively about the economic progress and related policies of the country being aided and to enable the aided country to know the level and kind of assistance it can expect. International institutions perform important intermediary services—provision of neutral chairmen for meetings, collection and presentation of basic data, stimulation of all parties to better efforts, and recording and monitoring of commitments made. Their services could be expanded to include the manning of small resident field missions in aided countries where appropriate, the inclusion in the consortium or consultative group of representation from other aid-receiving nations, and other devices to keep the coordinating mechanisms abreast of the times.

The trend toward multilateral planning or coordination coupled with bilateral financing deserves encouragement because it permits a merging of resources under politically acceptable auspices while permitting donor countries to finance specific undertakings, to tie their loans to domestic purchases if they insist on so doing, and to end up with identifiable monuments to their aid. It is a makeshift arrangement but in keeping perhaps with the transitional character of all international relations in this era of modified sovereignty for nation-states.[9]

9. For one of the most recent and best contributions to the growing literature on consortia and consultative groups, see Michael L. Hoffman, "The Scaffolding of Aid," *Finance and Development*, Vol. 5, no. 4 (1968), pp. 14–19.

Capital Assistance from the United States

Should bilateral capital assistance from the United States be provided on a grant basis or a loan basis, or both? On the assumptions
spelled out earlier in this chapter about the growth of the U.S.
economy and the net outflow of long-term resources from the
United States to less developed lands, the size of the supplementary
bilateral program will rise from a disbursement level of less than $3.5
billion in 1968 to $5 billion in 1975. The bilateral program, in brief,
will not be so insignificant as to make the grant-loan issue a quibble.

The foreign debt situation of the less developed countries suggests
that grant aid will be badly needed. Moreover, the case for putting
U.S. supplementary assistance on a grant basis will be reinforced if
it is the U.S. national interest in the narrower sense that is being pro-
moted by our bilateral aid. Why should other countries pay us for
directly promoting our own interests? On the other hand, loans give
both parties the illusion of being businesslike and in so doing discourage naked politics. If they can be made available on the same
basis as the credits of the International Development Association,
they will be only slightly more costly to the borrower than grants,
and borrowers will not be tempted to come to the United States simply because they can get easier terms from it than from the multilateral IDA. A grant program involving capital assistance would probably have to be justified at least annually to the Congress; a loan
program would have a better possibility of obtaining its funds on a
multiyear basis, with some part perhaps coming from the private
sector.

Although the Export-Import Bank, which is firmly established and
well managed, might seem a likely candidate to handle the bilateral
loan program, it is not a development bank and, in my view, almost
incapable of becoming one. Its basic purpose is to serve the commercial export interests of the United States. It makes some moderately
long-term loans to low-income countries at rates of interest that reflect the cost to the U.S. Treasury of borrowing the funds that the
Bank, in turn, lends. The Export-Import Bank normally does not

seek to finance projects of the highest priority from the point of view of the low-income countries or accumulate data on country development prospects or review country development programs. Typically it finances the purchase of fairly sophisticated mining and manufacturing equipment, commercial jet aircraft, and other additions to capital stock. It also finances the purchase of defense articles by governments of "friendly countries." It has participated in international consortia organized for India, Pakistan, Colombia, and Ghana and extended loans or lines of credit to some other low-income countries during exchange crises. All credits are subject to its usual proviso that the proceeds of the credits be used entirely for the purchase of U.S. goods and services. Thanks in part to the offsetting effects of a rising level of repayments, its net contribution to the flow of resources from the United States to the less developed countries has been very modest.

The establishment of the Development Loan Fund (DLF) in 1957 represented an attempt by the administration to separate the function of making development loans from other aid and credit functions, insulate it somewhat from short-run political considerations, and authorize it on a multiyear basis. Congress was reluctant to cooperate, the Kennedy administration was eager to have the DLF in the AID, and by late 1961 the DLF as a separate Washington agency (it never had a field staff) was out of business. Project lending again became an integral aspect of AID work, dependent on annual appropriations from the Congress. In practice it has been easier to integrate program than project loans into the annual program planning cycle of the AID. The theoretical advantages of having one agency responsible for technical assistance, investment guarantees, program lending, and project lending have to a considerable extent remained theoretical.

It takes a long time to develop a loan proposal to the point where it satisfies technical and economic criteria. In most countries only a handful of capital projects are ready for financing at any given time. . . . Therefore, in many countries A.I.D. is likely to finance a capital project which looks economically and technically sound and for which funds on suitable terms are not available from other sources, even if the project has little or no relation to the goal structure of the rest of the United States assistance program in the country. As a result, six years after the Development Loan Fund has been incorporated into the rest of the United States economic assistance effort, capital project assistance remains poorly integrated with other A.I.D. activities.[10]

A new U.S. development bank (or U.S. development cooperation fund, to use the name suggested by the Perkins Committee in a report released early in 1969) would have many advantages over the present AID, not the least of which could be an authorization to tap the private capital market. Its bonds, of course, would be salable only if principal and interest payments were guaranteed by the U.S. government. Since it would be lending the bulk of its capital at far below commercial rates of interest, it would need frequent injections of public capital. Provided congressional approval were obtained, some of this capital could consist of amortization and interest payments on outstanding public sector loans already made by the AID and predecessor agencies.[11] Appropriated funds would also be needed and a renewed effort to obtain them on a multiyear basis (three or five years at a time) should be made. John Pincus has suggested, for an institution such as the proposed U.S. development cooperation fund:

A modest interest subsidy fund appropriated by the Congress could cover the differential between the Government guaranteed market borrowing rates and the lower rates that some underdeveloped countries could afford to pay.... As nations receiving these loans progressively develop their economies, the activities of such a proposed relending agency might be limited simply to guaranteeing bond issues of these countries without subsidy provision, and in the longer run, without intervention by the U.S. authorities.[12]

The best known and most tireless recent advocate of interest subsidization is David Horowitz, a governor of the World Bank and the IDA (for Israel), who made personal presentations on behalf of the idea at both the 1964 and the 1968 sessions of the UN Conference

10. Joan M. Nelson, *Aid, Influence, and Foreign Policy* (Macmillan, 1968), p. 64.
11. In Chapter 8, I mention the suggestion of the International Private Investment Advisory Council that interest income generated by the AID portfolio of prior dollar and local currency loans *to private and mixed public-private borrowers* be assigned to a U.S. overseas private investment corporation.
12. Statement of John Pincus of the RAND Corporation, in *The Future of U.S. Foreign Trade Policy*, Hearings before the Subcommittee on Foreign Economic Policy of the Joint Economic Committee, 90 Cong. 1 sess. (1967), Vol. 1, p. 250.

on Trade and Development. The World Bank, which was asked by UNCTAD I to make a staff study of the proposal, appears to consider it a "non-starter." The AID, too, is ardently unenthusiastic. The interest subsidy would go, not to the poor countries, but to the bondholders, who would be located in rich countries, in order to give them a reasonable rate of return on capital invested in less developed countries. The costs of the subsidy would mount rapidly under a constant or rising level of lending. A subsidy scheme would therefore be more helpful if the problem of inadequate appropriations for aid proved to be a short-term problem—a problem of the next 5–10 years—than if it proved to be a long-term problem. In the latter event, inadequate appropriations for subsidies could become an equally acute problem.

The cost of the subsidy for ¾ percent loans over 50 years will, of course, be greater than the cost of the subsidy for loans of lesser duration or loans at higher rates of interest. The inability of a current Congress to commit the U.S. government to appropriations for 50 years ahead raises questions of sound budget management which align the U.S. Bureau of the Budget with other opponents of interest subsidies for long-term loans. Moreover, less developed countries that can afford 25-year loans at 3 percent interest should not get 50-year loans at ¾ percent. What is needed is acceptance of the principle of interest subsidization for foreign lending; authority to tailor loan terms to a variety of debt-servicing prospects, including authority to lend on IDA terms; and a more secure source for the subsidy fund than annual congressional appropriations—for example, a once-and-for-all assignment of certain government revenues to the subsidy fund.

Interest subsidization schemes have been successfully employed domestically for housing, rural electrification, and small business loans. Italy, Germany, and other nations subsidize their international lending and the United States could also if it became convinced that no alternative method was equally likely to maintain an adequate flow of development finance.[13] Once it has been agreed that loans to less developed countries should be made at less than commercial rates

13. Presumably aware of the official misgivings about interest-subsidization schemes, the President's General Advisory Committee on Foreign Assistance Pro-

of interest, government lending versus private lending under a viable interest-subsidy scheme boils down, in the bilateral program, to a choice between (1) carrying the loan on the government budgetary account, and subsidizing it by the difference between the government borrowing rate and the lending rate to the less developed country; and (2) carrying the loan in the private economy's account, with the subsidy for the borrowing–lending differential carried in the government account.

Supporting assistance, the grant aid that now goes almost entirely to Vietnam, Laos, and Thailand but also in small amounts to Korea and one or two other countries, could, I hope, be phased out within the next five years. Development assistance from the United States should not be used primarily to enable countries to maintain larger military establishments than would otherwise be possible, but rather to give an extra boost to peaceful, forward-looking regimes committed to promoting "social progress and better standards of life in larger freedom."[14]

As for the contingency fund, this has already been reduced by the Congress to a negligible total, less than $30 million in fiscal year 1968 and $5 million in fiscal year 1969. Consequently, it can no longer be regarded as a source of capital assistance for emergency needs in the low-income world. If the proposed U.S. development cooperation fund is given sufficient flexibility in the allocation of credits for development assistance among regions, countries, and purposes, it should not need a contingency fund.

---

grams (the Perkins Committee) in a report dated Oct. 25, 1968, and released Jan. 9, 1969, nevertheless called attention to the possibility of financing "at least part of a future IDA replenishment through government commitments to subsidize interest payments on IDA bonds sold in private capital markets. . . . If, for example, a government undertook to provide an additional $100 million a year for ten years in this manner and to reimburse IDA for six percent a year on the amount borrowed, the budgetary burden would grow gradually from $6 million in the first year to $60 million in the tenth and succeeding years. If this were done prudently, expanding capital markets ought to be able to absorb both new issues and re-issues of such securities" (p. 41). The American share of the subsidy, it might be added, could conceivably be met or partially met by allocating to the IDA subsidization fund the service payments on loans by AID and predecessor agencies, thereby eliminating or reducing the need for appropriating the U.S. share.

14. Quotation is from the Preamble to the Charter of the United Nations.

Technical Assistance from the United States

Let us turn now to technical assistance, or technical cooperation, as it is frequently called in order to stress the mutuality of the relationship. If there had never been a European Recovery Program or a Mutual Defense Assistance Program, and American aid to the less developed countries had evolved more organically from President Truman's original Point Four proposal, the potentialities and limitations of technical assistance might today be better known. Financial and commodity assistance would doubtless also have been provided, but they would probably have become available primarily within the framework of technical assistance efforts, as adjuncts to programs of teaching and training. Speculation about what might have been is not necessarily fruitful, however, and realism requires us to accept the fact that technical assistance, although popular among donors, has been regarded by receivers not as the heart of development assistance but as a fringe benefit.

Neither the promise of technical assistance nor the threat to withdraw it will impel the receiving nation to incur the political and financial risks involved in introducing major changes in policy. Nevertheless, technical assistance is reported with growing frequency to be the most productive form of assistance per dollar spent, to be essential at all phases of the foreign aid cycle (not just at the beginning), and as reported in Chapter 3, to be needed after the "trade limit on growth"—the inability to earn enough through exports to finance necessary imports—has been overcome.

United States technical assistance has consistently been concentrated in three sectors, agriculture, health, and education, although this fact has from time to time been revealed with all the éclat of a brand new discovery. A background document prepared in July 1949 for the House Committee on Foreign Affairs said, "Among inhabitants of least-developed areas, basic improvement[s] in education, health, and agriculture are essential before there can be an increase in production or a rise in the standard of living."[15]

15. *Point Four, Background and Program*, prepared by the Legislative Reference Service, Library of Congress, largely from materials supplied by the Department of State (July 1949), p. 5.

Seventeen years later, in the proposed economic assistance program for the fiscal year 1967, the government announced, with a certain amount of fanfare, that "major changes in U.S. foreign assistance programs are proposed for fiscal year 1967.... [To meet the challenge of hunger, disease, and ignorance] AID assistance will be directed toward maximum progress in agriculture, health and education."

My purpose at this juncture, however, is not to discuss the content of technical assistance programs but rather their financing and organization. It was noted earlier in this chapter that increasing amounts of technical assistance are being supplied by international lending agencies in conjunction with their regular capital assistance loans and credits. A U.S. development cooperation fund should also cover the financing of technical assistance that is integrally related to the capital assistance it provides.

In addition to the kind of technical assistance that can be furnished in connection with multimillion dollar loans for capital improvements, I suggested that the 1970s ought to see more loans and credits in the $1 million to $10 million range made available to poor countries specifically for technical assistance. Loan arrangements of this kind would permit borrowers to hire their own experts, supervise their work, get their money's worth out of them, and remove them from U.S. embassy compounds and "little Americas" in foreign capitals. Technical assistance loans should be obtainable not only from international lending agencies but from the United States as well; in fact, it would be desirable for the United States to do some pioneering in this type of lending.

My proposal to put much more technical assistance on a loan basis (with very soft loans for very poor countries) could result either in some reduction in the flow of technical assistance to less developed countries or in a much slower rate of increase in this fastest growing component of aid. The reductions, if they occurred, would take place in the types considered least valuable by the less developed countries and would thus become part of the process of giving them a stronger voice in the shaping of aid programs.

Judging from the fact that the IDA considers the poorest of poor countries capable of servicing an IDA credit, I would not be excessively worried about the capacity of the low-income world to pay service charges on technical assistance loans provided by the United States during the 1970s. Even a billion dollars' worth of technical assistance (three times the present U.S. level) at ¾ of 1 percent means an interest charge of only $7.5 million per year.

Although I see no real justification for the conventional distinction between the financing of technical assistance and other forms of aid, I would not urge other donors to follow suit in placing their bilateral technical assistance programs on a loan basis. The first concern of the United States should be to provide something more closely resembling a market test for technical assistance from the United States and to facilitate the integration of its own technical and capital assistance.

The high cost of American technical assistance could discourage less developed countries from spending loan proceeds in the United States unless the desired service were unavailable from anywhere else in the world or the cost were partially subsidized. The subsidy could consist of resources to "top off" salaries of specialists for which less developed countries are unable or unwilling to pay in full and to reduce the cost of sending qualified nationals of less developed countries to the United States for training.

Technical assistance comes in many shapes, sizes, and varieties and is peculiarly difficult to administer effectively. American government agencies tend to be too cumbersome, inflexible, and regulation-ridden to fulfill the bilateral role well, especially for technical assistance in the fields of science and education.[16]

What is needed, it seems to me, is a government-subsidized techni-

16. "Since Point Four days...the traditional concept of an American expert showing an Asian farmer how to plow a straighter furrow, or demonstrating to an African villager how to dig a deeper well, has changed somewhat. Such advisory activity continues, but it is now much more complex and broader in scope.

"Technical assistance now includes research, both here and abroad, in a widening range of fields, such as projects to develop nutritious, high-protein grains, or a better method to exterminate rats. Technical assistance also provides limited funds to strengthen [the] competence of U.S. universities to carry on specialized programs, such as land tenure, water resources and food from the sea, in the developing countries. It encourages experimental or pioneering projects, as in family planning motivation, the role of special interest groups in economic development, or rural leadership training." AID press release of Sept. 24, 1969, announcing the establishment of a Technical Assistance Bureau within the agency.

cal cooperation foundation or institute capable of performing a number of functions. First of all, it should be an intermediary to help aid-receiving countries buy the technical assistance they want from the United States. Aid receivers should not be discouraged from going directly to the General Electric Company, the University of Utah, or the Bureau of the Census to spend the proceeds of their loans. Often, however, they will prefer to deal with a foundation or institute that already knows something about their problems, their procurement procedures, and their idiosyncrasies.

In the second place, it should be a center for continued educational, scientific, and technical cooperation with countries like Taiwan and Iran after the need for capital assistance on concessional terms has ended. A 1967 U.S. mission to Taiwan noted,

> With the closing out of its economic assistance in 1965, AID made generous arrangements for providing capital assistance as a cushion against the shock of the termination of the AID program. Furthermore, through the Export-Import Bank and PL 480, the U.S. Government offers the opportunity for continued U.S. capital assistance through non-AID channels. No similar arrangement was made for continuing technical cooperation between the two governments in the post-AID period. The end of AID meant the termination of university contracts and the withdrawal of U.S. technical personnel whose advice and support the Chinese Government had used to such good effect.[17]

The AID now has within it a Private Resources Development Service set up on a modest experimental basis to act as a broker in helping AID "graduate and phaseout countries" locate non-AID U.S. resources, public and private, and get them used in the developing countries. The latter are expected to pay the direct costs of the assistance requested. Lack of funds for topping off the salaries of U.S. technical personnel is one of the major handicaps of the Private Resources Development Service.[18]

17. Donald F. Hornig, special assistant to the President for science and technology, "Report to the President on the Mission to Survey Scientific and Technological Aspects and Needs in the Republic of China," Sept. 17–24, 1967 (processed), p. 5.

18. See Agency for International Development, Manual Circular 1000.3 of May 31, 1968, "U.S. Technical Cooperation with non-A.I.D. Countries."

Recently, a sizable interagency working group on technical co-operation, aware that "a country's capacity to earn enough foreign exchange to pay for essential imports does not necessarily mean that it no longer needs technical assistance," produced a comprehensive report on American technical cooperation with non-AID countries.[19] It recommended a topping-off program of around $5 million, which would initially be appropriated to and allocated by the AID, but after one or two years would be distributed among federal agencies according to their normal domestic functions. If the topping-off fund were to cover countries still receiving capital and commodity assistance on concessional terms as well as recent graduates of such assistance, it ought to total at least $25 million per year. I would prefer to have the topping-off fund administered by a quasi-governmental foundation or institute which could be more neutral about topping off salaries from the private as well as the government sector.

A technical cooperation institute should be authorized to accept private contributions. It should be concerned with the improvement of educational, training, and research facilities in the low-income world. One of my friends has suggested the need for a mechanism that would collect information on new processes, practices, products, and ideas potentially useful to less developed countries and would send them promptly to appropriate receiving stations in the less developed countries; a technical cooperation institute could perform this function. It could also be concerned with cultural exchanges and measures to discourage the brain drain and with arrangements and subsidies for training in the United States specialists and leaders from less developed countries. Finally, it could form some judgments about the services of the heterogeneous array of American voluntary agencies that are probably spending twice as much per year as the U.S. government in technical assistance to less developed countries. The technical cooperation institute could remain in close touch with the proposed U.S. development cooperation fund (which would be the principal development financing agency of the U.S. government)

19. Interagency Working Group on Technical Cooperation, "U.S. Technical Cooperation With Non-A.I.D. Countries" (Report of Subgroup I; revised February 1969; processed).

by sharing space with the latter and by having the director of the fund on the board of directors of the institute.[20]

The Nixon administration's plan to reorganize and revitalize U.S. technical assistance is to create a technical assistance bureau headed by an assistant administrator within the AID and to have the technical assistance program authorized for a two-year period. While this would be an improvement over the existing arrangements, it would not represent progress toward another goal that seems to me at least equally important, namely, making the technical assistants hired hands of the nations expected to benefit from their presence.

Technical assistants who have previously enjoyed the comforts, prestige, and administrative services of a sizable U.S. aid mission may feel orphaned when attached instead to agencies and institutions of the host country, as individuals or as part of a team, as employees or consultants, with housing and transportation provided or not provided. The adjustment can surely be made, however, and in the process the average effectiveness of U.S. assistance raised rather than lowered.

Other Organizational Changes

An area of AID work that must remain bilateral but is also ripe for different handling during the 1970s is the work performed by the

20. The idea of a semiautonomous government institute to handle certain aspects of technical assistance is not new with me; it was proposed in numerous reports during the 1960s. The 1964 report, *A.I.D. and the Universities*, by John W. Gardner, for example, devoted its closing chapter to such a proposal. The chief factor, said his task force, "that leads us to propose this [a semi-autonomous government institute] is the absolute *necessity* that certain technical assistance activities be relieved of the pressures for early termination that Congress and the public impose on other aspects of foreign aid.... We believe that if Congress and the American people were given the opportunity to see certain technical assistance activities in an organizational setting somewhat apart from the rest of the foreign aid package, they would readily grasp the essential long-term character of these activities. They would see that they are to be thought of on a par with our other long-term, international educational efforts—efforts which the nation has no intention of terminating" (p. 47). For a thoughtful recent statement of what a "Technical Assistance and Development Research Institute" should do and how it might be financed, see National Planning Association, *A New Conception of Foreign Aid*, Special Report 64 (Washington: March 1969), pp. 14–18. See also Chapter 10, below.

Office of Private Resources. Problems associated with stimulating the flow of private capital to less developed countries and investing it productively within those countries are discussed in a subsequent chapter. Although it would be an illusion to think that the flow of investment will be significantly altered in the short run by the establishment of a federally chartered overseas private investment corporation, there are good reasons for going along with the current sentiment in favor of such a corporation, and the idea is endorsed in Chapter 8 below.

The establishment of a U.S. development cooperation fund or bank, a technical cooperation foundation or institute, and an overseas private investment corporation and other changes required by the altered domestic and international environment will eliminate or redistribute most of the functions currently performed by the Agency for International Development. The AID now shares responsibility with the Department of Agriculture and others for the Food-for-Freedom program authorized by Public Law 480. Given a continuation of the encouraging agricultural trends of the last few years, the importance of food shipments from the United States to less developed countries should diminish during the 1970s. So long as Public Law 480 remains on the books, it should be administered with a view to maximizing its potentialities for humanitarian ends, famine relief, and agricultural development abroad. This implies some easing of its present credit terms. It would not appear necessary, however, to keep the AID alive in order to perform the Public Law 480 functions performed by the Office of the War on Hunger.

At the field level, I envisage drastically reduced aid missions, primarily because most of the technical assistance personnel would be employees of aid-receiving nations, but also because of greater reliance on the less developed countries and on international agencies for the establishment of priorities and requirements and the monitoring of performance. I would not expect the principal U.S. bilateral agency, the development cooperation fund or bank, to be as concentrated in Washington as the Development Loan Fund of 1958-61, particularly since it should be engaged in program and sector lending as well as project lending, but I would keep its resident field staff very small—large enough only to prevent the State Department from having a monopoly in field personnel and therefore exclusively able to tip the scales at policy councils in Washington with the weight of real or fancied firsthand data on the local situation.

Some arrangement will be needed to give overall policy guidance to the development cooperation fund, the technical assistance foundation or institute, the private investment corporation, the Public Law 480 program, and the U.S. participants in consortia and consultative groups. The loan program will be the guts of the U.S. bilateral effort and a case could therefore be made for vesting coordinating responsibility in the proposed development cooperation fund or bank. More logical, however, in view of the wide range of U.S. foreign policy interests to be served by bilateral programs, would be coordination by a White House office comparable to the Office of the Special Representative for Trade Negotiations.

Do these recommendations for phasing out the AID add up to a peculiarly American recipe for chaos: when activities are centralized, decentralize them; if they are decentralized, centralize them? Do they constitute an ironic thanks to David E. Bell, William S. Gaud, and others for their tireless efforts to build an effective, all-inclusive American development agency and for their dedicated service to the cause of development?

In 1950, the case for a powerful U.S. Economic Cooperation Administration was overwhelming, and in 1960 the case for the Agency for International Development was strong. At the dawn of the 1970s, the situation at home and abroad is quite different. The reasons for shifting to a predominantly multilateral effort have been given. That shift will inevitably be hindered rather than helped by retaining a bilateral agency with a large field staff, equipped to offer a full range of capital and technical assistance as well as investment guarantees, wedded to the present U.S. way of doing things, subconsciously if not consciously resisting multilateralization, and burdened with an unshakable heritage of legislative restrictions. Moreover, it seems to me highly unlikely that the Congress could be persuaded to free the AID of its shackles, fund it for several years at a time, authorize it to tap the private capital market in various new ways, and reinvest it with glamour and status.

In the circumstances, the conclusion I reach—not without occasional pangs of regret—favors phasing out the AID while seeking to provide a new organizational framework, a fresh lease on life, and additional autonomy for the three principal functions that should continue to be carried on bilaterally: development lending over and above multilateral efforts, a broker's role in procuring from a variety of sources technical assistance that the United States can advantageously provide, and the promotion of private U.S. foreign investment in areas prepared to receive it. These functions will have to be performed throughout the 1970s.

CHAPTER SEVEN

Trade Policy

EIGHTY PERCENT OR MORE of the foreign exchange of less developed countries is earned through exports of goods and services. Three-quarters of those exports are taken by the industrialized countries of the world. Changes in trade policy that would permit even modest increases in the export earnings of less developed countries are very important to them. If, for example, exports of goods and services account for 85 percent of a country's foreign exchange receipts while public grants and loans account for 10 percent of the inflow and private investment for 5 percent, then a 6 percent increase in the goods and services account would produce more foreign exchange than a 50 percent increase in public grants and loans or a 150 percent increase in private funds. This is not to say that the 6 percent increase would produce more development; the problems of converting increased export earnings into economic growth are fairly formidable in a less developed country.

Higher export earnings can easily be dissipated in imports of luxuries, in exports of capital to private accounts in Swiss banks, in inability to mobilize capital for domestic investment, and in general waste. It takes little talent to absorb additional resources without achieving additional development and to run a constant or growing balance-of-payments deficit, even in the face of increased export earnings.

Given the importance and respectability of foreign trade, however, it is essential that sympathetic examination be given to (1) policies that the United States could adopt, alone or in concert with other industrialized countries, to provide low-income nations with opportunities to earn more from foreign trade; and (2) policies and programs that the less developed countries might adopt, with or without foreign aid, in order to capitalize more fully on existing and future opportunities in international trade. Among such policies are elimination of tariffs on imports into industrialized countries; temporary tariff preferences for manufactured products from less developed countries; a beginning of the dismantling of agricultural protectionism; better treatment for less developed countries under "buy American" legislation; multilateral arrangements for compensatory financing of unavoidable shortfalls in the export proceeds and unavoidable increases in the import requirements of less developed countries; international financing of buffer stocks and other methods of stabilizing trade in certain primary commodities; more technical assistance to low-income countries in expanding their exports and developing rational tariff structures; more adjustment assistance to help management and labor in rich countries move out of activities in which comparative advantage rests with poor countries.

My own view of priorities in the trade field to facilitate development of the low-income countries in ways that would also serve the long-run interests of the United States would give top places to tariff abolition in high-income countries, to easier recourse to adjustment assistance for adversely affected activities, and to programmed decreases in the protectionist agricultural policies of such countries, including the subsidies they give to agricultural exports that compete with agricultural exports from poor countries.

Tariffs and Other Aspects of Commercial Policy

Tariff barriers to international trade are slowly but steadily being reduced. Their full elimination (zero tariffs) for imports into industrialized countries has become a practical goal of economic policy. Nominal, or legal, U.S. tariff rates are, on the average, already rather low—around 10 percent of wholesale prices on dutiable imports of manufactures after the Kennedy Round reductions become effective. The average, however, is a composite figure and many of the individual rates are well above the average. It is in some of these latter products that the less developed countries are most interested. Moreover, the nominal tariff rates usually understate substantially the true effect of the tariff in protecting processing.

From the point of view of the domestic producer, the protection of value added (the effective tariff) rather than the duty on the product itself (the nominal tariff) is relevant since his main concern is whether, and to what extent, tariffs permit him to produce at a direct cost (value added) higher than that obtained in a free trade situation. Conversely, effective tariffs indicate the extent to which producers in developing countries will have to operate with a direct cost lower than their counterparts in developed countries in order to gain access to the protected markets of the latter.[1]

And, "The effective protection afforded to processing of raw products in the developed countries by the combination of a tariff on the processed product with free entry of the raw material may be very high indeed, because the cost of processing may be small by comparison with the cost of the raw material."[2]

Tariff rates in developed countries tend to rise with the amount of processing done abroad. Noncompetitive raw materials enjoy the most favorable rates, semifinished goods come next, while products manufactured abroad are subject to the highest tariffs. The labor-intensive manufactured products in which the less developed countries would appear to have the greatest comparative advantage, at least during the initial stages of their industrialization, are the most heavily protected.

The preferable course of action would be for all the more developed nations to move in unison toward the complete elimination of tariff barriers in high-income countries. If it is true that the present

1. Bela A. Balassa, "Tariff Protection in Industrial Nations and Its Effects on the Exports of Processed Goods from Developing Countries," *Canadian Journal of Economics* (August 1968), p. 584.

2. Harry G. Johnson, *Economic Policies Toward Less Developed Countries* (Brookings Institution, 1967), pp. 90–91.

tariff structure is rigged against the less developed countries, then elimination of tariffs should be of particular benefit to them, even if no special preferences are received. The less developed countries appear to believe, however, that in order to obtain a foothold in international markets for their processed goods, they need better terms than equality with countries that are already highly industrialized.

Consequently, the trade proposal that has evoked the most enthusiasm in the low-income world is for temporary tariff preferences in all the industrialized countries for processed products from all the nonindustrialized, less developed nations. This assumes that complete elimination of tarriff barriers is unlikely within the next five to ten years. Thus, if the legal duty on bicycles is now, say, 10 percent, it might be reduced, for less developed countries only, to zero, either in advance of a phased reduction negotiated among industrialized countries or for a fixed number of years. In principle, the United States has accepted the proposal. If agreement on product coverage could have been obtained at the second UN Conference on Trade and Development (UNCTAD) held in New Delhi in the spring of 1968, the gap between principle and practice might by now be narrower than it is.

The interval could perhaps be used advantageously to complete a careful study of zero tariffs versus tariff preferences. Is not the full elimination of tariffs by the industrialized countries of the world a practical policy goal for the 1970s? Would the complications of negotiating and administering a preference scheme hasten or impede attainment of that goal? What would be the advantages and disadvantages to less developed countries of a fairly rapid general lowering of tariff barriers, particularly the relatively high tariffs on products reported to be of special interest to less developed countries, as compared with temporary preferences which might or might not be followed by reimposition of the prepreference rate at the end of the preference period?

In his excellent chapter on tariff preferences for less developed countries, Harry G. Johnson reports: "The clear implication of the theoretical considerations and empirical evidence is that, despite impressions to the contrary derived from contemplation of nominal tariff levels, preferences in developed-country markets for exports of manufactures and semimanufactures might well exercise a powerful influence in expanding the export earnings and promoting the industrialization of the less developed countries."[3]

His view is supported by a subsequent unpublished State Department study, based on 1966 trade. The study assumes the complete elimination of duties on exports of manufactured and semimanufactured goods from less developed to developed countries, except for duties on textiles, clothing, and precious stones. Total exports of the less developed lands in the categories covered amounted to $3.2 billion. The minimum benefits to less developed countries from zero tariffs on 1966 trade would be $193 million, the tariff revenue forgone by the developed countries. The maximum benefits (on the basis of the elasticities used in the study) would be $712 million. The higher figure, which is believed to reflect the real tendency, would be distributed among regions as follows: the Far East would be the principal regional beneficiary, with a net increase in exports of about $440 million, of which roughly half would go to Hong Kong; Latin American exports would rise by about $183 million, African exports by $60 million, and those of the Middle East by $28 million. Projecting past trade trends into the future, the benefit of preferences by 1972 is estimated to rise to nearly $1.3 billion.

Apart from shifts in the pattern of international trade, the impact on the U.S. trade account would appear to be an increase in U.S. imports of $228 million and an increase in exports of $176 million, or a net impact of minus $52 million (which would rise to about $100 million by 1972). If Hong Kong were excluded from the preference system, the cost to the U.S. trade account would be reduced from minus $52 million to minus $20 million, which is also the estimated cost of a scheme applicable only to Latin America.[4]

Despite the substantial benefits that could accrue to less developed

3. *Economic Policies*, p. 173.

4. Roger A. Sorenson, "The Effects on World and U.S. Trade of a Generalized System of Preferences," U.S. Department of State, Office of International Trade (March 1969). Calculations based on the inclusion of textiles in the preference system would raise the above estimates of benefits and costs; calculations excluding additional categories of goods, or based on partial instead of complete elimination of duties, would reduce the estimates.

countries from a generalized system of preferences and the modest cost to the more developed countries, little progress is being made in implementing the scheme. At the March 1969 meeting of the Organisation for Economic Co-operation and Development (OECD) member governments were to submit lists of products on which they were prepared to consider granting preferences, but the United States failed to produce a list and could only say that the new administration needed more time for a review of American trade policy in all its aspects. Other OECD members were glad to have an excuse for delay, and the momentum resulting from President Johnson's 1967 endorsement of the proposal in Latin America is being lost.[5]

Better access to the American market for processed goods and manufactured products of less developed countries will benefit primarily the most advanced among the low-income nations, some of which are penetrating the market admirably without special concessions. Preferences cannot be expected in the short run to reduce significantly the aid requirements of the least industrialized countries, though they might enable more of the available aid to be concentrated on the neediest areas.

Less developed countries, it should also be noted, do far too little trading with each other. The experience of the Central American Common Market, where international trade has risen spectacularly since the CACM came into being in 1961, is proof that preferential systems among less developed countries can be advantageous to them. Even without preferences, much can be done to increase trade among less developed countries through export promotion drives and export credit arrangements.[6] India, for example, is beginning to suspect that

5. For a reminder of some policy issues not mentioned by me in this chapter—for example, the preferences already accorded to some African countries by members of the European Economic Community and the "reverse preferences" granted to these developed countries—see "Future United States Foreign Trade Policy," Report to the President submitted by the Special Representative for Trade Negotiations (Jan. 14, 1969; processed), pp. 62–63; and Hal B. Lary, "Tariff Preferences for Less Developed Countries," in John H. Adler (ed.), *International Development, 1968* (Dobbs Ferry, N.Y.: Oceana Publications, 1969), pp. 253–62.

6. "Developing countries have found that competition is not confined solely to the range of exportable products available, nor to their quality, reasonable cost ratios and dependable delivery schedules, but also encompasses the capacity to offer

other less developed countries, despite their fragmentation into ninety or so political jurisdictions, constitute a promising market for Indian exports. The most recent trade statistics show a substantial increase in Indian exports to them.

If tariff barriers were lowered by the industrialized countries only to be replaced by nontariff barriers—arbitrary quotas, costly labeling requirements, unnecessary health and sanitation regulations, and "arrangements" as questionable as the Long-Term Cotton Textiles Arrangement—the incentives to less developed countries to export more processed goods to industrialized countries would be vitiated.[7]

"Buy American" restrictions represent a special internal tariff. They include both the federal "Buy American" Act adopted in 1933 as an antidepression measure and the laws and regulations of more than twenty states which impose significant additional restrictions on the purchase of foreign goods for public projects. Where foreigners are not prevented entirely from bidding on the billions of dollars' worth of goods bought by public authorities, they are required to underbid Americans by substantial percentages in order to be awarded contracts.

Authorization for foreigners to compete on the same terms as domestic producers would benefit other industrialized countries more than less developed countries. Concessions to less developed countries only would be analogous to tariff preferences for them and justifiable on the same grounds. Without a detailed analysis of government purchases and of the ability of less developed countries to supply the items needed—particularly in circumstances more normal than when

---

prospective buyers deferred payment terms similar to those tendered by competitive suppliers of comparable export products." *Survey of International Development*, Vol. 6, no. 2 (Washington: Society for International Development, April 15, 1969), p. 2.

7. Whatever temporary justification they may have had, the tendency of the cotton textile restrictions to become permanent features of the commercial landscape and ever-present models for proposals restricting imports of other products is distressing. If the United States were appropriately serious about development of the low-income countries, it would have given much higher priority to easing the transfer of American resources out of fields in which they no longer enjoy a comparative advantage and into fields in which goods made in America can be fully competitive without special protection.

so many American troops are in Asia—it is impossible to estimate in dollars the costs and benefits of "buy American" regulations more favorable to the less developed countries. The psychological effect of putting less developed countries on the same footing as domestic bidders would be considerable.[8]

Since 80–90 percent of the export earnings of the less developed countries still comes from primary products, measures that enable such exports to be increased would have the greatest immediate effects on the foreign exchange earnings, though not necessarily on the industrialization, of the exporting country. With certain exceptions among the minerals and metals, however, the market for exports of primary products is not dynamic. It grows slowly and sluggishly and is subject to considerable price fluctuations. Most of the primary products exported by poor countries have to compete with commodities produced and exported by rich countries. Taken as a group, exports of primary products during the 1960s expanded at a much slower rate in both value and volume than exports of manufactured goods.

In the rich countries, agriculture has been virtually exempt from the trade liberalization movement of the postwar years. Domestic producers of sugar beets and sugar cane, cereals, and many other primary products are sheltered from foreign competition. Elimination of agricultural protection in the highly developed countries could be an enormous stimulant to the exports of the less developed countries. Full elimination during the foreseeable future is unlikely,

8. Under Executive Order 10582 of Dec. 17, 1954, covering federal but not state and local procurement, domestic bids are considered unreasonable if they exceed the foreign bid price by 6 percent—or 12 percent if the domestic product is made by a small business firm or in an area of substantial unemployment. Since July 1962, however, the Defense Department (by far the largest purchaser) has been using a "national interest" exception in the executive order and applying a differential of 50 percent in order to protect the U.S. balance of payments. The "Buy American" Act applies only to procurement for use in the United States, but the Defense Department also gives the 50 percent price preference to domestic producers in its procurement for use overseas. The AID used to permit a limited amount of procurement in less developed countries but now goes to great pains to show that the proportion of AID-financed goods purchased in the United States is coming closer and closer to 100 percent. See William Kelly, Jr., "Nontariff Barriers," in Bela A. Balassa (ed.), *Studies in Trade Liberalization* (Johns Hopkins Press, 1967), pp. 278–79.

but a prompt follow-up on the modest beginning made in the 1963–67 Kennedy Round of trade negotiations would be helpful. In New Delhi in 1968 the less developed countries shelved their previous insistence on the elimination of agricultural protectionism and asked instead for a share of the increase in domestic demand for primary commodities in industrialized countries.

More attention can be given to ways of meeting this request. The U.S. policy on sugar, for example, favors domestic producers and requires consumers to pay far more than the world market price for sugar. Foreign nations that are allocated quotas, however, benefit from the high domestic price. All are less developed countries; together they receive "aid" amounting to half a billion dollars or so a year which is unrecorded in aid statistics.

Pending genuine diversification of production and exports by the less developed countries—that is, pending development—one of the remedies they have sought most persistently is a series of international commodity agreements to stabilize and step up earnings from those primary products that they do export in quantity—coffee, cocoa, tea, bananas, rubber, tin, copper, lead, and zinc, among others. The list of commodity agreements in operation is very short; sensible arrangements are inordinately hard to work out and seldom very successful after having been put into effect. The International Coffee Agreement, with its new fund for diversification, appears to represent a breakthrough, however. Since it went into effect in 1962, world prices for coffee have remained relatively stable, while the annual foreign exchange proceeds from coffee exports have risen by about $400 million. Emergent African interests in the world coffee market have been accommodated and Brazil has undertaken a sizable diversification program.

The International Coffee Agreement can include a significant volume of "aid" to less developed countries because coffee is one of the handful of commodities meeting certain criteria. It is produced only in less developed countries. It is important in the export trade of a number of those countries. It has no close substitute. Demand is not so sensitive to price that earnings fall off as prices approach the upper reaches of the levels selected for support. Applying these criteria, John Pincus concluded a few years ago that coffee, tea, cocoa, bananas, and sugar (although sugar is produced in developed as well as less developed countries) "should receive priority attention."[9]

A sugar agreement of sorts is in operation, but without the participation of some key countries. A cocoa agreement is in the offing, though as of this writing, the cocoa-producing countries appear to be doing fairly well without it. The previously mentioned International Cotton Textiles Arrangement, though disadvantageous to low-income countries that export textiles and to consumers in the countries that import them, does at least illustrate the fact that many inherent technical difficulties in working out agreements vanish when powerful countries are determined to surmount them.

During the 1950s and early 1960s, the less developed countries were on the whole more interested in import substitution than in export promotion. Import substitution meant producing at home, behind a hastily erected tariff wall and almost regardless of cost, goods that previously were purchased abroad. By the mid-1960s, however, import substitution had run its course in a number of countries and many of the more obvious opportunities had been seized. In a number of cases, the new monopolies were making a questionable contribution to development.

The literature on economic development contains little advice on what constitutes a rational tariff structure and domestic antitrust policy for a country desiring to increase the number of its citizens employed in industry without undue sacrifice of the principle of comparative advantage.[10] Technical assistance presumably could be helpful in devising suitable tariff schedules and represents one more way in which trade and aid could be better integrated. Is it feasible,

9. John Pincus, *Economic Aid and International Cost Sharing* (Santa Monica: RAND Corporation, July 1965), p. 159. The criteria are discussed on pp. 157–59. I am also indebted to Bart S. Fisher, Brookings research fellow in 1968–69, for information on the International Coffee Agreement.

10. C. A. Cooper and B. F. Massell shed some light on this subject in "Toward a General Theory of Customs Unions for Developing Countries," *Journal of Political Economy*, Vol. 73 (October 1965), pp. 461–76.

for example, to design a schedule under which the effective rates of protection would provide some cushion for domestic manufacturing but market forces would play a greater role in determining which industries survive and which fall by the wayside? Can declining protectionism be built into the tariff structure from the beginning?

Not only had import substitution run its course by the mid-1960s, but analysis of successful development programs had revealed that success was rare without sizable absolute increases in export earnings.

The growth of exports is an essential element of a healthy development program. It enables poor countries to benefit from rapidly growing external markets and to overcome a slack caused by any slowdown in the growth of domestic markets.... An expansion of exports provides the resources to pay for the larger imports required by a successful development program, or for the debts incurred to finance part of these requirements. It is now generally recognized that imports must rise as development proceeds, particularly if industrialization is to play a strategic role. Increased industrial output—either through better utilization of existing plants or by the start of new industries—often requires an increase in imports of raw materials and intermediate goods. Even where a policy of import substitution has succeeded in suppressing imports, the lag in import growth behind output growth has often proved temporary; if prolonged, however, it may harm industrial expansion by imposing a limit on the supplies of new capital goods and raw materials. Over the longer term, export growth is the only satisfactory solution to the problems posed by a high burden of debt incurred to finance development.[11]

Although concerted action to lower tariff and nontariff barriers to exports from less developed countries would be preferable, unilateral reductions on the part of the United States should not be ruled out. Unilateral action would help the United States politically in the less developed world. At home, American consumers might benefit from lower-priced supplies, to the extent that the less developed countries succeeded in taking advantage of the enlarged opportunities for sales abroad, and inflation in the United States could be countered.

The export opportunities thus provided could not translate them-

11. Barend A. de Vries, *The Export Experience of Developing Countries* (International Bank for Reconstruction and Development, 1967), p. 6.

selves into export earnings unless the underdeveloped countries were in a position to take advantage of them. This requires realistic exchange rates that do not artificially overvalue exports. It also requires control of the kind of domestic inflation that in a number of poor countries provides a ready market for the national output and reduces drastically the residue available for export. In addition, it usually requires a positive program to promote exports. The problem is to make production for a world market profitable and attractive without extending the array of subsidies that, if present trends continue, will make it cheaper for the whole world to import than to produce at home. Technical assistance and other forms of foreign aid could be more helpful than they have been in generalizing the postwar experience of Japan, Italy, Hong Kong, Taiwan, and Korea in expanding exports.[12]

Safeguards against flooding the American market could be erected and American producers whose future was threatened could be helped by better adjustment assistance programs or other means. Adjustment assistance—government aid to U.S. firms and workers in meeting injury caused by imports—can upgrade the U.S. economy while having several times the impact abroad of a comparable amount of foreign aid.

What I have tried to suggest in this section is that more rational trade policies on the part of the industrialized countries can not only facilitate in a thoroughly respectable way the economic development of the less developed countries but also reduce to some extent their need for foreign aid. The United States should begin to consider systematically the various adjustments in its economic structure necessary for it to absorb substantially more imports from the less developed world during the 1970s and thereafter. It could invite other high-income countries to engage in similar introspection and it might take the initiative in proposing a post-Kennedy Round conference on the problem, beginning perhaps with primary products.

12. See Amicus Most, *Expanding Exports: A Case Study of the Korean Experience* (Agency for International Development, 1969), especially pp. 163–72. Note might also be taken of the work of the export promotion division of the U.S. AID mission in India.

The Persistence of Protectionism: A Sample

No one should labor under the illusion that the U.S. Congress or the American public is at the moment any more inclined to meet the needs of the less developed countries through trade concessions than through aid. In both areas, strenuous efforts are being made to repudiate or retreat from the policies of the first two postwar decades—efforts that would not enjoy a clear field if there were imaginative new programs for further advances.

Although tariffs and import quotas are the best-known manifestations of the protectionist spirit, resistance to a restructuring of the world economy on the basis of comparative advantage takes many other forms. One such form is to prevent aid funds from being used to build up economic activity abroad that might compete with vocal interests at home. For example, less developed countries wishing to modernize their textile industries find it extremely difficult to finance the import of textile machinery from AID allocations.[13] Because textile machinery can readily be obtained from Japan, Great Britain, and other countries, the chief result of the policy is not to protect American textile producers but to penalize American makers of textile machinery.

The fisheries industry provides an almost classic example of the constraints within which the U.S. aid program is compelled to operate. During the 1960s, the AID encouraged Korea, a major recipient of U.S. aid, to invest in fisheries in the plausible belief that expansion of Korea's high-seas fisheries would help that low-income country to become self-supporting. Although the expenditures of the AID were modest, Senator Gruening of Alaska soon wrote to Secretary of State Rusk:

Data obtained from the Agency for International Development disclose that the Government of Korea has developed a second Five Year Plan which envisages a substantially increased investment for fisheries....

13. AID policy is to limit its financing of textile equipment to replacement and repair material, except where it can be shown that machines for new or expanded capacity will not produce textiles for export to the United States.

I need hardly point out the adverse effect this tremendous growth in Korea's deep-sea fishing capability will have on our country's fishing industry when Korea sends its fishing fleets to the salmon and other fishery grounds of the North Pacific. I am particularly disturbed by evidence that the Agency for International Development is supporting Korea's plans for expanding its deep-sea fishing. It appears that AID has approved or otherwise endorsed the second Five Year Plan of the Korean Government and has specifically endorsed Korea's plans to expand its high seas fishing. . . .

I also noted that AID has given the Koreans a considerable amount of assistance in past years for the development of that country's fishing industry. Some $5 million has been given to Korea in the last twelve years for a variety of purposes connected with the development of its fishing industry. This included $3.4 million for construction of fishing boats; $300,000 for research; and over $1 million for plants, markets, and processing facilities. Current economic assistance to Korea for its fishing industry amounts to over $200,000 for 1966–68 and includes a team of United States technicians to "provide technical advice on processing and management to various agencies and organizations in the fishing industry. . . ." It is also planned to assist the Korean fishing industry by a program of training Koreans, at U.S. expense, in various aspects of fisheries management. . . .

I suggest you reappraise AID's present policy which supports expansion of the Korean deep-sea fishing industry and consider terminating any assistance to that industry unless firm assurances are received that such expansion will not be in competition with the United States.[14]

The reply written on behalf of the secretary of state said that since the department had become aware that the Republic of Korea might be entering the North Pacific salmon and halibut fisheries, it had been "very active in pointing out to the Korean authorities the severe difficulties that would arise from such action on their part." It had invited the general who headed Korea's fisheries to the United States for face-to-face talks and sought to steer Korea away from the salmon and halibut stocks of the North Pacific toward tuna and mackerel. One difficulty was that the Koreans were finding it possible to secure

14. *Economic Aid for Development of Foreign Fishing Industries in Competition with Domestic Industries*, Hearing before the Subcommittee on Foreign Aid Expenditures of the Senate Committee on Government Operations, 90 Cong. 2 sess. (1968), p. 3.

capital in Europe and Japan. "The Korean fishing industry, therefore, will expand with or without our help. We believe that we will have greater influence on the direction of Korean fishing policy by assisting it than by withdrawing and leaving assistance to other nations (whose influence might lead the Koreans in other directions than we would wish)."[15]

Two letters from Howard W. Pollock, the congressman from Alaska, reporting on his negotiations with key Koreans, indicate that the story might have a happy ending: Korea would provide economic aid to Alaska!

My primary concern in these negotiations has been twofold: (1) to divert the Korean fishing fleets from fishing for salmon, king crabs, halibut, shrimp, and other products of the sea which are now being harvested by Alaska fishermen, and (2) to create new industries and new jobs in Alaska by encouraging the Koreans to invest in new business ventures in our State. . . . As you will note, the Chairman has agreed not to fish in Alaskan waters for salmon, king crab, halibut, shrimp and scallops (which are now being newly harvested by Alaska fishermen), but instead to purchase these seafood products from Alaska fishermen at prevailing market prices. This is a major victory. In addition, Chairman Choung evidenced an interest in building a fish protein concentrate plant in Alaska, and to use Alaska bottom fishermen to supply the fish resources. The Koreans also showed interest in a number of other possible new businesses in Alaska, utilizing Alaskan labor and Korean financing. The prospects are bright indeed, and I urge that we render every possible assistance to this international friend.[16]

The "assistance" was supposed to include port privileges in Kodiak for the Korean fishing fleet. Senator Gruening and the fishermen of Kodiak agreed, however, that "it would not be in the interests of the Alaska fishing industry to invite the South Koreans to establish a base for fishing operations in Alaska in competition with the fishing industry of our own State."[17] The agreement negotiated by the congressman therefore languished.

15. *Ibid.*, p. 4.
16. *Ibid.*, p. 9.
17. *Ibid.*, p. 10.

Trade-Related Measures: Compensatory and Supplementary Financing Schemes

All countries suffer fluctuations in export earnings, but shortfalls in anticipated earnings due to circumstances beyond the control of the exporting nations are more serious for the less developed countries. Development programs on which people are counting heavily may be interrupted or slowed down. Foreign aid can compensate for the shortfall, but so can drawing rights from an international fund or an insurance scheme. There is a trend toward these latter, more businesslike techniques.

Because of historical accident rather than logic, the problem of dealing in businesslike fashion with shortfalls in export earnings has tended to become two problems, one short term and the other long term.

The International Monetary Fund (IMF), established in 1946, has as one of its principal functions the provision of short-term credit (three to five years) to countries in temporary balance-of-payments difficulties. It created a special "facility" in 1963 to provide a more automatic access to credit for less developed countries suffering foreign exchange deficits caused by reductions in export proceeds below the level of the medium-term trend and beyond the control of the exporting country. Originally, such compensatory drawings could not normally exceed 25 percent of the country's quota in the IMF and were repayable within three to five years. In September 1966, "the amount of drawings that could be outstanding under this policy was increased from 25 to 50 percent of a member's quota although the second 25 percent would be available only if the IMF was satisfied that the member was cooperating in an effort to find an appropriate solution for its payments difficulties."[18]

During the fiscal year ending April 30, 1968, the first full year of operations under the September 1966 decision, compensatory

18. Edward M. Bernstein, "The International Monetary Fund," in Richard N. Gardner and Max F. Millikan (eds.), *The Global Partnership: International Agencies and Economic Development* (Praeger, 1968), p. 141.

drawings amounting to $194 million were made by nine members. This amount exceeds the amount drawn by members during the preceding four years of the facility's existence.[19]

The IMF scheme assumes that the adverse export trend will be relatively brief and consequently can be financed on a short-term repayable basis. There is also the problem of long-term declines in the projected export earnings of less developed countries. Pursuant to a request made by the UN Conference on Trade and Development in 1964, the staff of the World Bank devised a scheme that would help to relieve commodity agreements of the burden they have been least successful in carrying, namely, the maintenance of the total export earnings of producing nations. The scheme would provide less developed countries with an accessible source of foreign exchange to enable them to maintain internationally approved development programs in the face of unforeseen adverse export movements that are beyond their control and beyond their ability to offset from reserves or to finance on three- to five-year terms. Isaiah Frank has suggested that the Bank's proposal might be adapted to cover not only unanticipated export shortfalls but also unanticipated increases in import requirements caused by drought or other adverse conditions beyond a country's control.[20] The World Bank's plan is predicated on the assumption that it would be supplementary to, not a substitute for, existing forms of aid.

France has opposed the plan on the ground that "market organization" is a superior method of averting shortfalls in the export proceeds of developing countries. The United States, for quite different reasons, has been less than lukewarm to the proposal. If a separate supplementary financing program seems at the moment a question-

19. International Monetary Fund, *1968 Annual Report* (Washington: IMF, 1968), pp. 101–02. During the fiscal year ending April 30, 1969, primary product prices were somewhat more favorable and only Afghanistan and Iceland had recourse to the facility.

20. Isaiah Frank, "Foreign Trade Policies and Latin American Development," statement of March 1, 1968, to the Subcommittee on American Republic Affairs of the Senate Foreign Relations Committee (mimeographed), p. 14. The Bank and the Fund, it should be noted, are also better prepared than heretofore to provide some initial multilateral financing for buffer stocks established in connection with international commodity agreements.

able proliferation of international machinery, would it not be possible to experiment with the idea through existing forms of aid—in other words, to make program lending flexible enough in some carefully selected cases to encompass the kind of foreign exchange difficulties the supplementary financing scheme is intended to overcome?

The compensatory financing facility of the IMF and the supplementary financial measures designed by the World Bank staff (but not yet adopted by governments) strengthen the case for a line of action that seems inevitable in any case: an international review of country development programs to find some consensus, not only about each country's needs, but also about the policies it will follow to attain its goals. However highly nation-states may value their sovereignty, if they desire outside assistance on a significant scale, they are going to have to satisfy potential sources of assistance that they can make good use of the available resources. The process of presenting and defending a development program need not be demeaning or humiliating if aid receivers as well as aid providers have had a voice in developing the principles governing the review.

CHAPTER EIGHT

Private Investment

As in various other aspects of international finance, discussion of the role of private investment has covered familiar ground and managed to come almost full circle in the course of twenty years. Public investment in reconstruction and development became necessary because private investment was inadequate for the massive task at hand; now private investment is being lured with renewed vigor because public investment is inadequate. Both have been needed throughout the postwar era, and knowledgeable people have always urged that both channels be used. As additional devices to stimulate private investment have gained acceptance, the line between private and public finance has grown dimmer. The problem at present, in the context of this study, is twofold.

1. How much more can governments of aid-giving countries do to stimulate, encourage, manage, or underwrite productive private investment in less developed countries without favoring special interests at home, loading the receiving countries with insupportable debt burdens and remittance obligations, creating fresh political tensions, or otherwise betraying the public interest they are expected to protect?

2. Because full responsibility for promoting private foreign in-

vestment in less developed countries cannot soon be transferred to multilateral auspices, should U.S. responsibility be lodged in a public corporation, thereby permitting a more flexible, longer-range approach to the problem than can be taken by a subordinate unit of a government agency—the Office of Private Resources of the Agency for International Development (AID)—which is unlikely to survive unless it is radically streamlined?

For purposes of discussion, it is useful to separate the task of enlarging the flow of funds emanating from the private sector in rich countries and destined for poor countries from the closely related problem of freeing up the private sector in poor countries, encouraging entrepreneurship in the low-income world, and relieving overburdened governments of responsibilities they need not carry. This chapter is addressed primarily to the problem of facilitating the export of capital from rich countries to needy poor countries. Within this sector of the problem, a further distinction should be made between capital transferred via such intermediaries as the World Bank and the Inter-American Development Bank and capital and technology movements resulting from the efforts of American and European enterprises to establish or enlarge their footholds in Asian, African, or Latin American markets.

The less developed countries tend to want funds that they can draw on for the fulfillment of their development ambitions *as they see them.* Private investors want opportunities for profit attractive enough to justify investing abroad. Many of them take a very long view indeed; others are looking for quick returns. Given a modest amount of goodwill, numerous compromise arrangements that would raise the flow of private capital can be envisaged.

The private capital obtained by the World Bank and regional development banks from private bond-purchasers and institutional investors creates relatively few problems at the receiving end. The U.S. development cooperation fund recommended in Chapter 6 would also have authority to tap the private capital market for funds to lend to less developed countries. Private capital of this kind can be invested in the public sector, just as appropriated public funds can be used to strengthen the private sector. Interest payments on borrowed capital have to be met, of course, and amortization of principal is required; as previously noted, many less developed countries face major debt-servicing problems.

Direct private foreign investment, which has largely superseded portfolio investment in private international finance, offers some advantages over loan capital but gives rise to a host of problems. Among its advantages are the managerial skills, technology, organizational and institutional links, familiarity with world markets, and other special knowledge brought in by the investors. While equity investments mean that dividends need not be declared until there are profits from which to pay them, most of the underdeveloped countries "are convinced that the cost of capital is greater when obtained in the form of foreign equity investments than when secured through long-term loans. Earnings on equity investments continue indefinitely and increase as the investment increases in value. Interest payments are generally less than equity earnings and, after a fixed period, a foreign loan will be repaid with no further obligation."[1]

There are, to be sure, ways of limiting equity earnings, phasing out foreign management and personnel, and selling foreign holdings to domestic buyers. They tend, however, to operate as disincentives to the investment that one is trying to promote.

The inevitable tensions between foreign direct investors and less developed countries have been perceptively analyzed by Raymond Vernon. Issues of control are at the heart of the controversy. Less developed countries want control over their resources, their industries, their economy; foreign investors want freedom to manage their investments, to deal with unforeseeable problems that are bound to arise, and to solve the problems in ways that serve their total interests. Vernon concludes that whatever the initial position of the parties to a negotiation may be, the likelihood is that the interests of each will change over time.

There are two projections commonly made as to the outcome of these changes. One projection, popular among the less developed countries, is that it is only a matter of time before foreign investors can be disposed

1. Stefan H. Robock, "It's Good for Growth, But Who's Swallowing?" *Columbia Journal of World Business*, Vol. 2, no. 6 (1967), p. 18.

of; another, popular among the investors, is that it is only a matter of time before foreign direct investment is accepted in the less developed countries with tolerance and appreciation. If my analysis is correct, both projections are wrong. According to the analysis, the position of the foreign investor will continually change, according to the external needs of host governments for capital, markets, and technology. Tensions will rise and fall in patterns that are partly predictable, reflecting the relative strengths of the parties concerned and the changing nature of their interests.

My guess is, however, that the tensions could be reduced measurably if (1) both parties were agreed that the initial arrangements would remain undisturbed for some fixed period of time; and (2) the termination date of the arrangement, although distant, was not remote. Agreements along these lines might well provide the investor with the prospect of the clear run necessary to justify his initial commitment, while yet providing the host government with the option of reacquiring control at some tolerable future date. Agreements of this sort, however, are not easily framed; among other things, they have to provide for the contingency that renewal negotiations, when they become due, might break down. To deal with that contingency, one would have to envisage a procedure that promised liquidation of mutual commitments on a reasonable basis. From a technical point of view, these problems can be difficult; but they are far from impossible.[2]

Means of Stimulating Private Investment in Less Developed Countries

The flow of private capital is almost inevitably erratic. During the period 1960–67, net new U.S. direct private long-term investment in less developed countries ranged from a low of $195 million in 1962 to a high of $807 million three years later, in 1965. The average per year was about $470 million. Petroleum accounted for more than half the total, but the trend in investment in other than the oil industry was modestly upward. Reinvestments of earnings result in larger figures for changes in total direct investment. The average annual increase in net capital outflows plus reinvested earnings was approxi-

2. Raymond Vernon, "Conflict and Resolution Between Foreign Direct Investors and Less Developed Countries," *Public Policy* (Harvard University, John F. Kennedy School of Government, 1968), pp. 350–51.

mately $800 million during 1960–67 (about $1 billion per year during 1965–67). Until quite recently, usable figures on the net outflows of U.S. funds for portfolio investment in less developed countries have not been available. The average during the 1960s was below $200 million per year.

As of the end of 1967, direct investments by U.S. business in less developed countries totaled almost $17 billion (as compared with $36 billion in Canada and Western Europe). Of the total for less developed countries, $8.8 billion, or more than half, was in petroleum and mining, slightly over $4 billion, or about 25 percent, was in manufacturing, and slightly under $4 billion was in other branches of activity. Although the increase in the value of U.S. direct private investment in less developed countries between 1960 and 1967 is not negligible and may look large to some of the less developed countries, the fact is that the level of U.S. private investment in most of the low-income countries is increasing rather slowly.

According to an analysis by Stefan H. Robock, the income received by the United States on foreign investments in the less developed countries totaled $23 billion during the years 1950–65, against an outflow over the same period of only $11 billion.[3] The $11 billion represents new investment; that is, net capital outflows from the United States plus undistributed earnings of subsidiaries, whereas the income of $23 billion represents the sum of dividends, interest, and branch profits after foreign taxes but before any applicable U.S. taxes. Juxtaposing the figures in this fashion implies that the less developed countries have inadvertently provided $12 billion in foreign aid to the United States.

This is a little bit like implying that it was a mistake for Sears, Roebuck or the American Telephone and Telegraph Company to issue stock because over the years they have paid out more in dividends than they have obtained in capital through the sale of shares and more than they would have paid in interest and amortization on bank loans. The inflow and outflow of foreign exchange which result from the original investment and its subsequent service in the

3. Robock, "It's Good for Growth," p. 14.

form of dividends, interest, and amortization are often taken as primary measures of the value of the investment to a less developed country.

While the cost of this service tends to be higher than for corresponding amounts of public aid, the comparison is not generally valid, if only because for most projects there will not be a ready choice between one or the other form of financing. Moreover, the balance of payments effect of private investment includes the additional foreign exchange earnings or savings resulting from the production of the enterprise—a result many public-aid-financed infrastructure projects reach only over the long term. It is thus difficult to draw meaningful conclusions from a straight comparison of over-all foreign investment inflows and service-payment outflows.[4]

The most respected source of loan capital for less developed countries is the World Bank (more formally, the International Bank of Reconstruction and Development). In his closing address to the Bretton Woods Conference in 1944, Henry Morgenthau, Jr., secretary of the treasury and president of the conference, said, "The chief purpose of the International Bank for Reconstruction and Development is to guarantee private loans made through the usual investment channels. It would make loans only when these could not be floated through the normal investment channels at reasonable rates. The effect would be to provide capital for those who need it at lower interest rates than in the past, and to drive only the usurious money lenders from the temple of international finance."[5]

Private investors, still smarting from the experiences of the 1930s with defaulted foreign loans and distrustful of governmental and intergovernmental institutions, were not noticeably interested during the 1940s in lending money to foreign governments, even with the safeguard of a guarantee by the World Bank. A bond, guaranteed by an institution whose own creditworthiness was not yet firmly established, would have been considered an inferior piece of paper by the financial community. It seemed more sensible to use the Bank's

4. United Nations Department of Economic and Social Affairs, *Foreign Investment in Developing Countries* (UN, 1968), p. 17.
5. Closing address to the United Nations Monetary and Financial Conference, July 22, 1944. Department of State *Bulletin*, Vol. 2 (July 30, 1944), p. 113.

creditworthiness directly. Accordingly, the Bank, on the advice of its management and without objection from its membership, decided to issue its own bonds and devote the proceeds to project loans.[6]

The purchasers of World Bank bonds are usually private investors, and the Bank has gradually become a kind of publicly managed investment fund whereby money raised in the private capital markets of the United States, Canada, and Western Europe is invested for productive purposes in other regions. The World Bank today engages in joint operations with investment banking houses, floats bond issues in the capital markets of industrialized countries to obtain resources for its public loans, and sells to institutional investors the early maturity portions of previously made loans. The Inter-American Development Bank engages in a similar range of activities.

Despite the hopes expressed at the end of World War II, there is as yet no procedure by which a bond issue can be floated in the New York capital market by a less developed country with the backing of an international agency or a U.S. government guarantee. Even though guaranteed paper normally turns out to be highly negotiable, experts have more or less convinced themselves that an international agency or U.S. government guarantee, unless combined with an interest subsidy program, will be given only to countries that are already demonstrably creditworthy and hence not in need of the

6. The capital structure of the World Bank, it will be recalled, was designed to provide it with some loan resources of its own (the 20 percent of their capital subscriptions that members would pay in) and a guarantee fund four times as great (the other 80 percent) to enable the Bank to mobilize private capital, either through the sale of its obligations to private investors or by guaranteeing international credits privately financed. Under its articles of agreement, the capital subscription of each member government is divided into three parts: (1) a small fraction, 2 percent, is payable in gold or U.S. dollars and may be used freely by the Bank for any of its activities; (2) another 18 percent is payable in the currency of the subscribing member and may be used for lending only with the consent of that country; (3) the remaining 80 percent is not available to the Bank for lending, but is subject to call if and when required to meet obligations of the Bank arising out of its borrowings or guarantees. No call has been made against this third portion of the subscribed capital. The uncalled portions of the subscriptions "constitute in effect a guarantee of the Bank's obligations by the Bank's members, with the members sharing proportionately in the risks of the Bank's loans and each member putting its own credit behind Bank obligations to the extent of the uncalled portion of its own capital subscription." (Quoted from The World Bank, IDA and IFC, Policies and Operations [World Bank, April 1968], p. 28.)

guarantee. By now, a few less developed countries have reached the stage where they can establish their own credit in a major capital market and have been able to borrow without such backing, although at alarmingly high rates of interest.

Investment Guarantees. Another type of private investment guarantee—the guaranteeing of direct investment by American firms—was pioneered by the U.S. government. The rationale is simple. Investment in less developed countries carries greater risks of loss due to currency depreciation, nationalization, and civil war than investment in developed countries. For a relatively modest premium, the risk can be made bearable. The program will need government backing in the form of a pledge of the full faith and credit of the United States and a reserve fund on which it is entitled to draw. As premiums accumulate, losses can be paid out of income and there should be no need for regular appropriations.

The United States has accordingly developed both specific risk insurance and extended risk guarantees. Under the former program, the AID may insure investors in developing countries against the political risks of expropriation, inconvertibility, and damage caused by war, revolution, and insurrection. The investors must be U.S. citizens, financial institutions, corporations, or other associations substantially owned (over 50 percent) by U.S. citizens, or a foreign subsidiary wholly owned by one or more such entities. The specific risk insurance program was in operation in 83 countries as of June 30, 1968. Between December 31, 1961, and June 30, 1968, outstanding coverage rose from under $500 million to more than $6 billion. More than $58 million had been collected in fees. Only seven claims, totaling $661,000, had been paid, but another seven, totaling about $6 million, were pending.[7]

7. Agency for International Development, Office of Private Resources. The per annum premium is ¼ percent for inconvertibility, ½ percent for expropriation, and ½ percent for war, revolution, or insurrection losses. Since the same investment is usually insured for all three risks (and can be partially covered also under the extended risk guarantee program), figures concerning the amount in outstanding coverage, such as the $6 billion figure above, greatly overstate, perhaps even treble, the amount of actual new investment covered by AID's investment insurance program.

Under the program of extended risk guarantees, the AID may protect 75 percent of long-term loans and 50 percent of equity investments against virtually all losses not due to investor fraud or misconduct. Risks for which commercial insurance is available are excluded, however. Recently liberalized, the plan now "permits institutional lenders to participate in the 75 percent fully guarantied portion of a loan without having to invest in the remaining 25 percent. The 25 percent portion, which can be insured by AID against specific risks, may be supplied by commercial banks and may mature first. This arrangement has made it possible for the first time to interest U.S. institutional investors in making long-term loans to important projects in developing countries."[8]

Under the extended risk guarantee program, premiums (including specific risk coverage) are not to exceed 1.75 percent of the outstanding amount of the loan investment or of the equity investment covered. From the inception of the program in fiscal year 1962 through June 30, 1968, the AID had issued $82.5 million worth of extended risk guarantees, covering projects with a total capitalization of more than four times that amount. Since most of the coverage was written in fiscal years 1967 and 1968, the potential of the extended risk guarantee program appears as yet to have been barely tapped.

Larger guarantees are available for the construction of new housing projects that would not otherwise have been undertaken. The AID "may not fully guarantee an investment, and, in fact, is now guaranteeing a maximum of 90 percent of an investment. The investor, however, may obtain from other sources security for that part of the investment not guaranteed by AID."[9] In Latin America, as of June 30, 1968, housing guarantees totaling $272 million had been authorized.[10]

In 1964 the AID requested authority to increase investment

8. Agency for International Development, *The Foreign Assistance Program, Annual Report to the Congress, Fiscal Year 1967* (1968), p. 14.

9. Agency for International Development and Department of Defense, *Proposed Mutual Defense and Assistance Programs FY 1964*, Summary Presentation to the Congress (April 1963), p. 75.

10. For balance-of-payments reasons and because of the legislative history of the proposal—it was intended to encourage housing efforts in Latin America—its use for housing construction outside the Western Hemisphere has been severely restricted.

guarantees by $1 billion for each of the next two years, and to expand war damage coverage to include civil strife. The latter request was denied by Congress. The overall ceiling, however, for the face amount of guarantees outstanding at any time under the program has by now been raised to $8.5 billion.

Official concern with private enterprise was given considerable impetus by the excellent report issued in 1965 by the Advisory Committee on Private Enterprise in Foreign Aid authorized by an amendment to the Foreign Assistance Act of 1963. Better known as the Watson Committee after its chairman, Arthur K. Watson, its 33 recommendations provided a concrete program of action for administrative and legislative consideration.[11]

At the time of its report, the statutory ceiling on outstanding guarantees against inconvertibility, expropriation, and military hazards was $2.5 billion; a substantially higher ceiling was recommended. (The present ceiling, as noted above, is $8.5 billion.) The Watson Committee also recommended that the law be relaxed to permit coverage of foreign corporations jointly owned by more than one U.S. company. This has been done. On the administrative side, the committee urged that the AID be permitted to use income from the guarantee program not only for the management and custody of assets but also for certain other operational costs associated with the guarantee program. This, too, has been done.

The early caution exercised by AID in administering extended risk guaranty authority is understandable [said the committee], especially in cases where the business commitment involves a direct investment (that is, an investment coupled with management and control). Businessmen managing the enterprises in which they invest cannot expect to be protected from all the hazards of their operation. Nevertheless, the Committee believes that a really significant potential may be in the extended risk idea. Through it we can see a way to make investment in less developed economies attractive, or in many cases even legally possible, for many United States institutional investors. The Committee recognizes that such insurance may one day result in large claims against the U.S.

11. See Agency for International Development, *Foreign Aid Through Private Initiative: Report of the Advisory Committee on Private Enterprise in Foreign Aid* (July 1965).

Treasury. It accepts this as preferable to alternative ways in which development can be stimulated.[12]

Its recommendations for expansion of the extended risk guarantee program have in large degree also been accepted. The proposal that portfolio investors be offered extended risk guarantees which would make selected securities of private enterprises in less developed countries competitive with the alternative opportunities open to such investors has been partially met by a recent liberalization of that program.[13]

Because the guarantee program is novel, complex, and ill understood, the AID has included in one of its brochures on private investment incentives a hypothetical example of how the program might be utilized by the XYZ Food Company, a U.S. corporation interested in establishing a broiler chicken enterprise in a less developed country. The XYZ Company is assumed to have decided to establish the LDC Broiler Corporation as a joint venture with a local firm as partner, XYZ owning 51 percent and the local firm 49 percent of the equity. The financial plan of the LDC Broiler Corporation is as follows:

XYZ Food Company's equity investment	$102,000
Local firm's equity investment	98,000
Loan from U.S. bank for purchase of U.S. equipment, materials, and services	350,000
Local currency loan for land and construction costs (U.S. dollar equivalent)	200,000
	$750,000

In attempting to put together this investment package, XYZ encountered several problems. Unfamiliar with overseas operations, it was unwilling to make the requisite equity investment unless its

12. *Ibid.*, p. 17.

13. For some limitations of the new arrangement, especially congressional failure to confirm the AID's liberal interpretation of the 75 percent restriction and the handicap of AID and Export-Import Bank insistence on 100 percent U.S. procurement in the face of alleged European willingness to permit up to 20 percent of its financing to be spent in the host country, see Peter A. Hornbostel, "Investment Guaranties: Bureaucracy Clogs the Flow," *Columbia Journal of World Business* (March–April 1969), pp. 37–47.

possibility of loss was reduced. It was also concerned about the possibility of loss due to expropriation, war, revolution, insurrection, or inconvertibility of its local currency earnings into dollars. Furthermore, the LDC Corporation was experiencing difficulty in obtaining a dollar loan for the purchase of U.S. equipment and had been unable to obtain the necessary local currency loan in the country in which it wished to operate.

The XYZ Food Company obtained an extended risk guarantee covering 50 percent of its $102,000 equity investment against loss from any cause other than its own fraud or misconduct. The remaining 50 percent was protected against the political risks of expropriation and so forth. Since the AID's extended risk guarantee program can also protect 75 percent of a lender's investment in less developed countries, XYZ found a U.S. bank that, with this protection, was willing to make the $350,000 loan to the LDC Broiler Corporation for seven years at 6 percent interest. In addition, through AID's local currency loan program (the so-called Cooley loans), the LDC Corporation was able to borrow $200,000 worth of local currency, on terms approximately equal to loans made by development banks in the host country.

As the AID says in the brochure "Private Investment Incentives," from which the above example has been taken almost verbatim, it is of course very unlikely that any one firm would be able or eligible to benefit from all of the assistance obtained in the hypothetical example. Still, the amount of assistance available through the guarantee program is by now remarkably comprehensive.

Tax Concessions. Tax concessions constitute another technique for stimulating private investment in less developed areas. In the words of the Watson Committee: "It is axiomatic that any measure which increases the prospective yield on an investment increases the investors' inclination to make the investment. As a result, there have been numerous proposals to stimulate investment in the less developed areas by reducing the tax burden on the income from such ventures."[14]

14. *Foreign Aid Through Private Initiative*, p. 21.

The committee's first recommendation in the field of tax relief arose from the fact that, when U.S. enterprises operate subsidiary undertakings in the United States, they can offset losses in such subsidiaries against gains in their other operations. When the subsidiary venture is located abroad, however, American enterprises are generally prevented by U.S. tax laws from offsetting foreign losses against domestic gains. The committee recommended that "United States tax laws and regulations be amended so that the United States taxpayer's right to offset losses in subsidiaries against taxable income from other sources would be the same for subsidiaries in less developed countries as it is for subsidiaries in the United States."[15] Although the AID has been sympathetic to the proposal, there are no plans afoot for its implementation. From the standpoint of equity among American taxpayers, the right to be taxed only on repatriated profits introduces a preference for the firm investing abroad, which would be increased by adoption of the loss-offset privilege.

The committee also endorsed proposals that would allow the U.S. taxpayer, in the calculation of his U.S. tax liability, to receive a credit for taxes normally payable to a foreign government but from which he has actually been spared by tax exemption or holidays under the laws of the foreign government. The executive branch, which initially favored the principle of tax sparing, subsequently changed its mind. Tax-sparing provisions would increase the incentive of American corporations to invest in less developed countries. By permitting credits for taxes that have not been paid, they would add to the inequities in the U.S. tax system. They might also encourage unproductive competition among less developed countries in offering exemptions and lead to unnecessary revenue losses to both the United States and the less developed countries. Less developed countries that offer tax relief in order to attract foreign investment strongly favor tax sparing on repatriated earnings because, without it, their own concessions lose most of their value. A fresh appraisal of the pros and cons of tax sparing could be one of the research tasks of the public corporation herein proposed as a successor to the AID Office of

15. *Ibid.*, p. 22.

Private Resources. The U.S. tax system at present includes a tax incentive not to repatriate the profits of foreign subsidiaries; tax sparing would eliminate or reduce this incentive by eliminating or reducing the U.S. tax on repatriated profits.

"Among the boldest" of the tax reforms proposed to stimulate U.S. investment in less developed countries, in the eyes of the Watson Committee, was the proposal to allow American firms to reduce their total tax bill in the United States by an amount equal to 30 percent of certain investments made in a less developed country. This discriminatory device, though opposed by one member of the committee, was considered justifiable and therefore endorsed by the others because of the "compelling need to increase the flow of private investment to the less developed countries." The committee furthermore recommended that U.S. tax credits extended to the direct investments of the U.S. investors in less developed countries be extended also to the portfolio investments of U.S. corporate or institutional investors.[16]

A still bolder, refreshingly unrealistic scheme has recently been floated by Albert O. Hirschman and Richard M. Bird.[17] Their proposal, in brief, is that every individual taxpayer be permitted to credit some of the federal income tax he would otherwise have to pay to a special bank account. The fund thus accumulated would then be available for investment in less developed countries. The fund would not belong to the Treasury and could be made to flow to the less developed countries along lines different from either bilateral or multilateral aid as presently known. Their tax credit proposal would require legislation, but not on an annual basis.

The principal agents for disbursing the funds received through the tax credit would be a group of ten to twelve independent private organizations called "development funds." The taxpayer, if he so desired, could indicate a preference as to which fund should receive his tax credit. Each fund would be managed by competent professionals recruited internationally from the growing group in both

16. *Ibid.*, pp. 23 and 32.
17. *Foreign Aid: A Critique and a Proposal*, Princeton University, International Finance Section, Essays in International Finance, no. 69 (July 1968).

rich and poor countries who have relevant experience in the problems of investment and development. The principal aim of these funds would be to transfer available moneys efficiently and quickly to less developed countries. "In the last resort the [United States] government would of course still be the donor to developing countries, in that its tax revenue would be reduced by the amounts that individual taxpayers were earmarking for foreign aid, but the resulting funds would not belong to the government and their allocation and uses—and, to some extent, their amount—would no longer be determined by it."[18]

Financial Intermediaries. Financial intermediaries, such as the World Bank and its affiliates, the International Development Association (IDA) and the International Finance Corporation (IFC), the various national development banks, savings and loan associations, local stock exchanges, and other institutions, have been established to mobilize and invest capital with a view to enlarging the domestic output of low-income countries. Most of them, like the IFC, have been slow to get under way and are only beginning to come into their own. The question is, How much more institution building in this area is feasible and desirable?

The United States already has an Export-Import Bank, and if the recommendation made in Chapter 6 of this study is adopted, it would establish a U.S. development cooperation fund as a national equivalent of the World Bank and the International Development Association and as the principal replacement for the Agency for International Development.

If a U.S. development cooperation fund or bank were established and empowered to raise money in the private capital market, it would be competing with other international lending institutions for capital resources. Some restrictions on this competition might have to be imposed for consistency with the recommendation made earlier in this study that the United States rely predominantly (though not exclusively) on the World Bank Group, the Inter-American Development Bank, and the Asian, African, and Central American development

18. *Ibid.,* p. 15.

banks as intermediaries for making development loans. How quickly the world's principal capital markets would be saturated by bond issues from all these institutions is not yet known.

There is a range of functions connected with stimulating and mobilizing American capital for investment in less developed countries which cannot readily be assumed by development banks and funds. Part, but only part, of the gap is filled by the IFC, which is not, for example, engaged in investment insurance.[19]

Aware of the existence of the IFC and in favor of expanding its role, the Watson Committee nevertheless reviewed a proposal by Senator Jacob Javits for an American peace-by-investment corporation which would "channel equity funds into less developed countries, using United States Government credit as its source of financing in the initial stages, and relying partly upon funds from private investors in late stages."[20] It recommended "careful consideration" of the idea.[21]

More recently, the Subcommittee on Foreign Economic Policy of the House Committee on Foreign Affairs has urged that studies be initiated

on the feasibility of establishing a quasi-public corporation dedicated solely to private industrial development work in less-developed countries. Although this corporation would be supported in the beginning by public funds such assistance should be tapered off and, if possible, means should be adopted for making the corporation self-supporting, in whole or in part, including the possibility of funding from private sources. . . . Its activities, though, should be kept consistent with U.S. foreign policy commitments and with development programs.[22]

Just as the IFC operates as an affiliate of the World Bank, so the subcommittee has suggested that the proposed national corporation

19. The staff of the World Bank, however, has prepared draft articles of agreement for an international investment insurance agency to insure new private foreign investment in developing countries against losses resulting from noncommercial risks. No rush to adopt these articles is detectable among the Bank's member governments.

20. *Foreign Aid Through Private Initiative*, pp. 30–31.

21. For a brief summary of the functions, financing, and management of the proposed corporation, see *The Involvement of U.S. Private Enterprise in Developing Countries*, Report of the Subcommittee on Foreign Economic Policy of the House Committee on Foreign Affairs, H. Rept. 1271, 90 Cong. 2 sess. (1968), p. 31.

22. *Ibid.*, pp. 3–4.

could be an affiliate of an agency of the U.S. government. Why not assign the functions directly to the Office of Private Resources in the AID?

A separate entity would offer greater organizational flexibility, direct involvement of private enterprise, and singleness of purpose.... As it is, the Office of Private Resources ... operates as part of the AID. In turn, AID operates in conjunction with the Department of State. The Office of Private Resources is only one of the many subfunctions competing for the time and money of the parent agency. Since this office is an integral part of AID, it must justify its existence every year before Congress, and this past year saw the lowest foreign aid appropriation in history. Additionally, from a purely internal operation view, it is governed by agency allocations and by personnel and recruitment policies.[23]

Other Means Used by AID. It would be an injustice to the Agency for International Development as it currently functions to close this summary of means of stimulating private investment in less developed countries without making clear that the agency does this in a variety of other ways not yet mentioned in this section. It persistently seeks to improve the overall climate for such investment. It encourages completion of the necessary economic and social infrastructure in transportation, communication, employment services, and other essential facilities. It provides program loans that ease access to materials and supplies for the indigenous private sector in less developed lands. It assists local development banks and rural credit banks which in turn make loans to the private sector. From local currency holdings, it has lent the equivalent of more than $250 million during the 1960s to private enterprises in less developed countries, almost all of them U.S.-owned or -affiliated enterprises.[24] It finances, in whole or in part, feasibility studies, and acts as "honest broker" in bringing opportunities to the attention of potential investors. The investment insurance and guarantee program, however, is now its most important and fastest-growing technique for promoting American private investment.

23. *Ibid.,* p. 30.
24. Foreign firms using American agricultural products are also eligible for these so-called Cooley loans.

Conclusions and Recommendations

Much has been written about the ambivalence and hostility to foreign private investment at the receiving end, the political and economic problems associated with high rates of foreign investment, and the techniques for overcoming specific difficulties. Representatives of capital-exporting and capital-importing nations have spent endless hours in vain efforts to develop acceptable multilateral codes for the treatment of private foreign investment. A Convention on the Settlement of Investment Disputes was ratified in 1966 and an International Centre for the Settlement of Investment Disputes has been established within the World Bank. To date, it has not been overwhelmed with business. Its business, moreover, is not related to the volume of investment but to the number of disputes between governments and foreign investors who voluntarily submit their differences to the Centre for conciliation or arbitration.

Analysts of the world scene have noted a decline in ideology which is producing a generation of leaders in less developed countries who are more pragmatic and less dogmatic about how to develop an economy than were their predecessors. This is resulting in larger roles for the private sector of the domestic economy and new ways of associating domestic capital and management, private and public, with foreign capital and management. Despite some improvement in the investment climate, thunder still rumbles and lightning still strikes. International investors in the 1970s will have to continue to put up with restrictions that would have been thought intolerable before World War II. A tremendous shift in bargaining power has taken place since then, and with every fresh increment of strength, the so-called host countries are tempted to reopen negotiations.

There appears to have been very little high-quality empirical study of the role private foreign investment is in fact playing in countries that are reasonably hospitable to it. Does it normally or frequently bring, in a single package, patents, know-how, sources of supply, markets, quality controls, and related items that could not otherwise be obtained without exorbitant effort? If so, does the package rather than the net financial transfer constitute the principal benefit to the less developed country and hence the real rationale for programs to promote direct foreign investment? Is it inevitably heavily concentrated in a few export industries with little spillover to other sectors of the economy? What kinds of backward and forward linkages does private foreign investment tend to have at the receiving end? What standards of performance is it setting? To what extent can it be stimulated? Should it be stimulated to the extent that it can be? What political problems does it create? Should it be phased out deliberately in certain exposed activities in order to minimize the jeopardy to other less prominent activities? Because little is as yet known about the net benefits of private foreign investment in less developed countries, research on the subject deserves a high priority.[25]

Since resources raised in the private capital markets of rich countries and funneled to poor countries through the intermediary of the World Bank Group and the regional development banks are eminently acceptable and consciously directed toward development, I favor much greater reliance than at present on these institutions for capital transfers. As a corollary, various minor improvements should be made in capital markets in order to reduce issuing costs and facilitate distribution of the bonds of the World Bank and other multilateral lending institutions.

Less developed countries that have good growth records and are beginning to be creditworthy in a commercial sense may need what has been called "a sponsored introduction" to capital markets—the opportunity to issue bonds of their own with the guarantee of the U.S. government or the World Bank behind the issue. In the process, the issuing government would become more familiar with and better integrated into the principal capital markets of the world and it

25. In this connection, see the pamphlet series, *Case Studies of U.S. Business Performance Abroad*, published by the National Planning Association, Washington, 1953–68. In his monumental study, *Asian Drama: An Inquiry Into the Poverty of Nations* (Twentieth Century Fund, 1968), Gunnar Myrdal considers the role of Western business interests in feeding corruption in less developed countries to be a problem requiring collective attention; any single company seeking to maintain high standards of integrity finds itself up against "the unfair competition of companies that resort to large-scale bribery" (p. 958).

might—though this is uncertain—obtain greater autonomy in spending the proceeds of the loan. Since the World Bank has eschewed the guarantee role, this could become a function of the U.S. development cooperation fund proposed in Chapter 6 as a vehicle for the provision of bilateral capital assistance from the United States.

The less developed countries prefer to receive foreign capital in the form of long-term loans; investors who forget this do so at their peril. To date, however, investment guarantee schemes have created relatively few problems at the receiving end; they are unilaterally undertaken by the capital-exporting nation and involve a public and private partnership in sharing certain risks inherent in investment in less developed lands, without significantly changing the obligations of the capital-importing nation.

Guarantee authority transfers to the U.S. government, at least until the actuarial soundness of the premium charges has been convincingly demonstrated, risks that would otherwise be borne solely by private investors. While most citizens are by now reconciled to a government role in underwriting income losses from unemployment, sickness, fluctuating agricultural prices, and other adverse developments, they are still understandably squeamish about underwriting risks directly associated with the search for private profit in foreign lands. The device, however, appears capable of mobilizing more capital than would otherwise be forthcoming. It can avoid legislative restrictions and administrative regulations that would inhibit government lending for similar objectives. It reduces the pressure to appropriate public funds for development assistance and is in accord with a time-honored principle of American politics that appropriations should be avoided if the same result can be achieved by other means. How far to carry the investment guarantee program thus deserves careful consideration.

My impression is that it would be desirable to raise the ceilings on the amounts of outstanding coverage that could be written. The International Private Investment Advisory Council recommends, somewhat exuberantly perhaps, $10 billion of additional issuing authority for specific risk insurance to cover another five years. It recommends $1 billion of additional issuing authority for extended risk guarantees. Since the guarantees are backed by the full faith and credit of the United States, the appropriated reserve would also have to be raised. Specific risk coverage ought, I believe, to be broadened to include losses from riots and civil disturbances. With respect to extended risk guarantees for potentially viable ventures important to development, the ceiling on the insurable portion of a loan could be raised from 75 percent to 90 percent and the insurable portion of an equity investment from 50 percent to 75 percent. Safeguards against losses due to devaluations and exchange rate changes should be provided, if feasible.

One kind of guarantee not yet used by the U.S. government, though successfully employed by the USSR and certain other countries, is the long-term contract guaranteeing a market within some stipulated price range for some proportion of the output of a new productive facility in a less developed country. Commercial financing of the facility itself ought to be possible if a foreign market for a reasonable proportion of its output is assured. In offering such assurances, however, state trading agencies have considerable advantages over private enterprises. Some experiments with this type of guarantee might nevertheless be undertaken.

In the discussion earlier in this chapter of tax concessions as a method of stimulating foreign investment, it was pointed out that the potentialities of this device have not been exhausted. At the same time, it was noted that when tax concessions to U.S. taxpayers are made, the aid giver is in reality not the taxpayer but the U.S. government. Since the government forgoes the revenue it would otherwise collect, proposals for tax concessions are peculiarly vulnerable to the charge of "back-door financing." They are, it is alleged, a disguised form of government spending over which the government has no control. While the principal opposition comes from Congress, tax experts also are usually unhappy about the inequities and potential inequities created by new loopholes. Proponents of concessions argue in their more philosophical moments that the taxpayers will employ the resources in question at least as wisely, productively, and imaginatively as the government.

Major breakthroughs in the use of tax concessions, it seems to me, are more likely to come in order to stimulate private domestic investment in urban renewal, housing, or mass transport than to stimulate private foreign investment. Some of the same methods may subsequently be found suitable for promoting foreign investment.

Having reached some tentative conclusions about the means of stimulating more private investment in low-income countries, and having mentioned the desirability of creating at least one new intermediary—a U.S. development cooperation fund or bank—I return to the question of machinery. The Foreign Assistance Act of 1968 not only invites the President to make a comprehensive reappraisal of U.S. foreign assistance programs, but in that connection to analyze and consider

proposals concerning the establishment of a Government corporation or a federally chartered private corporation designed to mobilize and facilitate the use of United States private capital and skills in less developed friendly countries and areas, including whether such corporation should be authorized to—
  (1) utilize Government guarantees and funds as well as private funds;
  (2) seek, develop, promote, and underwrite new investment projects;
  (3) assist in transferring skills and technology to less developed friendly countries and areas; and
  (4) invest in the securities of development financing institutions and assist in the formation and expansion of local capital markets.[26]

The International Private Investment Advisory Council of the AID responded with alacrity to the invitation and issued a brochure entitled "The Case for a U.S. Overseas Private Enterprise Development Corporation."[27] The report is singularly oblivious of the problems connected with private foreign investment. Its underlying assumption seems to be that the more U.S. private investment is pumped into the less developed countries, the better off everyone will be. I favor the creation of a U.S. overseas investment corporation specializing primarily in investment guarantees, but not a zealous investment-promotion agency that will be inviting expropriations costly to the U.S. government (diplomatically as well as financially),

26. Sec. 502(b).
27. Issued in December 1968 and obtainable from the AID Office of Private Resources (22 pages; processed).

partly because they are relatively costless to the insured, protected private investor.

The AID is harried and unloved by the Congress. Its private investment programs suffer accordingly. A federally chartered corporation should be salable to Congress and to the public. It could have not only the organizational flexibility and singleness of purpose already alluded to in this chapter, but also the opportunity to develop a professional staff of experienced, business-oriented career personnel, together with continuity of operations and an appropriate expansion of existing programs. The corporate form of organization would be justified on the ground that the principal activities—investment insurance and some financing of private enterprise—are business operations. The investment insurance programs produce revenue which would permit the corporation to be partly if not wholly self-supporting—$14.8 million in fiscal year 1968 against claims of $438,000. A corporation, moreover, can sue and be sued, enter into contracts with greater freedom than an ordinary government agency, acquire and dispose of property more readily, and generally act with greater autonomy. Its board of directors could consist of both private citizens and officials of the U.S. government.

The report of the International Private Investment Advisory Council envisages a corporation empowered not only to insure loans and equity investments but also to make loans directly to private enterprises, to take equity positions in enterprises in which there is also a U.S. private equity participation, to sell off its loans and equity positions in the U.S. capital market, and to provide technical assistance.[28] It reminds readers that interest income generated by the AID's portfolio of prior dollar and local currency loans to private and mixed public-private borrowers and industrial development banks—$27.5 million in fiscal year 1968—might be transferred to the new corporation, which would also need Treasury borrowing authority and some appropriated funds.

The principal problems in creating a corporation are how to keep

28. However, the overseas private investment corporation proposed to the Congress by the Nixon administration in June 1969 would not be authorized to make direct equity investments.

its development objectives as prominent as its desire to turn in a good profit-and-loss statement and how to avoid exaggerated expectations of what it can accomplish. In addition to the previously mentioned functions, it can in various ways identify, screen, and publicize investment opportunities and bring together potential investors. As a newly chartered corporation, it could operate with a self-confidence and a continuity denied to the AID. Unless all of the risks are transferred to the U.S. government, however, it cannot in the short run greatly increase the rate of foreign investment by American companies.

In summary, one encounters a good deal of wishful thinking in the United States today to the effect that (1) the vigorous promotion of private investment can reduce drastically the need for aid; (2) a dollar of direct private investment, with the managerial skills and technology that accompany it, is almost by definition more valuable than a dollar of aid; (3) private investment serves the U.S. national interest; and consequently, (4) the more of it, the better.

The recent report of the Perkins Committee refers to a more rapid expansion of U.S. private investment as "an essential complement" to public development assistance. The latter, it says, "is needed to support the framework within which private investment can do its part. *The vast majority of less developed countries will continue to need public grants and loans on liberal terms.*" [29] The policies recommended by that committee for promoting private investment will, in its view, be effective in supporting a cumulative 10 percent a year expansion from the 1963–67 average of $1.37 billion for less developed countries to $2.4 billion by 1973.

The optimistic calculation used in Chapter 6 of a 15 percent a year expansion, inclusive of private purchases of the bonds of multilateral development financing institutions, would raise the private flow to $4.5 billion in 1975, a figure that, though respectable, would come nowhere near meeting the estimated requirements for development assistance in that year.

29. *Development Assistance in the New Administration,* Report of the President's General Advisory Committee on Foreign Assistance Programs (Oct. 25, 1968), p. 26. (The italics are mine.)

A dollar of private resources wisely invested is more valuable than an aid dollar unwisely invested, but the reverse is also true. Even when both are wisely invested, closer examination might (or might not) reveal the superiority of the aid investment from various developmental points of view. Both can carry with them advanced technology, training programs, arrangements for competent management, and other modernizing ingredients. Expanded private investment alone will almost certainly harden the average terms of the total capital flows to less developed countries despite the fact that a number of those countries will be unable to service additional debt on present terms.

Moreover, there is no assurance that private investment will serve the national interest by going to the right places in the right amounts at the right times, and some danger that incentive systems will encourage it to go to the wrong places at the wrong times. Since the most successful private investments may become the best targets for angry demonstrators, there is much to be said for the same "low American profile" in the investment field as in the aid field.

CHAPTER NINE

Balance-of-Payments Restrictions

and Nonnational Sources of

Development Finance

SINCE THE EARLY 1960s, persistent large deficits in the U.S. balance of payments have created a crisis atmosphere and operated as progressively greater constraints on this country's development assistance efforts. The deficits have affected both the willingness of the Congress to appropriate funds and the ways in which the Congress and the executive branch have permitted appropriated funds to be used and private investment to flow. They have also hampered trade liberalization and strengthened protectionist forces. The administration has consistently tried to distinguish between the rich trading partners of the United States and its poor ones, with a view to minimizing the adverse effects of restrictive measures on those countries most in need of foreign capital, low-cost sources of supply, and export markets.

It may seem incongruous to discuss measures to stimulate capital assistance to less developed countries in the middle of a balance-of-payments crisis in the capital-exporting country. Though I deplore the practice of restricting aid purchases to the country financing the purchases, it is true that through aid-tying the United States can escape most of the adverse balance-of-payments effects of its aid efforts. Moreover, the reforms in the international monetary system that have already been agreed to will to some extent relax balance-of-payments constraints on the movement of goods, services, and capital, and further reforms are desirable. Finally, the tapping of certain nonnational sources or potential sources of revenue for development programs seems to me an appropriate course of action for its own sake as well as for balance-of-payments reasons.

Tied Aid

The practice of tying aid-financed purchases to U.S. sources of supply, which may appear to the aid-receiving country as an effort to promote American exports without regard to their relative cost rather than as a device to save the aid program from deeper slashes, has been almost perfected by now. Tying helps to neutralize foreign aid as a factor in our international accounts. If all aid is tied and additional to regular exports, the Congress and the public can be reasonably confident that foreign aid programs will not reduce U.S. reserves—or not reduce them by more than the cost of the imports contained in the exported commodities and the cost of imports drawn in to replace exported commodities. Moreover, the domestic interests that benefit from the tied-aid policy enlarge the constituency for a program that, like other public programs in a democracy, needs a constituency in order to survive.

If aid were untied, the constituency might shrink, but it would not disappear. Those firms that did well under international competitive bidding procedures and added to their export sales would presumably view foreign aid with some favor. If substantially fewer U.S. firms received orders, the constituency might be reduced. Major U.S. firms, however, have many more irons in the federal fire than foreign aid, and one should not imply that the size or strength of the business constituency is simply a function of the amount of business obtained by U.S. firms from the aid program, or of the number of firms that obtain such business.

Aid programs have direct and indirect effects on the balance of payments. Direct effects are those resulting from the direct expenditure of aid dollars for goods and services outside the United States. Since 1959, development loans have been available only for the procurement of commodities and services from U.S. sources. In 1960, procurement under grants was restricted to the United States or the developing countries, and subsequently to the United States alone. "To qualify for inclusion as authorized sources for AID commodity procurement, the less developed countries must agree to accept payment through U.S. Source Letters of Credit under which the dollars are tied to financing imports from the U.S." As of June 30, 1967, only eight countries—six of them in Asia and two in Africa—qualified as authorized sources: India, Morocco, Pakistan, the Philippines, the Republic of China, the Republic of Korea, Singapore, and Tunisia. Excluded were Thailand, Nigeria, Senegal, all of Latin America, and various other aid-receiving areas.[1] In mid-1968, the AID reported that its contribution to the dollar drain "had been cut to nothing."[2] Unfortunately, so had its immediate contribution to the expansion of international trade on the basis of comparative advantage.

In fiscal year 1961, the overseas expenditures of the AID totaled $982 million. By fiscal year 1968, the direct outflow had been reduced to $178 million.[3] More than offsetting this was a direct inflow of $259 million in interest and amortization payments on previous loans by AID and predecessor organizations. It is fair to say, therefore, that the net direct effect of AID operations in fiscal year 1968 was a dollar inflow of about $81 million, an inflow destined to increase in fiscal year 1969 and, in all probability, in fiscal year 1970.

Tying purchases to U.S. sources does not forestall indirect outflows such as those that occur when recipient countries use AID credits for purchases they would have made with their own free dol-

1. Agency for International Development, *Operations Report, Data as of June 30, 1967* (1967), p. iv.
2. Agency for International Development, *Facts About AID*, undated attachment to Information Bulletin of Aug. 5, 1968.
3. For the composition of this $178 million, see William S. Gaud, administrator, Agency for International Development, statement of Jan. 14, 1969, before the Subcommittee on International Exchange and Payments of the Joint Economic Committee, 91 Cong. 1 sess. (processed), pp. 4–5 and Table 2. Gaud's statement is one of the best available on the balance-of-payments effects of AID assistance. It has been drawn on liberally in this chapter.

lars. "To the extent that this happens, some commercial U.S. exports will be displaced, and there will be an indirect loss on the trade account of our balance of payments."[4] To prevent this substitution and to gain full "additionality," the AID was forced, primarily by the Treasury and Commerce departments, into one of the most elaborate and irritating boondoggles in its history.

Financing policies were modified in 1965 to include the promotion of U.S. exports as an explicit criterion in selecting capital projects and commodities for AID financing. In 1966, the "negative lists," which had previously been used to prevent aid funds from being spent on items such as luxuries and contraceptives, were expanded to include items for which the United States was already a major supplier. The purpose of making these latter items ineligible for AID financing was to reduce the possibility of substitution by forcing the recipient to use AID funds for purchases other than those it normally made from the United States.

In 1967 we first used positive lists for additionality purposes—that is lists of commodities which were the only ones which *could* be financed with A.I.D. credits. . . .

Commodities on these lists are selected jointly by A.I.D., Commerce, and Treasury according to several criteria. We attempt to identify particular commodities where we believe we have a competitive advantage, but which are not yet well represented in the recipient country's markets. We also seek to finance items which will engender a follow-on demand, often for industrial spare parts. *For the most part, however, positive lists are made up of commodities in which the United States is relatively less competitive, and which we would otherwise be unlikely to export in any great volume.*

In order to ensure that A.I.D. credits restricted in this way are absorbed, recipient governments must take collateral measures to induce local importers to shift their purchases to U.S. suppliers. We try to bring about removal of any discriminatory barriers to the import of U.S. goods. *In addition, where credit is very scarce, recipient governments may give easier credit terms for imports from the United States or permit importers of U.S. goods to make smaller down payments. They may selectively reduce tariffs in such a way as to favor U.S. exports. In countries with import and exchange controls, licensing may be used to favor*

4. *Ibid.*, p. 6.

U.S. exports so as to ensure additionality. All of these efforts except the removal of discriminatory barriers are restrictions on the operation of free market forces.[5]

Latin American countries in particular, but other nations as well, were greatly offended by the efforts of the world's leading exponent of free enterprise to promote so blatantly U.S. exports that were noncompetitive. The additionality concept, they contended, distorted the development priorities of aid receivers and adversely affected their credit, exchange, and tariff policies.

If, in the absence of the additionality program, aid-receiving nations had used aid resources largely to replace imports they would otherwise have bought in the United States with free funds, the program might have had significant balance-of-payments effects. It appears, however, that the whole elaborate campaign made a difference of only about $35 million per year while in operation, as compared with U.S. worldwide exports of about $30 billion. In June 1969, in the face of mounting criticism of the United States in Latin America, President Nixon wisely decided to abandon formal additionality requirements. And on October 31, he announced that development loans to Latin America from AID funds could thereafter be used for purchases anywhere in Latin America as well as in the United States.[6]

Two other indirect balance-of-payments effects should be mentioned. The direct outflow resulting from the initial expenditure of U.S. aid funds for goods and services from sources other than the United States is not completely lost to the United States. About half of it comes back to the United States via increased purchases of U.S. goods by the recipient countries themselves or by third countries. In addition to U.S. inflows resulting from this "responding effect," some portion of U.S. exports, estimated at $75 million per year in fiscal years 1965–68, "can be attributed to that portion of income growth in recipient countries which stems from U.S. aid itself."[7]

The upshot of all the direct and indirect effects is a shift in the

5. *Ibid.*, pp. 8–9. (The italics are mine.)
6. The Foreign Assistance Act of 1968 had provided $255 million in new obligational authority for loans in this category for FY 1969. As of the time of the President's announcement, the appropriation for FY 1970 was still pending.
7. Gaud, statement of Jan. 14, 1969, p. 13.

overall impact of the AID program on the U.S. balance of payments from a negative impact of more than $300 million in fiscal year 1961 and of $14 million in 1965 (outflows of $517 million offset by inflows of $503 million) to a positive impact of $177 million in 1968 (outflows of $303 million offset by inflows of $480 million from respending effects, growth-induced exports, and receipts of interest and amortization on prior loans). Service payments on earlier loans and U.S. export earnings from aid-induced growth in less developed countries are, of course, functions of the U.S. aid expenditures of prior years and presumably would not disappear if the aid program were halted. But by far the major factor in stanching the direct outflow in any given year is the tying of procurement to U.S. sources.

If all aid-giving nations adhered to the practice of tying their bilateral aid, each would be deprived of the opportunity to earn funds from the expenditures of others, to the detriment of its most efficient producers. Effective tying inevitably procures less aid for the same amount of money, or raises the total cost of bilateral aid programs over what they would cost if purchases were made on the basis of international competitive bidding. The most serious study of the costs of tied aid to the receiver that I have seen deals with Pakistan in 1965, when it was obtaining aid not only from the United States but also from the World Bank, the International Development Association, and other sources. It therefore had greater flexibility and greater bargaining power than a country dependent entirely on French or American aid. The author of the study estimated conservatively that untying the $500 million Pakistan expected to receive in foreign aid that year would have saved Pakistan approximately $60 million. In a country receiving all of its external assistance from a single source and therefore without freedom to decide which aid-financed imports would be charged to which source of funds, the costs of tied aid might be considerably higher.

Tied credits come in all sorts of packages—they are tied to the country of origin, tied to individual projects, tied to specific end-uses. In most cases, all the three forms of tying are applicable. The most important form, however, is country-tying which makes it difficult for the recipient countries to take advantage of the competitive conditions in the international market. All forms of tying result, in one way or another, in higher prices. The adverse implications of tied credits extend, however, beyond the question of prices. Tied credits also limit the ability of the recipient country to choose an appropriate technology or international consultants of its own choice.[8]

If the higher-priced items are financed by grants, the receiving country would appear to have no complaint. Yet it is the dollar cost of the gift that shows up in aid statistics, and people in both donor and receiving nations tend to expect a larger development dividend from $100 million in grant aid than from $85 million. If in fact $100 million from the United States provides no more in goods and services than $85 million from Italy or Japan, is the United States in such circumstances providing any more aid?[9]

More important is that, even in the case of grant aid, the grant is to the government of the low-income country. The end-users normally pay in local currency for the equipment and supplies imported under aid programs. If manufacturers, utilities, railroads, or others pay more in rupees or pesos than they would if the imports came from a lower-cost source of supply, the costs of the goods and services they produce will, in turn, also be higher and less competitive.

As the U.S. bilateral program has moved away from grant aid and increasingly into loan aid, with a simultaneous hardening of loan terms, the governments of aid-receiving countries have become increasingly concerned about aid tying. Less developed countries can ill afford to borrow and pay interest on $100 million in foreign exchange in order to obtain equipment that could have been obtained elsewhere for $85 million on comparable loan terms:

it was partly the appreciation of this burdening effect of tying that led to the recommendation at UNCTAD [the 1964 UN Conference on Trade and Development] of reverse tying of repayments, that is, obliging

8. Mahbub ul Haq, "Tied Credits—a Quantitative Analysis," in John H. Adler (ed.), *Capital Movements: Proceedings of a Conference Held by the International Economic Association* (St. Martin's Press, 1967), pp. 326–27.

9. This sentence is not intended to suggest that Italy and Japan do not tie their aid (they do) or that they provide as much grant aid as does the United States. The point is that any nation able to supply on a grant basis for $85 million goods and services that would cost $100 million in the U.S. market is providing the same amount of aid for each $85 million in its grant column as the United States for each $100 million in its grant column.

the donor to accept repayment in the goods whose production facilities have been financed by aid. There is a certain element of rough justice in this suggestion, given the prevalence of aid tying and the barriers to imports of industrial products into developed countries from less developed countries. But a more efficient solution would be for the element of excess cost imposed by tying to be given in the form of a grant and charged to some domestic expenditure account (as export promotion, domestic transfer, or domestic production subsidy) rather than against foreign aid.[10]

The last thing Congress wants to do, however, is to reveal the true extent of the subsidies to industry, agriculture, and shipping that have crept into foreign aid programs. Quite the contrary. The Food-for-Peace Act of 1966, for example, is very specific in requiring that the President, in presenting his budget, shall classify expenditures under this act "as expenditures for international affairs and finance rather than for agriculture and agricultural resources."[11] The effect is to overstate the international affairs budget by the amount the Commodity Credit Corporation would have spent anyhow on Food-for-Freedom commodities.

The type of reverse tying of repayments referred to by Professor Johnson is virtually standard practice in trade-aid relations between communist countries and less developed countries. The Soviet Union regularly accepts goods—steel, fertilizer, sugar, and so forth—in repayment of loans for steel mills, fertilizer plants, and sugar mills. The United States dismisses this as barter and proclaims its willingness to pay dollars for the imports it needs. But because of an enormously productive economy and a panoply of protective measures, its imports of goods the less developed countries can supply are modest. This contributes to the difficulties of the less developed countries in repaying loans out of export earnings. In the long run, aid should

10. Harry G. Johnson, *Economic Policies Toward the Less Developed Countries* (Brookings Institution, 1967), pp. 124–25. The report of the Pearson Commission recommends that costs arising from tying aid to the use of donor shipping should be excluded from statistics of official development assistance; also, and more important, that donors untie their aid to permit aid-financed procurement anywhere within the less developed world. *Partners in Development*, Report of the Commission on International Development, Lester B. Pearson, chairman (Praeger, 1969), p. 174.
11. Sec. 403.

surely be untied; in the short run, there is some injustice in tying the outflow to relieve the balance-of-payments problems of the lending nations without mitigating correspondingly the balance-of-payments problems of the borrowing nations.

Although tied aid has harmful effects in both donor and recipient nations, simultaneous untying by all donors would leave the United States with the problem of an increase in direct outflows. Assuming the United States will continue to provide between half and two-thirds of the aid flow from the noncommunist developed countries, it cannot expect the less developed countries as a group, under free market conditions, to spend nearly that large a fraction of their aid receipts directly for U.S. goods and services. In a paper prepared for the 1968 session of the UN Conference on Trade and Development (UNCTAD), Jagdish N. Bhagwati therefore suggested two types of proposals: (1) proposals for the untying of aid, *while making due adjustments* for the difficulties, and (2) proposals based on the assumption that some aid tying would continue but the adverse effects on recipient countries could be reduced.[12]

Because international lending agencies adhere to the principle of competitive bidding and the principle results in a smaller proportion of expenditures for U.S. goods and services than the U.S. contribution as a proportion of total expenditures of those agencies, the greater reliance on multilateral lending agencies recommended in this study may appear untimely from a balance-of-payments point of view. If the United States contributes 40 percent of the funds of the International Development Association, while 25 percent or less of the IDA's disbursements are for goods and services of U.S. origin, whereas bilateral aid can be 100 percent tied, would not the United States worsen its balance-of-payments position by adding to the IDA's resources?

The IDA's limited resources have been concentrated heavily on India and Pakistan, which normally do not turn to U.S. sources of supply for as large a proportion of their imports as do, for example,

12. "Ways of Reducing Tied Aid and Its Real Costs," *Development Digest*, Vol. 6, no. 4 (Washington: National Planning Association, 1968), pp. 44–47, consisting of excerpts from Bhagwati's UNCTAD paper.

the nations of Latin America. If the resources of the IDA were substantially increased so that its credits could be more widely distributed, the proportion of its disbursements in the United States could be expected to rise. In addition to this "natural" correction, safeguards for countries in balance-of-payments difficulties can, as mentioned earlier, be negotiated—pending reform of the international monetary system in ways that would themselves help to alleviate the difficulties. Considerable thought is now being given to techniques for combining tied financing with the practice of international competitive bidding, and some interesting experiments are being tried.[13]

Restrictions on Capital Exports

Although the principal focus of this study is on aid rather than trade or private investment, brief mention at least must be made of the restrictions on exports of private capital introduced by the U.S. government for balance-of-payments reasons. Several years before the more acute balance-of-payments crisis of early 1968, the government undertook to restrict the outflow by (1) a 15 percent tax on certain types of capital raised by foreigners in U.S. markets; (2) a voluntary program by which U.S. parent companies try to improve the net balance-of-payments effect of the operations of their overseas subsidiaries; and (3) a program by which American banks would hold increases in their foreign lending to 5 percent a year. According to the Watson Committee,

From the start, official policy has sought to make clear that these restrictive measures were not directed at the less developed countries. For those countries, the United States aim of stimulating economic growth was to take precedence over its aim of controlling the outflow of United States capital. Accordingly, the 15 percent interest equalization tax was

13. See, for example, *World Bank, International Development Association, Annual Report 1968* (WBIDA, 1968), p. 20, describing the agreement reached by the Bank with Canada, the United States, and ten European countries for joint financing with the Bank of a $90 million Mexican power expansion program. Note also that the most recent IDA replenishment provides that other countries will accelerate their contributions so that expenditure of the U.S. contribution, to the extent required for other than U.S. procurement, can be postponed.

made applicable only to capital exports destined for the advanced countries. For the same reason, the voluntary program for improving the balance-of-payments performance of United States companies with foreign interests was limited to transactions with the advanced countries.

But the distinction was badly blurred in the Federal Reserve Board's voluntary program for curbing overseas bank lending. Here, the ceiling imposed on bank loan increases was global in nature. The only special recognition given to the less developed countries was a recommendation to banks that, within the global quota, priorities be given first to export loans and, second, to loans for the less developed countries.

A curtailment of this sort defeats the United States objective of encouraging the development of the less developed countries, and above all, of the private sectors in those countries. What is more, there is a real question whether the curtailment does much to help the balance of payments position of the United States.[14]

Under the "Action Program" introduced by President Johnson early in 1968 to surmount the heightened U.S. balance-of-payments crisis, the situation of the less developed countries was made still more difficult. The exemption from the interest equalization tax was continued, but new controls on direct investments (capital transfers plus reinvested earnings) were introduced. Although the restrictions on direct investment in low-income countries were less stringent than those on investment in more highly developed countries, they were intended to establish an investment ceiling below the level that might be reached in the absence of that ceiling.

The ceiling—110 percent of an investor's average investment in 1965 and 1966—left the investor free to juggle amounts and percentages to individual less developed countries, provided he stayed within the 110 percent limit for the less developed countries as a whole. (For purposes of the regulation, Hong Kong, Bermuda, the Bahamas, and the oil-rich countries of the Middle East were not classified as less developed countries and were therefore subject to more stringent controls.) The usual troubles and complaints nevertheless developed. Firms with carefully nurtured investment plans for 1968 but no base year investments in less developed countries had

14. Agency for International Development, *Foreign Aid Through Private Initiative: Report of the Advisory Committee on Private Enterprise in Foreign Aid* (July 1965), pp. 27–28.

no quotas. Firms with freakishly low investments during the base years needed quota adjustments. Others had special obligations or commitments. The system was somewhat liberalized by President Nixon in April 1969. The ceiling on the size of the foreign investment a firm could make without going through the reporting procedure was raised and quota adjustments were made easier to obtain.

If most U.S. direct investment in the less developed countries finances the purchase of machinery, goods, and services from the United States, a ceiling on direct investments may be doing more to curtail exports than to improve the U.S. balance of payments. In any event, the controls on capital outflows are obviously inconsistent with investment guarantees and other incentives to stimulate private investment in less developed countries. Eliminating the controls insofar as investment in poor countries is concerned would represent a small step forward, at negligible cost to the U.S. balance of payments.

International Monetary Reform

The most promising new source of development finance is through double-duty use of the special drawing rights (SDRs) created by the International Monetary Fund (IMF). Thereby, $1.5 billion or more per year could be provided. The SDRs, referred to earlier in this study in the discussion of changes in the international economic environment, owe their origin not to the export and import problems of the less developed countries, but to the need of the entire trading world for a reserve asset to supplement the gold and dollar balances held by central banks. All IMF members, it is hoped, will become participants in the new SDR account (the Special Drawing Account). Each participant has a quota, which is the same as its quota for regular IMF operations (the General Account). Its entitlement to share in any issue of special drawing rights—that is, to obtain some of the new "paper gold"—and its voting power in the Special Account are based on its quota. Countries receiving SDRs will be able to count them as part of their reserves. Although the creation of the SDR as a new reserve asset constitutes a genuine step forward, and the contemplated arrangements for access to this asset do not discriminate against less developed countries, an almost painless way of favoring them is being missed.

In the circumspect language of the managing director of the IMF:

a certain amount of disappointment has been expressed in some quarters that the agreed scheme does not provide for a specific link between reserve creation and development assistance. At one time a great deal of attention was paid to proposals of this sort, associated, in particular, with the name of Maxwell Stamp and elaborated by a committee of experts convened by the UNCTAD. The general conception was that the bulk of any new reserves deliberately created to meet a world need for liquidity would, in effect, be distributed through international investment institutions [for example, the International Development Association] in the form of development assistance and would be acquired by industrial countries—not given to them, but earned by them—in exchange for goods and services supplied to the developing countries.

While there was nothing technically impractical about this way of getting new reserves into circulation among monetary authorities, the idea was generally unwelcome to industrial countries who felt that the provision of aid and the creation of international liquidity called for two distinct decisions, each of which should be taken deliberately on its own merits by appropriate procedures, and that reserve creation should not provide a back door through which aid-giving could be freed, in some measure, from the restraints of parliamentary control over expenditure.[15]

After the first tranche of SDRs is in circulation and the time has come for a second issue of SDRs, the deliberate forging of a "link between reserve creation and development assistance" may seem more sensible, more urgent, and less insidious than it does today. Liquidity needs served as justification for the creation of SDRs in the amount of $9.5 billion for the three years beginning January 1, 1970, and requirements are not expected to diminish thereafter. Using only half of these newly created SDRs as a basis for IDA credits to poor countries could add more than $1.5 billion per year to the volume of aid resources without impairing in any way the task

15. Pierre-Paul Schweitzer, "New Arrangements to Supplement World Reserves and Their Implications for the Developing Countries," Supplement to *International Financial News Survey* (International Monetary Fund, Dec. 15, 1967), p. 417. (The italics are mine.)

of providing adequate international liquidity. The $1.5 billion per year for development assistance, moreover, would come in the form in which it is most needed—under the control of a competent multilateral agency, untied as to procurement sources, and available on a truly long-term, low-interest basis.

Early in 1965, in a report entitled "Guidelines for Improving the International Monetary System," the Subcommittee on International Exchange and Payments of the Joint Economic Committee of the U.S. Congress opposed any close link between the creation of new international monetary reserves and long-term aid to less developed countries, principally because it was thought that connecting them would increase the difficulty of reaching agreement on new monetary arrangements. By late 1965, at least two members of the committee—Representatives Henry S. Reuss and Robert F. Ellsworth—were urging that there be a link.

The World Bank should take the initiative in proposing a plan to link new reserve creation with the provision of additional assistance to the less developed countries.... There should be more discussion on how to develop two distinct but complementary sets of foreign aid formulations. One would be based on conventional contributions out of national budgets and financed by domestic taxation. The other would involve setting aside a portion of new reserve creation for the developing countries.

As an experienced and well-regarded multilateral instrument for extending aid, the World Bank should take the initiative in asking the IMF to dedicate some part of reserve creation to long-term aid. Once the IMF and the Group of Ten have tentatively agreed on a new mechanism for creating reserves, the World Bank should propose that the International Development Association be financed in part by the conventional national contributions and in part by IMF purchases of IDA bonds, guaranteed by the World Bank, with a portion of the new reserve assets.[16]

A similar recommendation was made by a group of UN experts in 1965, and by late 1967, the congressional Subcommittee on International Exchange and Payments was virtually unanimous in urging that the U.S. governors of the World Bank and the IMF, after activa-

16. Henry S. Reuss and Robert F. Ellsworth, *Off Dead Center: Some Proposals to Strengthen Free World Economic Cooperation*, Report to the Joint Economic Committee, 89 Cong. 1 sess. (1965), pp. 16–17.

tion of the new agreement on the creation of SDRs, "should start to direct thought and dialogue in both organizations to the possibility of linking the new reserve creation with the provision of additional assistance to the less-developed countries."[17] Given the conservatism of European central bankers and some of their theological distinctions between capital and liquidity, the debate may drag on for several years.

Fears that less developed countries, in order to increase the quantity of SDRs available for development assistance, would press for their creation in larger volume than necessary to serve liquidity needs could be met by agreement on an absolute ceiling on the quantity available for development assistance, for example, $2 billion per year during an initial period of five or ten years. In similar fashion, other risks inherent in trying to kill two birds with one stone can be reduced. Under the rules already in operation, countries with only 15 percent of the voting power in the IMF can veto any level of SDR creation that they consider excessive. This raises a real danger that too few rather than too many SDRs will be created.

In summary, it should surely be easier to persuade governments in developed countries to forgo a small part of the massive benefits from monetary reform than it is to accept the obvious costs of appropriated aid funds or tariff concessions or higher commodity prices. To maximize the amount of development assistance that can safely be provided via monetary reform and to make the building of international community a cooperative enterprise, all of the richer members of the IMF should agree to an allocation system that distributes the bulk of the SDRs to poor countries or permits them to be used as a basis for IDA credits. Pending a multilateral decision, however, there is nothing to prevent voluntary decisions by individual wealthy countries to increase their foreign aid appropriations or contributions by an amount equal to their share of SDRs or to some sizable fraction thereof. An announcement to this effect by the United States, which

17. *Guidelines for Improving the International Monetary System—Round Two*, Report of the Subcommittee on International Exchange and Payments of the Joint Economic Committee, 90 Cong. 1 sess. (1967), p. 8. For the recommendations of the UN group, see United Nations, *International Monetary Issues and the Developing Countries* (UN, 1965).

is entitled to almost 25 percent of all the SDRs issued on the basis of the present quota agreement, could have an important galvanizing effect on development financing.

Seabeds and Ocean Floors

More remote as a nonnational source of development finance than SDRs, but not to be ruled out, is international registration or licensing of the privilege of exploiting the seabeds and ocean floors beyond the limits of present national jurisdiction. Before this second possibility can become a reality, governments will have to agree on the limits of "present national jurisdiction," which they have not yet done, and on the type of international regime best equipped to regulate the exploitation of resources lying beyond those limits.

Vesting ownership of a revenue-producing resource in the United Nations or some other international agency, or conferring upon it the power to tax or license, would do more than provide a new source of development finance. It could represent a real breakthrough in strengthening the international community vis-à-vis national governments and transnational corporations. For that very reason, governments have not been enthusiastic about recurrent proposals to give the United Nations jurisdiction over the resources of the oceans and ocean beds, the right to levy a tax on international trade or international capital movements, or to tax transnational corporations.

Governments rich or poor, nevertheless, can hardly view with equanimity the prospect of a wasteful, anarchic scramble for petroleum and other mineral resources in seabed areas until recently considered to be unambiguously beyond national jurisdiction. The scramble is a real possibility. Until 1962, offshore oil and gas drilling was limited primarily to the Gulf of Mexico (off the Louisiana coast) and Lake Maracaibo in Venezuela. It has now spread to the waters of more than eighty countries.

Fifteen years ago offshore drilling was within 25 miles of the mainland; today some U.S. wells are more than 75 miles from shore. Fifteen years ago there were approximately 200 offshore U.S. wells in water depths not exceeding 70 feet; today there are more than 6,000 U.S. producing offshore wells, and some of the most recent are being drilled in water over 600 feet deep. . . . Some large oil and gas producing companies now have more than 50 percent of their lease holdings offshore. . . . Total investment of companies in offshore activities, according to some authorities, will have quadrupled by 1980, increasing from $13 billion in 1968 to $55 billion.[18]

Experts have predicted that by 1980 between 30 and 35 percent of the world's oil will come from offshore wells in waters up to 2,000 feet deep. If offshore drilling increases and extends farther out to sea to produce such a substantial proportion of the world's petroleum output, the less developed countries may suffer triply: (1) through the loss of income from decreased interest on the part of the big corporations in exploiting the more conventional sources; (2) from greater dependence on the developed countries for resource exploitation if, as is highly likely, claims to exclusive national jurisdiction over seabed resources extend far out from shore; and (3) from delay by the international community in setting up machinery to obtain and use for development purposes a portion of the value of the petroleum or other mineral production from deep-water exploitation beyond national jurisdiction.

Furthermore, investment in deep-water exploitation may be unnecessarily risky for the investors without the kind of legal safeguard provided by registration or agreement with, or license from, a recognized international authority.

President Johnson, in a speech at the commissioning of the research vessel *Oceanographer* in mid-1966, said that "under no circumstances, we believe, must we ever allow the prospects of rich harvests and mineral wealth to create a new form of colonial competition among the maritime nations. We must be careful to avoid a race to grab and to hold the lands under the high seas. We must insure that the deep seas and the ocean bottoms are, and remain, the legacy of all human beings."

The question is by no means merely an economic issue: the ocean floor and its subsurface can be put to a variety of military uses and governments have just begun to realize the strategic implications of

18. Dresser Industries, Inc., *Third Interim Report, 1968* (Dallas, Texas, Aug. 22, 1968).

this important fact. Specific recommendations concerning the control of the seabed are beyond the scope of this study. I am not arguing for vesting control in the United Nations proper, or in one of the specialized agencies, or in an international authority similar to the TVA. I am not proposing public instead of private exploitation. I am merely calling attention (forcefully, I hope) to the fact that commercial exploitation of seabed areas considered until recently to be well beyond national jurisdiction may begin soon and burgeon quickly into an economically significant activity. Payments for the privilege of exploitation, whether in the form of registration or licensing fees or on some other basis, can provide an important source of development finance.[19]

Other Nonappropriated Sources of Development Finance

Other nonnational sources of development finance may be equally promising. It is hard to envisage a substantially larger flow to the low-income countries without much greater recourse, not just to nonnational, but to all nonappropriated sources of assistance. Nothing will become available without a campaign strategy and a battle, but the battle for each source will need to be fought only once, or only once in a while, in order to keep the channel open. This argues strongly for further study of such sources, with a view to substituting

19. For recent general discussion of the seabed problem, see Daniel S. Cheever, "The Role of International Organization in Ocean Development," *International Organization*, Vol. 22, no. 3 (1968); "Marine Science Research: Problems and Challenges," *FAR Horizons*, Vol. 1, no. 5 (Government Printing Office, September 1968); Arvid Pardo, "Who Will Control the Seabed?" *Foreign Affairs*, Vol. 47, no. 1 (1968); and the report of the U.S. Commission on Marine Science, Engineering, and Resources, *Our Nation and the Sea* (January 1969), especially pp. 147–55. The commission proposed an international registry authority with which all claims to explore or exploit particular mineral resources in particular areas of the deep seas would be registered. "Every nation registering a claim to exploit should be required to pay a portion of the value of the production, if any, into an International Fund to be expended for such purposes as financing marine scientific activity and resources exploration and development, particularly food-from-the-sea programs, and aiding the developing countries through the World Bank, UN Development Program and other international development agencies" (p. 149).

them to the maximum feasible extent for annual appropriations. Among those already mentioned in earlier chapters of this book are (1) the foreign exchange that could be earned by less developed countries through trade liberalization by the developed countries coupled with export promotion by the less developed countries; (2) commodity agreements and arrangements that cannot honestly be considered trade liberalization measures but constitute a thoroughly respectable means of increasing the export earnings of less developed countries and protecting them from excessive year-to-year fluctuations; (3) private capital raised through bond issues of various types (with and without interest subsidies), investment guarantees, and tax concessions; (4) reuse of interest payments on earlier loans to subsidize subsequent bilateral and multilateral lending; (5) under certain circumstances, debt relief or write-off to reduce the burden of service charges on foreign loans previously obtained by less developed countries, together with measures to forestall recurrent crises in accident-prone areas.

In addition one might consider the earmarking of customs revenues from the products of less developed countries for so long as such revenues continue to be collected (though this might operate to discourage trade liberalization); the imposition of import taxes on coffee or other duty-free products for which demand is relatively inelastic and allocation of the revenues to a development financing agency; and the taxation of international movements of capital or of transnational corporations.

The big money is surely in trade liberalization consciously undertaken to facilitate a more rational structure of world production in agriculture as well as industry. It is in no sense a new source of development finance nor one that will necessarily yield quick economic results, but it is a mutually beneficial imperative for the 1970s. Whereas trade liberalization will be resisted by entrenched interests, it is the absence as yet of firmly vested interests in SDRs that makes urgent and attractive a system for sharing the windfall from their creation with less developed countries in a manner better calculated to promote development than the sharing arrangement initially adopted.

CHAPTER TEN

America's Authorizing Legislation:
A Basic Act
for International Development?

THE INTERRELATIONS AMONG trade, aid, and investment policies have long been known but are now more widely appreciated than at any time since the end of World War II. Changes in each are required. The Foreign Assistance Act of 1961 need not, and probably should not, be replaced by another aid bill. The time has come for the United States to adopt a basic act for international development designed to integrate aid, trade, and investment policies and educational and scientific cooperation into a broad, long-range strategy for facilitating growth in the low-income countries.

Specialists may recall that in 1950 the United States did adopt, as Title IV of the Foreign Economic Assistance Act, an Act for International Development. Intended only to establish the machinery for the Point Four Program, that act dealt almost exclusively with technical assistance. It was amended by the Mutual Security Acts of 1951, 1952, and 1953, and repealed by the Mutual Security Act of 1954. Specialists may also recall that the report of President Kennedy's Task Force on Foreign Economic Assistance was published under the title, *An Act for International Development*, and was subtitled, *A Program for the Decade of Development.*[1] Although in

1. Department of State Publication 7205 (June 1961).

many respects a landmark report, it dealt largely with proposals for more effective use of the familiar ingredients of foreign aid programs—grants, loans, and technical assistance—to support country development programs.

The legislation subsequently adopted was entitled the Foreign Assistance Act of 1961. (In the field of trade policy the Kennedy administration's great achievement was the Trade Expansion Act of 1962.) Amended almost beyond recognition, the Foreign Assistance Act of 1961 was still in effect in mid-1969. As someone has said, "Aid today is like a little donkey that's piled so high with burdens it can hardly stagger."

In the absence of any widespread demand for truth in legislative labeling, it will always be possible for the United States to superimpose grandiose titles on modest and inadequate legislative efforts. A new act for international development is suggested here, not as a public relations device, but as an opportunity to change the nature and time frame of the U.S. commitment to development and to provide an authorization for a broad range of development-oriented efforts.

Basic Ingredients of the Act

The basic ingredients for a new act for international development are summarized below.

1. A statement of purpose should indicate the interest of the United States in the economic, social, and civic development of low-income countries which are themselves seriously interested in development, and the desire of the United States to contribute appropriately to the process. Because the American concept of development embraces social justice as well as economic growth, the act for international development could refer explicitly to the U.S. desire to improve the lot of the most disadvantaged groups, to the importance of popular participation in development planning and execution in low-income countries, and to the need for an equitable internal distribution of productivity gains achieved with external assistance.

In fulfillment of its broad objectives, the United States should announce its willingness to accord certain types of financial and technical assistance, trade opportunities, preferences, and the like to low-income countries, and various guarantees, incentives, and facilities to American private investors ready to put some of their resources to work in the less developed world, insofar as these actions can be taken without damaging the legitimate interests of other high-income countries or seriously disrupting the American economy.

2. Without legislating specific changes in commercial policy, the act could stress the desirability of enabling less developed countries to earn more from exports of both primary and processed products. It could express, as the sense of Congress, the view that more strenuous efforts ought to be made to reduce tariffs on products of special interest to low-income countries and the view that concessions such as temporary tariff preferences for manufactured products from less developed countries appear warranted.[2]

3. In the private investment field, the principal object of the legislation would be the creation of a federally chartered corporation to take over the role of the Office of Private Resources in the Agency for International Development (AID) and to perform other functions connected with (a) facilitating the flow of private capital to less developed countries that want it, and (b) investing such capital productively within those countries. The specific concerns of the proposed corporation, preferably not spelled out in detail in the legislation, would be administration and liberalization, to the extent feasible, of the U.S. investment guarantee program; relaxation insofar as possible of restraints introduced for balance-of-payments reasons on outflows of U.S. capital to less developed countries; positive incentives for individual and corporate investment in such countries; judicious use of authority to make loans directly to private enterprises and to take equity positions in enterprises in low-income countries in which there is also a U.S. private equity participation—all

2. A more comprehensive list of desirable measures in the field of commercial policy is carried in the introductory portion of Chapter 7 above. Including the full catalog in the authorizing legislation, however, would doom the bill before the practicality of the proposals had been adequately tested.

with full consciousness of the shifting attitudes of poor countries toward direct investment from abroad.

4. Because no foreseeable combination of trade and private investment policies will eliminate the need for technical and capital assistance during the 1970s, the proposed act for international development would have to authorize financial and technical assistance to low-income countries. In terms of channels, the act should, as proposed earlier in this discussion, provide for a phased transition to a predominantly multilateral capital lending program within a five-year span; there are international agencies well equipped to administer larger loan programs than they now operate. Bilateral capital assistance should also be authorized, with the loan portion administered by a U.S. development cooperation fund which would be a cross between the Development Loan Fund of 1958–61 and the present Agency for International Development, less project oriented and Washington centered than the former and less visible and prominent in the low-income countries than the latter.

The U.S. development lending agency should be authorized to draw on Treasury funds as the Export-Import Bank now does and to issue its own securities with principal and interest guaranteed by the federal government. In order to borrow at market rates and lend at less than market rates, it would need an interest subsidization fund. To reduce dependence on appropriations for that subsidy, the U.S. development cooperation fund should be permitted to use repayments on U.S. loans to the public sector made by the AID and predecessor aid agencies.

5. Technical assistance includes a number of services that the United States, if it organizes itself to do so, can more readily provide than can the UN Development Program, the Organization of American States, or the regional institutions of Asia and Africa. Insofar as possible, however, the practice of putting technical assistants on the payroll of the U.S. government (or keeping them there if they are already on it) should be discouraged in favor of making them consultants to or employees of agencies in the low-income countries. This seems to require establishing the kind of autonomous or semi-autonomous, government-subsidized technical cooperation founda-

tion or institute described in Chapter 6. The institute would serve chiefly as an intermediary to help aid-receiving countries buy the technical assistance they want from the United States, whether financed by U.S. loans or from other sources. It would serve also as a center for continued technical cooperation with other countries after the need for capital assistance on concessional terms had ended. Other activities would include administration of a topping-off fund to enable qualified Americans to accept positions in less developed countries without suffering serious loss of income. (Twenty-five million dollars would permit $5,000 subsidies to 5,000 American technicians.) Subsidies would also be needed to bring within the realm of economic feasibility training in the United States of nationals from low-income countries. The general policy, however, should be to build up educational, training, and research facilities in the less developed world and thus reduce the brain drain from low-income countries. Finally, some technical assistance might have to be provided on a grant basis.

In proposing an analogous technical assistance and development research institute, a special report of the National Planning Association recommended that the institute

be chartered by act of Congress as an autonomous, nonprofit tax-free institution, like the National Academy of Sciences, for an initial period of 10 years, after which its charter could be renewed if desirable. . . . Its negotiating, contracting and auditing procedures should be modelled on those of the large private foundations and not of AID. The Institute's directors would be appointed by the President for staggered terms, and should include the administrator of the U.S. foreign aid agency and other appropriate government officials; persons from foundations, corporations and other private contributors; and professionals from the various social science and technological disciplines pertinent to the development process.[3]

The technical cooperation institute that I envisage should be related to the U.S. development cooperation fund, through an interlocking directorate and a space-sharing arrangement, in a manner resembling the relationship of the International Finance Corporation

3. National Planning Association, *A New Conception of U.S. Foreign Aid*, Special Report 64 (Washington: March 1969), p. 17.

to the World Bank. The objective, in short, is not to separate technical and financial assistance, but to make technical assistance a more businesslike relationship, to transfer more of the responsibility for integrating technical and capital assistance to the less developed countries, and to make it easier for countries no longer receiving capital aid from the United States to maintain programs of educational and scientific cooperation with the full spectrum of American governmental and nongovernmental agencies.

6. Supporting assistance in its present form—grant aid intended to improve the defense posture of certain low-income countries— has been justified on national security rather than development grounds. It goes primarily to Vietnam and, in smaller amounts, to Korea, Laos, and Thailand. In the new act for international development, supporting assistance as such should be terminated gradually. The principal form of assistance should be the very soft loan, and the vehicle for giving an extra measure of U.S. support to countries whose development the United States particularly wished to promote would be the U.S. development cooperation fund or bank.

7. The act for international development should not include a military assistance title. If military assistance to certain less developed countries is considered essential, either in the form of equipment and supplies or to enable the receiver to strengthen its defense posture in other ways, it should be provided out of defense appropriations and administered by the Department of Defense, subject to such political guidance from the Department of State and elsewhere as seems necessary. Development assistance should be separated conceptually, legislatively, administratively, and almost every other way from military aid, not because security and development are totally unrelated, but because development promotion is a basically civilian, increasingly professional enterprise that requires an independent, unambiguous authorization of its own.

8. The contingency fund for the President traditionally provided by the Foreign Assistance Act has by now been reduced to a minuscule sum. Common sense suggests that authorizing legislation for a new act for international development should provide for contingencies not foreseen at the time of enactment, but common sense

tends to be an early victim of the never-ending controversy between the executive and legislative branches of the U.S. government. If sufficient flexibility can be built into the other appropriation categories, a contingency fund as such will not be essential.

9. Since nothing will be gained by making the proposed act for international development more far-reaching and comprehensive than it needs to be, little or nothing should be said in that act about Food-for-Freedom or the Peace Corps. Indeed, the more that straight relief operations, teaching of the English language, exposure of well-motivated Americans to life in unfamiliar parts of the world, and other worthy nondevelopmental objectives can be excised from the act for international development, the more credible the true objective of the proposed act will become. The effectiveness of Food-for-Freedom and Peace Corps programs as instruments for promoting development can surely be increased, but the heart of the problem lies elsewhere.

10. By way of guidelines for appropriation acts, the authorizing legislation might include as a target figure the familiar 1 percent of gross national product (GNP) by specifying the willingness of the United States to raise the net flow of long-term resources from this country for development of the low-income world to 1 percent of GNP by 1975, and to provide two-thirds or three-fourths of the 1 percent in the form of "official assistance." Alternatively, it might state the intention of the United States, in combination with other high-income countries, to provide a total flow of resources that would meet validated requirements and permit low-income countries, with reasonable efforts on their part, to forge ahead at maximum feasible rates. (By total flow, I mean the flow inclusive of credits resulting from a future decision either to link special drawing rights in the IMF to development assistance or to tap any other new source of development finance. By validated requirements, I mean requirements endorsed by a consortium in which the United States has participated, or by an expert group such as the Inter-American Committee of the Alliance for Progress, or by a less-developed-country replica of the Organisation for European Economic Co-operation as it functioned during the Marshall Plan period. For reasons given

in Chapter 4, fractions of the GNP of rich countries are inadequate indexes of what those countries ought to provide; a conviction that development is worth fostering, plus analyses of "requirements" built up from careful country-by-country studies of performance and potentiality, would provide a better measure.)

The authorization act might limit the U.S. contribution to some proportion of the total contribution of high-income countries. It could perhaps include broad guidelines for classifying receiving countries according to income status or other standards of eligibility for U.S. bilateral aid, and it could make clear that certain international standards of behavior and decency should be observed by receivers.

To summarize, the act for international development should make it evident that the United States recognizes international development as the long-term job that it is, is eager to make development assistance primarily a multilateral enterprise, will contribute its full share to a cooperative effort, will administer its residual capital assistance through a development cooperation fund or other appropriate mechanism, and will carry on activities such as the promotion of private investment and the satisfaction of needs for technical assistance through quasi-governmental entities designed for the long pull.

A White House office of development coordination could be assigned responsibility for keeping interested organizational entities from working at cross-purposes, for speaking up on behalf of the multilateral development agencies when their coffers required replenishment from appropriated funds, and for seeing that, as far as possible, multilateral and bilateral activities were mutually reinforcing. The hand of the coordinator could be strengthened by establishing under his chairmanship a strong interagency committee on development policy. An undersecretary of state for economic affairs could serve as deputy chairman. For formulating policies toward less developed countries, the Treasury's long-standing domination of the National Advisory Council on International Monetary and Financial Policy established by the Bretton Woods Agreement Act of 1945 ought to be modified in favor of the interagency committee on development policy.

Questions of Political Acceptability

Must the social scientist who proposes a new program and a legislative technique to legitimize it then become master tactician and demonstrate how the Congress can be persuaded to accept his proposals? My hat is off to those who take on both assignments and discharge them with honor, but I reject the notion that it is irresponsible or dishonorable to tackle the first assignment without also taking on the latter. The principal obligation of the policy-oriented social scientist is surely to analyze the issues and indicate directions in which solutions might be sought.

I am not unaware that congressional committees are incredibly jealous of their jurisdictions and inhospitable to proposals that reduce their role or bargaining power; that the Congress has previously refused to give development assistance a long-term authorization, to liberalize lending, or to permit "back-door financing"; that a Congress hypersensitive to issues of control will hesitate to strike a radically altered balance between bilateral aid "controlled" by the United States and multilateral aid not "controlled" by the United States; that sense-of-Congress provisions of laws are often like preambles to UN resolutions—convenient receptacles for disposing of sentiments too noble to be incorporated into the operational portions of the resolutions.

Nevertheless, the development business needs the kind of "great debate" and legislative fresh start that trade negotiations received under the Trade Expansion Act of 1962. For nearly thirty years, tariff-cutting authority had been obtained by amending the Trade Agreements Act of 1934. In the early days of the Kennedy administration, a number of the economists and lawyers who were consulted thought that new authority should again be obtained within the same rickety framework by minimal changes in the legislation inherited from 1958, because they could not see how Congress could be persuaded to accept anything more fundamental. The President's message, however, stated that "in order to meet the challenges and opportunities of a rapidly changing world economy" the reciprocal trade agreements program initiated in 1934 and extended and amended eleven times after that should be replaced by "a wholly new instrument." Numerous concessions had to be made to obstructive interests, but a new framework was obtained.

I do not pretend to know what timing, tactics, concessions, and trade-offs will be needed to secure a new framework for development assistance. I know only that the badly battered Foreign Assistance Act of 1961 needs to be replaced with legislation that will make plain a five- or ten-year U.S. commitment to the development of the low-income world through a variety of interrelated long-term measures, implemented by machinery appropriate to the task. Some of the struts for a fresh framework have been described in this study.

Machinery without the fuel to make it run will never be more than a museum piece. A resounding act for international development unaccompanied by an adequate flow of resources to the less developed countries will not advance the cause of development or the interests of the United States.

Concluding Thoughts

This study has argued that a fresh approach to development assistance is needed for reasons more fundamental than that new administrations like to take the initiative and are in a better position to do so than they will be after two years in office. The basic reason for a new approach is that the world of today is very different from the world of 1945–55; the creaky apparatus inherited from an era in which the United States was virtually the sole provider of aid on a significant scale will no longer suffice.

Two decades of experience with development assistance have taught us a number of practical lessons that have significant implications for aid policy in the 1970s. The most important lesson is that aid works. Despite widespread frustration among donors and receivers of aid and the almost universal conviction that existing arrangements for helping it work are no longer appropriate, rates of growth impressive by any historical standards have been achieved in aid-receiving countries. Capital assistance, by providing some 20 percent of the investment resources of low-income countries and lubricating their economies in various ways, has shown that significant increases in gross national product can be achieved within a short span of years. With reasonably good management, the broadly shared 4-percent-per-person-per-year rate of growth favored herein as a target for the poor countries as a group during the 1970s can be obtained with inflows of long-term resources approximating 1 percent of the GNP of rich countries.

Not all of the 1 percent, moreover, needs to be obtained by resource transfers from rich countries. New sources of assistance not now the property of any national government—income from registering or licensing the exploitation of petroleum and other seabed resources beyond the limits of present national jurisdiction and, in the monetary field, paper that is as good as gold—constitute potentially important supplements to "levies" on national governments. Use of the newly created special drawing rights in the International Monetary Fund as a basis for credits to poor countries from the International Development Association could readily add $1.5 billion per year to the volume of aid resources during the 1970s. For the aid that ought to come by way of transfer from the United States, more could come from the private community if mechanisms were set up to guarantee bond issues floated by less developed countries or by new lending agencies, and if various other incentives to foreign investment by individuals and corporations were adopted. The government contribution could go further than it does if part of it could be used as an interest subsidy.

Other sources of funds that can be authorized on a once-and-for-all or once-every-few-years basis should be used to the greatest possible degree; several such sources are suggested in Chapter 9. Congressional ability to review American public programs, to expand or curtail them, or to give them new directions must be preserved but is not dependent on appropriating annually the full contribution labeled "official development assistance" if the stream can be fed in part from nonappropriated sources.

Whereas per capita incomes in less developed countries can be increased fairly rapidly, the attainment of comparable social and civic progress appears to require both longer time horizons and better arrangements for international technical cooperation after the need for capital assistance on concessional terms has subsided. The payoff on high-quality technical assistance—the kind that has been provided by the Ford and Rockefeller foundations, the government of Israel, and many individual U.S. government projects and missions—has been greater than is generally realized. Arrangements that facilitate long-term technical cooperation through institutions more flexible than the standard U.S. government agency deserve a high priority.

At present, there is little in international law that requires high-income countries to come to the aid of low-income countries; the obligation is at most a moral obligation arising from the fact that "we are rich and they are poor," that we are firmly committed to the mitigation of poverty at home and therefore cannot be totally indifferent to its prevalence abroad. With all of the rich countries, most of the middle-income countries, and many of the poor countries themselves in the aid-providing business, the moral obligation may gradually be transformed into a legal one by the strengthening of existing institutions, by the reinforcement of arrangements of the Alliance for Progress type, by the sheer momentum of continued experience with programs that once were novel. As development takes root and more countries move into the middle range of the spectrum in at least some aspects of development, the task of helping those in lower ranges will be more widely shared.

The long-range objectives of the United States and the gradual convergence of U.S. objectives with those of other donors, plus other factors, provide justification for a phased transition from an overwhelmingly bilateral development assistance program to one that is predominantly multilateral. While the study recommends a 40 percent bilateral/60 percent multilateral mix by 1975 instead of the current 85 percent bilateral/15 percent multilateral program of the United States, the emphasis is intended to be on purposeful movement at a rapid rate rather than on the exact dates and percentages mentioned.

The World Bank Group is the most dynamic force in the development sphere at the present time and should receive at least half of the resources allocated to multilateral auspices. (As a result of the sharp increase in its investment activity in the year ended June 30, 1969, the World Bank Group has already become a larger provider of development assistance than the AID.) More technical assistance, it has been urged in this study, should be provided on a loan basis in order to encourage borrowers to hire experts of their own choosing, integrate them into their own agencies and enterprises, and take greater advantage of their expertise.

The thrust of the study, in brief, has been twofold. On the one hand, it has been toward vesting more responsibility in the less developed countries themselves for programming their development, deciding on their priorities, and putting the priorities into effect. On the other hand, it has been toward vesting more responsibility in international bodies, including consortia and consultative groups, for developing standards and criteria, receiving and appraising country programs, and arranging for agreed requirements to be met. I am under no illusion that miracles can be wrought through organizational changes, but I have some hope that the proposed reallocations of responsibility will permit the explosive relationship between rich donor and poor recipient to be placed in a more modern political context. The resultant reduced presence and lower political profile for the United States in the less developed world may be difficult to reconcile domestically with a high priority for foreign aid.

Substantively as well as organizationally, numerous changes in aid policies and procedures seem to be required. The most important policy change is to reverse the downward trend in U.S. assistance or, more broadly, to increase the foreign exchange receipts of the less developed countries. In part, this means easing the debt burdens of countries like India so that less of what they now receive will be needed for interest and amortization payments on previous borrowings. In part, it means changes in trade policy that would permit the more advanced developing countries to earn through trade more of the foreign exchange they need. It also means, however, sizable increases in the volume of new aid and considerable easing of the financial terms on which fresh loans and credits are made available. Project aid need not be abandoned, but more of the increases in available capital assistance should be allocated to sector and program assistance; for example, to coordinated efforts to improve the agricultural or educational sector or to bring in a range of imports needed throughout the economy instead of at some single project site.

The agricultural breakthrough that is under way must not be allowed to lag. The campaign for family planning should be stepped up, not as an alternative to mass starvation in the 1980s, but for a variety of equally compelling reasons. The number of jobs opened up as a concomitant of investments in development must be increased in order to provide remunerative employment for new entrants to the labor market.

Fellow-feeling between man and man is conspicuously absent in many of the less developed countries. There, the few who are rich are often very rich indeed and distressingly reluctant to pay taxes or decent wages, or to assist in other ways the many who live in abject poverty. So long as rich citizens in poor countries remain blind to their obligations, average citizens in rich countries will find it difficult to support ungrudgingly programs for the transfer of resources to poor countries. In this respect, tax reform, social justice, and the extension of substantial benefits to the neediest elements in less developed countries deserve high priority. However, since less developed countries almost by definition have been neglecting actions that would speed their development and reduce domestic disparities in privileges and income, it will always be easy for the highly developed, more egalitarian nations to cite reasons for niggardliness in foreign aid.

On the basis of the most relevant criteria—ability of the United States to supply development assistance without denying itself resources needed for higher priority purposes; requirements for those resources to expedite growth and change in the low-income world; probability that they will be put to productive use, that the efficiency with which they are used will increase as more is learned about the development process and how to influence it, and that the end results will be less detrimental to the interests of the United States than refusing to give assistance or supplying it sporadically and in inadequate volume—the U.S. effort should be considerably larger in the

1970s than it was in the last half of the 1960s. However, in proportion to GNP, which will exceed $1 trillion in 1971, foreign aid can be less than half as large as it was in the late 1940s and early 1950s and probably still be large enough.

Urgent social needs, it seems, consistently go unmet while marginal private needs—for second and third family cars, color television sets, summer homes at the beach—can be indulged. Because of parochial attitudes about the size of the public sector and the purposes for which public funds may be spent, and because of the magnitude of the defense budget, the war on poverty at home is being waged penuriously and inconclusively. While this is so, the war on poverty abroad is bound to suffer. Even a generous and vigorous prosecution of the domestic war will not secure a generous flow of foreign aid but will, initially at least, simply increase the competition for available resources within the perennially short-changed public sector.

Psychologically, the need to fight a two-front war has some redeeming features and can blunt the self-righteousness of a rich country that might otherwise think it had much to teach and little to learn. Today the richest of the so-called developed countries is acutely aware of its depressed areas, its domestic misery, its concentration of privilege, its inability to cope with many domestic problems—in short, its own underdevelopment. Denis Goulet can rightly ask, "But who will teach the 'developed' countries how to run a leisure society, how to humanize personal relations . . . how to elicit solidarity not by fiat, but inner conviction? . . . Perhaps understanding will become possible now that self-satisfaction has begun to ebb because of the growing awareness that our performance has been so poor."[4]

For how long must the United States continue supporting a sizable development assistance effort? On the basis of economic criteria, Latin America is the most advanced of the underdeveloped continents, but social and political tensions there appear to be mounting at a rate that makes economic prediction particularly perilous. In some parts of that continent, self-sustaining growth has been achieved; in others, it ought to be attainable during the 1970s. Self-sustaining

4. Denis Goulet, "That Third World," *The Center Magazine*, Vol. 1 (Santa Barbara: Center for the Study of Democratic Institutions, September 1968), p. 50.

growth in the least developed portions of Latin America, Asia, and Africa is probably several decades further away. While the initial objective of development assistance should be to help poor countries reach the point where they can grow rapidly without encountering balance-of-payments crises, it hardly seems probable that in the long run the United States will be satisfied—or indeed permitted—to leave to their own devices countries that are still quite poor.

Poverty, like development, is relative. A per capita income of $1,000 today is enough to put a nation into the upper middle-income group. A nation that now has a $200-per-person-per-year income and increases it at the excellent rate of 4 percent per year will take more than forty years to reach the $1,000 level. By then, however, a nation now at the $1,000 level and growing only half as rapidly will have surpassed the $2,200 level, thereby widening the dollar gap and leaving the first country still poor not only in relative terms, but probably in absolute ability to ensure the survival, in good physical and mental health, of its inhabitants. The same forces that result in income transfers from richer to poorer citizens and from richer regions to poorer regions within a progressive nation-state like the United States will work toward institutionalizing income transfers in the world as a whole and reducing the extremes between nations.

To what extent should future income transfers be a part of a foreign aid program? Can one appropriately think of the "foreign aid period" as the more heavily subsidized era preceding achievement of five to ten years of growth at an overall average rate of 6–7 percent per year, and the subsequent period (in which the principal need may be for sponsored introductions to the private capital market, topped-off technical assistance, more sophisticated industrial processes, and a large influx of tourists) as somewhat different in conception and financing?

How far ahead should one attempt to see? In the perspective of human history, the twenty-odd years since the close of World War II constitute but a moment. A beginning has been made on the promotion of orderly growth and evolution in a disorderly world. The foundations for a more sustained effort have been laid. But commitment to that effort is lacking. The voices crying for action on the home front to make our cities habitable and enable our own people to live in harmony are loud and clear.

Ignored for far too long, they are now drowning out the claims of lands across the seas. If the United States can hold down its defense budget after extricating itself from the morass in Vietnam, it can devote more of its resources, ingenuity, and know-how to the solution of urgent domestic problems. The United States can also, if it considers it important enough, devote more of its growing wealth to the relief of poverty and the reward of self-help in low-income countries beyond its borders. An impatient world awaits its decision.

Selected Readings

Books, pamphlets, and articles on aspects of the development process and on the theory and practice of foreign aid are being published in all languages and in all parts of the world at a rate that makes it impossible for the individual reader to keep abreast of the flow. The following highly selective list of readings omits many valuable publications and may give undue prominence to American source materials, but seeks to include references that readers of this book should find particularly informative and relevant.

Adler, John H. *Absorptive Capacity: The Concept and Its Determinants.* Washington: Brookings Institution, 1965.
——— (ed.). *Capital Movements and Economic Development.* New York: St. Martin's Press, 1969.
Agency for International Development. "AID Manual." Continually updated; processed.
———. "Development Assistance in the New Administration." Report of the President's General Advisory Committee on Foreign Assistance Programs (Perkins Committee), October 25, 1968. Processed.
———. Discussion papers. Issued periodically; processed.
———. *Foreign Aid through Private Initiative: Report of the Advisory Committee on Private Enterprise in Foreign Aid* (Watson Committee). Washington: AID, July 1965.
———. *The Foreign Assistance Program, Annual Report to the Congress.* Washington: Government Printing Office, various years.
———. "Operations Report." Issued quarterly; processed.

Agency for International Development. *Principles of Foreign Economic Assistance*. Washington: Government Printing Office, 1963 and 1966.
———. *Summary Presentation to the Congress*. Washington: Government Printing Office, published annually.
American Assembly, The. *International Stability and Progress: United States Interests and Instruments*. New York: Columbia University Graduate School of Business, June 1957.
Asher, Robert E. *Grants, Loans, and Local Currencies: Their Role in Foreign Aid*. Washington: Brookings Institution, 1961.
———. *International Development and the U.S. National Interest*. Planning Pamphlet 124. Washington: National Planning Association, 1967.
———. "The United States and the Developing Nations," in Hans J. Morgenthau (ed.), *The Crossroad Papers*. New York: Norton, 1965.
Avramovic, Dragoslav, and others. *Economic Growth and External Debt*. Baltimore: Johns Hopkins Press, 1964.
Balassa, Bela A. *Trade Prospects for Developing Countries*. Homewood, Ill.: Irwin, 1964.
Black, C. E. *The Dynamics of Modernization: A Study in Comparative History*. New York: Harper & Row, 1966.
Cairncross, A. K. *Factors in Economic Development*. London: Allen & Unwin, 1962.
Chenery, Hollis B., and Alan M. Strout. "Foreign Assistance and Economic Development," *American Economic Review*, Vol. 56, no. 4, pt. 1 (1966).
Coffin, Frank M. *Witness for Aid*. Boston: Houghton Mifflin, 1964.
Economic Assistance Programs and Administration. Third Interim Report Submitted to the President of the United States by the President's Committee to Study the United States Military Assistance Program (Draper Committee), July 13, 1959. Washington: Government Printing Office, 1959.
Economic Development and Cultural Change. Chicago: University of Chicago Press, published quarterly.
Effective Aid: Report of an International Conference Held Jointly by the Ditchley Foundation and the Overseas Development Institute, 3–6 June 1966. London: Overseas Development Institute, 1967.
Finance and Development. Washington: International Monetary Fund and World Bank Group, published quarterly.
Gardner, Richard N., and Max F. Millikan (eds.). *The Global Partnership: International Agencies and Economic Development*. New York: Praeger, 1968.
Geiger, Theodore. *The Conflicted Relationship*. New York: McGraw-Hill for the Council on Foreign Relations, 1967.

————. "Why Have a U.S. Foreign Aid Effort?" in *Looking Ahead* (Washington: National Planning Association), Vol. 16 (January 1969).

Goldwin, Robert A. (ed.). *Why Foreign Aid?* Chicago: Rand McNally, 1962.

Hirschman, Albert O. *Development Projects Observed.* Washington: Brookings Institution, 1967.

————. *The Strategy of Economic Development.* New Haven: Yale University Press, 1958.

Huntington, Samuel P. *Political Order in Changing Societies.* New Haven: Yale University Press, 1968.

International Development Review. Washington: Society for International Development, published quarterly.

Jacoby, Neil H. *U.S. Aid to Taiwan: A Study of Foreign Aid, Self-Help, and Development.* New York: Praeger, 1966.

Johnson, Harry G. *Economic Policies Toward Less Developed Countries.* Washington: Brookings Institution, 1967.

Kaplan, Jacob J. *The Challenge of Foreign Aid: Policies, Problems, and Possibilities.* New York: Praeger, 1967.

Kuznets, Simon. *Postwar Economic Growth.* Cambridge: Harvard University Press, 1964.

Lary, Hal B. *Imports of Manufactures from Less Developed Countries.* New York: National Bureau of Economic Research, 1968.

Lewis, John P. *Quiet Crisis in India: Economic Development and American Policy.* Washington: Brookings Institution, 1962.

Lewis, W. Arthur. *The Theory of Economic Growth.* Homewood, Ill.: Irwin, 1955.

Little, I. M. D., and J. M. Clifford. *International Aid.* Chicago: Aldine, 1966.

Maddison, Angus. *Foreign Skills and Technical Assistance in Economic Development.* Paris: Development Centre of the Organisation for Economic Co-operation and Development, 1965.

Mason, Edward S. *Economic Development in India and Pakistan.* Cambridge: Harvard University Center for International Affairs, September 1966.

————. *Economic Planning in Underdeveloped Areas.* New York: Fordham University Press, 1958.

————. *Foreign Aid and Foreign Policy.* New York: Harper & Row, 1964.

Mikesell, Raymond F. *The Economics of Foreign Aid.* Chicago: Aldine, 1968.

Millikan, Max F. "The United States and Low-Income Countries," in

Kermit Gordon (ed.), *Agenda for the Nation*. Washington: Brookings Institution, 1968.

Millikan, Max F., and D. L. M. Blackmer (eds.). *The Emerging Nations: Their Growth and United States Policy*. Boston: Little, Brown, 1961.

———, and W. W. Rostow. *A Proposal; Key to an Effective Foreign Policy*. New York: Harper, 1957.

Montgomery, John D. *The Politics of Foreign Aid: American Experience in Southeast Asia*. New York: Praeger, 1962.

Morgenthau, Hans J. "A Political Theory of Foreign Aid." *American Political Science Review*, Vol. 56 (June 1962).

Myint, Hla. *The Economics of the Developing Countries*. New York: Praeger, 1965.

Myrdal, Gunnar. *Asian Drama: An Inquiry into the Poverty of Nations*. New York: Twentieth Century Fund, 1968.

———. *Beyond the Welfare State*. New Haven: Yale University Press, 1960.

———. *An International Economy: Problems and Prospects*. New York: Harper, 1956.

Nair, Kusum. *Blossoms in the Dust: The Human Factor in Indian Development*. New York: Praeger, 1962.

National Planning Association. *Case Studies of U.S. Business Performance Abroad*. Series published 1953–68.

———. *Development Digest*. Prepared quarterly for the Agency for International Development. Washington: NPA, 1962–.

———. *A New Conception of U.S. Foreign Aid*. Special Report 64. Washington: NPA, March 1969.

Nelson, Joan M. *Aid, Influence, and Foreign Policy*. New York: Macmillan, 1968.

Nurkse, Ragnar. *Problems of Capital Formation in Less Developed Countries*. New York: Oxford University Press, 1953.

Ohlin, Goran. *Foreign Aid Policies Reconsidered*. Paris: Development Centre of the Organisation for Economic Co-operation and Development, 1966.

Organisation for Economic Co-operation and Development. *Development Assistance Efforts and Policies*. Paris: OECD, annual reviews, beginning in 1961.

Owen, Wilfred. *Strategy for Mobility: Transportation for the Developing Countries*. Washington: Brookings Institution, 1964.

Partners in Development. Report of the Commission on International Development, Lester B. Pearson, chairman. New York: Praeger, 1969.

Pincus, John. *Economic Aid and International Cost Sharing*. Santa Monica, Calif.: RAND Corporation, July 1965.

————. *Trade, Aid and Development: The Rich and Poor Nations*. New York: McGraw-Hill for the Council on Foreign Relations, 1967.

Ranis, Gustav (ed.). *The United States and the Developing Economies*. New York: Norton, 1964.

Rostow, W. W. *The Stages of Economic Growth*. New York: Cambridge University Press, 1960.

Rubin, Seymour J. *The Conscience of the Rich Nations: The Development Assistance Committee and the Common Aid Effort*. New York: Harper & Row for the Council on Foreign Relations, 1966.

Schelling, Thomas C. *International Economics*. Boston: Allyn and Bacon, 1958.

Shonfield, Andrew. *The Attack on World Poverty*. New York: Random House, 1960.

Stern, Robert M. *Policies for Trade and Development*. International Conciliation Series 548. New York: Carnegie Endowment for International Peace, May 1964.

Sufrin, Sidney C. *Technical Assistance: Theory and Guidelines*. Syracuse: Syracuse University Press, 1966.

Tinbergen, Jan. *Shaping the World Economy: Suggestions for an International Economic Policy*. New York: Twentieth Century Fund, 1962.

United Nations. Annual *World Economic Survey*. New York: UN, 1948–.

————. *Foreign Investment in Developing Countries*. New York: UN, 1968.

————. *Towards a New Trade Policy for Development: Report by the Secretary-General of the United Nations Conference on Trade and Development*. New York: UN, 1964.

U.S. Congress. Senate. Committee on Foreign Relations. *Foreign Aid Program*, Compilation of Studies and Surveys Prepared under the Direction of the Special Committee to Study the Foreign Aid Program. S. Doc. 52, 85 Cong. 1 sess. Washington: Government Printing Office, July 1957.

U.S. Department of State. *An Act for International Development: A Program for the Decade of Development*. Department of State Publication 7205. Washington: Government Printing Office, June 1961.

Walinsky, Louis J. *Economic Development in Burma, 1951–1960*. New York: Twentieth Century Fund, 1962.

Wolf, Charles, Jr. *Foreign Aid: Theory and Practice in Southern Asia*. Princeton: Princeton University Press, 1960.

————. *United States Policy and the Third World*. Boston: Little, Brown, 1967.

Index

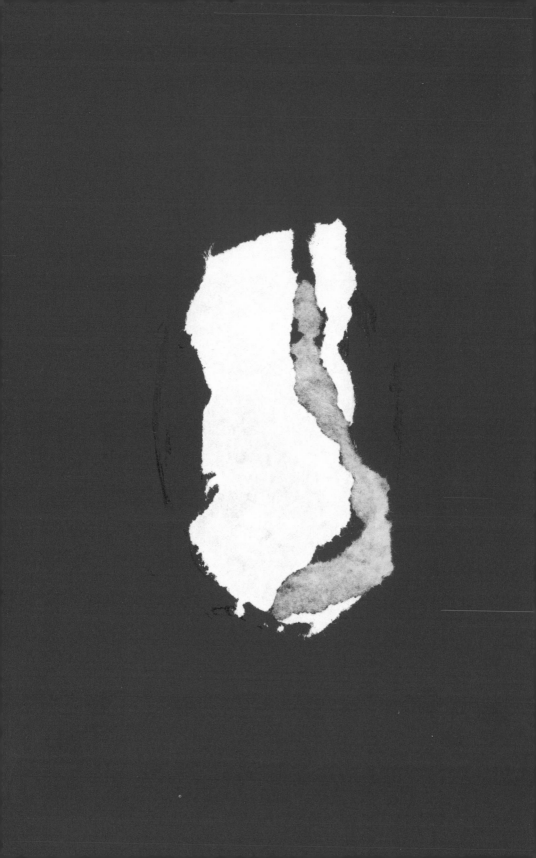